# PRINCIPLES OF
# DEVELOPMENTAL PSYCHOLOGY

# PRINCIPLES OF DEVELOPMENTAL PSYCHOLOGY

GEORGE BUTTERWORTH
*University of Sussex*

and

MARGARET HARRIS
*Royal Holloway University of London*

**A volume in the series**
***Principles of Psychology***

*Series Editors*
Michael W. Eysenck
Simon Green
Nicky Hayes

Reprinted 1994, 1998 and 2003


Psychology Press Ltd, Publishers
27 Church Road
Hove
East Sussex, BN3 2FA
UK


**British Library Cataloguing in Publication Data**
A catalogue record for this book is available from the British Library

ISBN 0-86377-279-X (hbk)
ISBN 0-86377-280-3  (pbk)
ISSN 0965-9706




Subject index compiled by Sue Ramsey
Cover design by Stuart Walden and Joyce Chester
Printed and bound in the UK by TJ International (Padstow) Ltd

*For Annetta, Harry and Francesca*
*—at different stages in their development*

# Acknowledgement

Thanks to Roger Goodwin for his perceptive comments on the text. Thanks also to Michael Forster for his patience, to the staff at LEA for their help and to Nicky Hayes, Usha Goswami and Simon Green for their encouraging and constructive criticism.

# Contents

# Preface

Developmental psychology is a science of broad scope which aims to explain how children and adults change over time. The discipline offers a particular method of scientific enquiry, unique in psychology, in that it focuses on the biological and social processes generating stability and change in people as they grow. The different forms of psychological organisation typical of different periods of the lifespan are the core phenomena to be explained.

This book is an introduction to a very wide field and we have had to be selective in order to illustrate some of the essential features of developmental psychology. We begin by situating the discipline in its historical context. We cover the influence and impact of evolutionary theory in order to help the student to understand the origins of the issues that still preoccupy developmental psychologists. Subsequently we focus on contemporary research with particular, critical, reference to three major developmental theorists: Piaget, Vygotsky, and Bowlby. Their theories overlap in some ways, but they also differ in their relative emphasis on intellectual, social, and emotional aspects of development.

Piagetian theory tends to dominate our book because so much contemporary research has been directed to a critical examination of his work. Piaget has set the agenda in developmental psychology but his is by no means the only voice. We draw attention to the way in which the child gains understanding through more immediate, intuitive processes than the reasoning abilities that Piaget emphasised. Perception, language, and social communication have their own important parts to play in acquiring knowledge. These psychological processes situate the child in a physical, social, and cultural context. At different ages, and in different cultures, the child may draw upon these abilities in different ways.

There is not yet a single "correct" theory of development. However, there are two distinctions that are often made, and which we chose not to pursue because they are misleading. First, we prefer not to polarise a distinction between "individual" and "social" development. Rather, we favour a view that sees the individual and the social as reciprocal domains. What the child knows of self is often a function of society, and what the child knows of society is, at least in part, a function of self. The inter-dependence of the individual and the social aspects of development should be apparent in our discussions of language acquisition, moral development, play, attachment theory, gender identity, and parenting, and in the many references to cultural factors that influence growth.

A second distinction, between biological and psychological aspects of development, is commonly made, but is misleading. These are not alter-native accounts; they are mutually embedded and it is important to make the effort to accommodate both levels of explanation. Biological aspects of psychological development are discussed at various points, notably in stressing the importance of a proper account of evolution and its implica-tions. The interdependence of biological and psychological processes also arises in pre-natal development, in motor development, in language acquisition in the chimpanzee, in the contribution of ethology, in the development of gender identity, and in ageing.

We have tried to be up to date and this has influenced the balance of topics. Most contemporary research has been on infancy and childhood, and the structure of the book reflects this. If space had allowed, we would have included more on adulthood and later periods of the lifespan. It would also have been fun to explore further such important issues as: the evolution of humans; the genetics of development; the development of the central nervous system; comparative development in different species, in different cultures and over different historical periods; and abnormal development. These omissions will at least alert the reader to some of the many fascinating topics to which further study of the principles of human development can lead.

George Butterworth and Margaret Harris
Brighton, April 1994

# PART 1

# History and Methods of Developmental Psychology

# The origins of developmental psychology 1

## Defining the subject

Developmental psychology is concerned with the scientific understanding of age-related changes in experience and behaviour. Although most developmental theories have been specifically concerned with children, the ultimate aim is to provide an account of development throughout the lifespan. The task is to discover, describe, and explain how development occurs, from its earliest origins, into adulthood and old age.

Two strands of explanation are involved in developmental psychology. The discipline takes some of its inspiration from the biology of growth and evolution, but other aspects of explanation are concerned with the ways in which different cultures channel development. Explaining human development not only requires us to understand human nature—because development is a natural phenomenon—but also to consider the diverse effects that a particular society has on the developing child. In truth, development is as much a matter of the child acquiring a culture as it is a process of biological growth. Contemporary theories of development make the connection between nature and culture, albeit with varying emphases and, of course, with varying degrees of success.

This book will examine modern approaches to human development with particular reference to children and their social, physical, and intellectual growth. Intellectual development is concerned with the origins and acquisition of thought and language. This field of study is known as cognitive development and it includes such important abilities as learning to read and write. Problems of cognitive development, for example mental retardation, or the effects of deafness or blindness on the child's understanding, also fall within this domain. Social development is concerned with the integration of the child into the social world, and explaining how the child acquires the values of the family and the wider society.

The balance of the book is towards the traditional study of the childhood years, but we will also introduce modern ideas about development in adulthood. However, most contemporary research concerns the period from birth to adolescence and this is the age range we have covered most extensively. We were concerned to provide adequate coverage of the important recent work on the origins of development and so there is rather more detail on the pre-natal period and infancy than other periods of the lifespan.

It will also become apparent that much contemporary research in cognitive development has been concerned with detailed criticism of the important theory of Jean Piaget, and so his work receives rather extensive critical consideration throughout the book. We also give fairly detailed consideration to the ideas of Lev Vygotsky, who emphasised the importance of social factors in development, and to the work of John Bowlby on establishing social relationships. Wherever possible we introduce evidence from different cultures to illustrate the important principle that human development is both a biological and a cultural process. In a final chapter, we consider how development continues even into adulthood with such important life-events as becoming a parent, moving in and out of employment, and the effects of ageing.

# The historical and social background

Human development as a biological process obviously has a long past but its systematic study has a short history. Our need to study development is often motivated by social and economic changes, even though the phenomena of reproduction and growth have always been available for observation.

Western societies did not study the childhood years—from the age of about seven to adolescence—until after the industrial revolution in the nineteenth century, even though early childhood had long been recognised as a distinct period in the life-cycle. Once the social changes in economic organisation induced by the industrial revolution such as population movement from the countryside to the towns were in place, the stage was set for the study of childhood. The industrial revolution led to a need for basic literacy and numeracy in the factories which was eventually to be met by universal primary education. This, in turn, made it important to study the mind of the child so that education itself could become more effective. No doubt other social factors such as increased wealth, better hygiene, and progressive control of childhood diseases also contributed to the focus on childhood.

Adolescence as a distinct stage interposed between childhood and adulthood can also be defined by biological, historical, and cultural changes. The distinctive biological changes of adolescence provide a visible means of demarcation of a further phase in the life-cycle, and this became an object of developmental study in its own right as twentieth-century Western society became wealthy enough to protect the child from adult economic responsibilities. It was possible to postpone the entry of the adolescent into the workforce and also necessary to increase the period of education.

Development in adulthood—*lifespan development*—is an even more recent object of study. Social and medical changes that have allowed survival into great old age, long after the elderly person has ceased to make a direct economic contribution, have drawn attention to the problems and possibilities of old age. These, in turn, raise questions about the psychology of ageing for the developmentalist to address.

In summary, there are biological and cultural aspects of development at many points in the life-cycle. Biological processes contribute to development and provide "markers" for particular stages. These often acquire significance for reasons of our social history, which provides the impetus to acquire a deeper understanding of the life-cycle. The social structure has an impact on development at all stages of the lifespan. It provides a framework in relation to which distinctive stages, or periods of life, may be identified and studied.

# Cultural and biological determinants of development

Present-day developmental psychology is a function of its recent ancestry. Obviously, people have always had children but it is only in the last century that we have moved away from anecdotal descriptions to systematic study of development. "Folk" explanations were very general and often rather prescriptive. For example, the English philosopher, *John Locke* (1632–1704), thought the child was born a *tabula rasa* (blank slate), whose every characteristic would be moulded by experience (Locke, 1690). On this view, the newborn is psychologically structureless and extremely malleable to the effects of the environment (Bremner, 1994). Locke's environmentalist view tends to deny that innate factors make any important contribution to psychological development. It places great emphasis on what can be learned as a way of explaining the acquisition of knowledge by the child.

In sharp contrast to the views of Locke, the Swiss philosopher, *Jean Jacques Rousseau* (1712–1778), was more inclined to a "natural" theory of human development (Rousseau, 1762). He considered that children are innately "good", requiring little by way of moral guidance or constraint for normal development, and that they grow according to "nature's plan". Rousseau's account emphasises "natural" propensities and minimises the effects of upbringing or experience.

Such very general views as those of Locke and Rousseau set the stage for rather misguided debates about the relative contributions of "nature and nurture" to development. Contemporary developmental psychologists avoid such dichotomous approaches to explanation in favour of "interactive" or "dialectical" accounts which attempt more adequately to capture the complex interplay of factors contributing to development.

# Scientific foundations of developmental psychology

One of the main differences between a commonsense or folk psychological understanding of development and a scientific understanding is the extent to which theories are subjected to systematic test. Systematic investigations are directed specifically at understanding how, why, and what course human development takes, and this in turn requires rather sophisticated methods. Although anecdotal accounts have always been available, and obviously there is folk wisdom in all societies about child rearing, the scientific study of childhood is really very recent. It begins as a serious scientific study in the nineteenth century with Charles Darwin's theory of evolution (see Cairns, 1983).

## Foundations: 1859–1914

Fig. 1.1 Darwin & his son Doddy. By permission of the Syndics of Cambridge University Library.

*Charles Darwin* is often credited with establishing the scientific approach to developmental psychology. Although his major interests were in evolutionary theory, he could be considered the first developmental psychologist because he published a short paper describing the development of his infant son, Doddy, in 1877. He was impressed by the playfulness of his baby son, and by his capacity for emotional expression.

Darwin's studies of his infant son were intended to help him understand, in particular, the evolution of innate forms of human communication. As we shall see, many basic developmental concepts, such as the idea that development can be understood as the progressive adaptation of the child to the environment, can be traced directly to Darwin and the influence of evolutionary theory. Another of Darwin's contributions was to introduce systematic methods to the study of development. The philosophical or anecdotal speculations of earlier theorists, such as Locke and Rousseau, were replaced by actual observations of developing children and this set the discipline on a scientific path.

The major biological foundations of developmental psychology were laid in the period between the publication of Darwin's theory of evolution in 1859 and the first decades of the twentieth century. Darwin's theory of evolution located man firmly in nature and raised questions about continuities and discontinuities between man and the animals.

Another effect of the Darwinian revolution was that people became curious about the biological origins of human nature. Evolutionary explanation led naturally to an emphasis on changes that occur as a function of time, both in the extremely long time-scale of evolution and over the individual lifespan. Darwin's books on *The origin of the species* (1859), *The descent of man* (1871) and *The expression of emotions in men and animals* (1872), raised questions about the origins of the human mind in the evolutionary past. They posed the challenging problem of the relation between individual development (*ontogeny*) and the evolution of the species (*phylogeny*).

The question of the relation between phylogeny and ontogeny was pursued vigorously by late nineteenth-century embryologists, such as Haeckel (1874), who was impressed by the similar form taken by the embryos of many different species at certain times in their development. Haeckel argued that the development of the human embryo recapitulates its ancestry. The embryo successively takes the shape of various more primitive ancestors, before attaining its final human shape.

Today, it is no longer believed that "ontogeny recapitulates phylogeny" as Haeckel had argued. The more sophisticated view of the resemblances between different mammalian embryos is that the similarities reflect biological structures we still hold in common with our remote ancestors (Gould, 1977). Thus, there is no simple translation from the evolutionary past into present-day development. Nevertheless, clear stage-like changes in biological form led to the idea that other aspects of biological growth, such as cognitive and social development in humans, may also show distinct age-related stages in organisation.

The emergence of an independent developmental psychology is generally dated to 1882, with the publication of a book by the German physiologist, *Wilhelm Preyer*, entitled *The mind of the child*. This book was based on Preyer's observations of his own daughter and described her development from birth to two and a half years. Preyer insisted on proper scientific procedures, writing every observation down and noting the emergence of many abilities in his daughter. He was particularly impressed by the importance of the extended period of curiosity evident in human infant development.

Fig. 1.2
Embryos of
different species
at three
comparable
stages of
development
(after Haeckel in
Romanes, 1892).

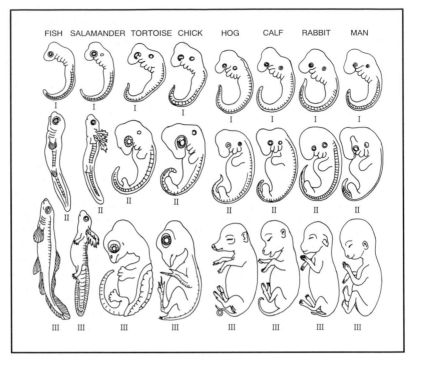

FISH  SALAMANDER  TORTOISE  CHICK      HOG       CALF      RABBIT     MAN

Wilhelm Preyer's work was translated into English in 1888, one of a burgeoning series of publications by then amounting to 48 full-scale empirical studies of children that had been carried out in Europe, Britain, and the United States. Developmental psychology as a discipline was now in full swing.

Among other famous pioneers was *Alfred Binet* (1857–1911), who was working on experimental studies of thinking in young children in France. He is best known for developing the first intelligence test. Binet had been critical of diagnoses of mental deficiency made by medical practitioners responsible for placing feeble-minded children in special schools in Paris. No single sign of mental deficiency could reliably differentiate mentally retarded from normal children. In fact, the same child might carry a different diagnosis, depending on which physician had made it. The urgent practical need for a valid and reliable test of intelligence led him to construct the Binet and Simon scale which was published in 1905.

The main early application of Binet's work was to provide guidelines on the relative intellectual abilities and educational potential of mentally retarded children, but his work was soon to find much wider application in education and training. Binet developed tests that were based on norms

## Mental age and IQ

The concept of mental age, which was first used by Binet, is best illustrated with some examples. Suppose that a child of 8 years 0 months is able to solve items in a test that are normally solved by children of the same age but is not able to solve items normally solved by older children. That child would be considered to have a mental age of 8 years. However, if the same child consistently succeeded on test items that were normally solved by 10-year-olds, he or she would clearly be functioning intellectually at a mental age level that was above chronological age. In this case, the child would be considered to have a mental age of 10 years. A child who is only able to solve items normally solved by younger children would have a mental age that was lower than his or her chronological age.

The psychologist *William Stern* (1871–1938) devised a formula for calculating the *intelligence quotient* (IQ) defining intelligence relative to age:

$$IQ = \frac{\text{Mental age}}{\text{Chronological age}} \times 100$$

In the example we have just considered, the 8-year-old with a mental age of 10 years would be credited with an IQ of: 10/8 x 100 = 125. Similarly, a 12-year-old with a mental age of 15 years would also have an IQ of 125 (15/12 × 100 = 125) because he or she would have the same relative standing in relation to age peers. A child who has a mental age that is the same as his or her chronological age is considered to be of average intelligence. This is because, on average, intellectual development in the population proceeds at the same rate as chronological age. Children of average intelligence have an IQ of 100.

of performance for a given age, and this soon led to the idea of a child's *mental age* as distinct from *chronological age* (see the panel above).

Binet's work was very influential in making careful measurement a basic part of modern psychology. His intelligence scale (which was only one of his contributions) laid the foundations for the extensive psychometric tests now so useful in educational, medical and other applied fields.

Among the most important, but perhaps least well-known, of the founders of present-day developmental psychology was the American, *James Mark Baldwin* (1861–1934). Baldwin made a major intellectual and administrative contribution to setting up scientific psychology. He was the founding editor of the first scientific psychology journal, *The Psychological Review* (1895), and he was later the editor of the important journal *Psychological Bulletin* and one of the first presidents of the American Psychological Association (1897). He was influential in many ways in the new science of psychology, including establishing an international group of scholars who contributed to a four-volume *Dictionary of Philosophy and Psychology* (Baldwin, 1905). In 1903, a survey ranked Baldwin in the top five contributors to international research (Broughton & Freeman-Moir, 1982).

Fig. 1.3 James Baldwin. Courtesy of the Department of Psychology, Indiana University.

One of Baldwin's most important contributions to the founding of developmental psychology was made in the period 1903–1908, when he was professor of philosophy and psychology at Johns Hopkins University. He published the first of a three-volume series on "Genetic Logic", a difficult work on the development of thinking in children. In this series, Baldwin set out the foundations of a theory of the progressive development of knowledge in childhood. He proposed that development proceeds in a series of distinct stages, beginning at birth with the innate motor reflexes, and progressing to the acquisition of language and logical thought. He proposed that moving through successive stages of development depends on feedback from the stimulating environment.

In Baldwin's terminology, the essential mechanisms for development are *assimilation* (incorporation of effects of the environment into the organism) leading to *accommodation* (plastic change) of the organism. He emphasised that the child is as much a product of social experience as of biological growth. From 1912 Baldwin lived in France and he made periodic visits to the University of Geneva in Switzerland. He established a warm friendship with the Swiss child psychologist Edouard Claparède. Baldwin's books were translated into French and he was a major influence on a student of Claparède, the famous developmental psychologist, Jean Piaget (1896–1980). Piaget's theory of development will be considered in detail at various places in this book.

Other early developmentalists, such as *G. Stanley Hall* (1844–1924) in the USA, based their ideas on a misreading of evolutionary principles. Hall proposed the *biogenetic law*, another way of stating that "ontogeny recapitulates phylogeny", which also supposed that the course of human development involves a repetition of the ancestral, evolutionary timetable. This led, for example, to his thoroughly mistaken idea that children love to swing in trees because they recapitulate their monkey ancestry; or that the child has a primitive "savage" mind (or conversely, that the savage mind is childlike). He even argued that there is a scale of mental abilities with children (and women) at the bottom and men at the top!

As we have already stated, developmentalists need to guard against misplaced analogies between evolution, heredity, and development. This remains a problem even today in discussions about the inheritance of intelligence. Hall did have one very important influence though: as the president of Clark University, he was responsible for inviting Sigmund Freud to the United States in 1909 and thus promoted Freud's psychoanalytic ideas. The Freudian influence is perhaps most clearly seen in theories of social and emotional development, especially in research concerning attachment between parent and child. We will be considering contemporary ideas influenced by Freudian theory, especially the work of John Bowlby.

## Formation of the major "schools": 1914–1927

From 1914 to 1927, the empirical basis of developmental psychology was established. This period coincided with an intense interest in theories of learning based on the work of the Russian physiologist, *Ivan Pavlov*. Pavlov's studies of learning in dogs established that some types of learning take place through the association of stimuli and responses, under conditions of reward and punishment. For example, in his famous studies of "classical conditioning" he showed that a hungry dog will readily learn that a signal, such as a bell, regularly predicts the arrival of food, and the dog will soon salivate in anticipation of food when the bell sounds. In this example, the dog has learned to associate the bell with food and the normal (unconditioned) response of salivation to food has become associated with (conditioned to) the sound of the bell.

This focus on the laws of learning led to the rise of a school of psychology known as *Behaviourism*, whose major figure was *John Watson* (1878–1957). Watson had distinct ideas about child development based on "learning" theory. He was very interested, for example, in whether infants naturally showed fear of animals or whether such fears were learned (see the panel on p. 12). He concluded that these fears were learned.

Fig. 1.4 John Watson. Photo courtesy of Ferdinand Hamburger, Jr., Archives of The Johns Hopkins University.

Watson believed so strongly in the potential of the child to learn through experience that he wrote:

> Give me a dozen healthy infants, well formed and my own specified world to bring them up in and I'll guarantee to take any one at random and train him to become any type of specialist I might select—doctor, lawyer, artist, merchant-chief and yes, even beggar man and thief, regardless of his talents, penchants, tendencies, abilities, vocations and race of his ancestors. (Watson, 1930, p. 104)

As this quotation vividly illustrates, "nature" took rather a back seat to "nurture" in Watson's explanation of the causes of development. He believed, for example, that whether a person is left-handed or right-handed was a function of early training rather than of genetic factors. (This

---

### Watson's studies of childhood fears

In his book, *Psychology from the standpoint of a behaviorist* (1919), Watson reported a study of three children who were introduced to novel birds and animals over a period of several days. In one case, Watson presented a 6-month-old baby called Thorne with a black cat, a pigeon, a rabbit and, later on, a whole series of animals at the local zoo including a camel and a zebra. He studied Thorne's reaction to their presence in a number of different conditions and found that, even in the dark, she did not display fear on any occasion, although she was very interested in all the animals and looked at them intently. She also reached out to touch the smaller animals.

Having shown that children did not have any innate fear of animals, Watson went on to study the acquisition of irrational fears through learning. He reports the case of a 6-month-old baby who had a small dog tossed into her pram. (How this came about Watson does not reveal.) The baby became terrified and subsequently showed a fear reaction not only to dogs but also to rapidly moving toy animals. At 18 months, the unfortunate baby was tested by having a tame white mouse placed on the floor near her. She responded by crying and rushing into her father's arms.

A similar—and more famous—study was carried out on a baby called "Little Albert", and reported by Watson and Rayner (1920). They showed that after Albert was frightened while playing with a furry toy, he also learned to be afraid of other furry objects (such as a beard) and animals.

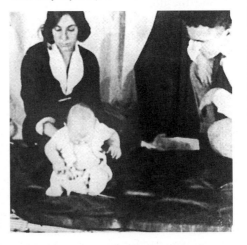

Fig. 1.5 "Little Albert" © Ben Harris, 1980.

theory receives rather less support today—see Chapter 5 on motor development.) Watson's views were partly based on inherent American optimism and partly on an extreme view of the extent of human plasticity. That is, the developing child was considered to be extremely malleable and highly susceptible to the effects of environmental influences.

Learning-theory approaches to development continued to exercise great influence, especially in the USA, until quite recently. They still find useful application in dealing with some developmental problems, such as bed wetting, or fears and phobias, where techniques based on the laws of conditioning first described by Pavlov, and developed by Watson, have been applied. However, the contemporary influence of learning theories on development is rather limited by comparison with other more recent schools of thought.

The diametric opposite to an extreme learning theory approach is the maturational school, led by *Arnold Gesell* (1880–1961). His main idea was that the time-locked processes of biological growth are particularly important for the appearance of various abilities. Gesell was most interested in motor and perceptual development, which he saw as inevitable and rather automatic under normal circumstances.

Unlike the environmentalists, such as Watson, maturationists tended to emphasise "nature" at the expense of "nurture" as a cause of development. The nativist view of Gesell—and his insistence on the importance of evolution in shaping the course of development—is illustrated by the following quotation which stands in stark contrast to the earlier quotation from Watson:

> The child grows … . The capacities and, to no small extent, the directions of growth are the end products of ages of evolution. (Gesell, Ilg, & Bullis, 1949, p. 44)

As a comparison of the views of Watson and Gesell reveals, the middle period in the founding of developmental psychology produced a polarisation between, on the one hand, an extreme environmentalism—somewhat similar to Locke's view of the child as a *tabula rasa* on which experience would have a major effect—and, on the other, an extreme maturationist view. The influence of maturation was most strongly espoused by those interested in such aspects of development as hand–eye coordination and the acquisition of motor skills like walking, which seemed to proceed according to a strict biological timetable. (It should be noted, however, that Gesell recognised the significant individual variation in the age at which children reached particular developmental milestones.)

These sharply polarised views of nature versus nurture, although out of date now, were important because they led to distinct fashions in child-rearing and education each based on the rival views. The environmentalists emphasised habit training as a means of teaching children, for example, in toilet training or the acquisition of basic skills like reading and writing. Maturationists emphasised the biological need for the child to be "ready" for particular types of experience before learning could occur.

## Conclusion and Summary

Developmental psychology is concerned with age-related changes in experience and behaviour. The origins of the discipline are in philosophy but the scientific study of children was founded on the insights of evolutionary biology in the nineteenth century. Social and economic changes since then have made it imperative to understand better the processes of growth and development in children, adolescents, and adults.

By the 1920s, developmental psychology was well established as a scientific discipline, although by then it had broken up into various schools, each emphasising a different aspect of nature or nurture. The field had become fragmented and needed synthesis, so that the biological and social factors which actually interact in development could be more adequately understood. This work of synthesis was mainly accomplished by the "grand" theories of the middle twentieth century, which will be described in the next chapter.

### Further reading

Cairns, R.B. (1983). The emergence of developmental psychology. In W. Kessen (Ed.), *Handbook of child psychology, Vol. 1*, (pp. 41–101). (Series editor: P.H. Mussen). New York: John Wiley.

# The modern synthesis 2

U ntil quite recently, developmental psychology has been dominated by grand theories. These have attempted to interrelate "nature" and "nurture" in a manner more appropriate to the post-Darwinian age than the extreme maturationist or environmentalist accounts that preceded them (see Chapter 1). The major influences to the present-day can be summarised by considering the work of three developmental psychologists, each of whom offered very broad theories.

Although grand, all-encompassing theories of development have now given way to more circumscribed, detailed examination of particular developmental phenomena, the best way to introduce late twentieth-century developmental psychology is still in terms of the major historical figures who have shaped contemporary ideas.

## The main twentieth-century developmentalists

The three major developmental psychologists are the Swiss psychologist Jean Piaget (1896–1980), the Russian psychologist Lev Vygotsky (1896–1934), and the English child psychiatrist John Bowlby (1907–1990). Each of these theorists, in his own way, offered a more satisfactory account of development than any before. All were influenced by biological and evolutionary theories and each takes a particular focus on the developmental process.

Piaget sought to show how logical thinking in children develops out of its biological roots; Vygotsky was preoccupied with the special role that language plays in human society and social thought; Bowlby was most concerned with the role of social relationships between parent and child in the formation of personality and mental well-being. Much current research continues to be influenced by these three theorists.

### Jean Piaget

Jean Piaget has had the most profound influence on our understanding of development. He lived such a long and productive life that he straddled the whole of the modern history of developmental psychology, almost from its foundations to the present. He based his ideas on the work of James Mark Baldwin and, over the years, developed a major centre devoted to developmental psychology research at the University of Geneva, in Switzerland.

Piaget's ideas have been the focus of much controversy and empirical investigation. One measure of how much impact ideas have in science is how much new research they generate. There can be no doubt that Piaget had a major influence by this criterion. Even though a lot of contemporary workers disagree with the detail of his theory, there is no doubt that he has acted as a catalyst for some of the most exciting work in the field.

In 1921, Piaget returned from France to Geneva, to begin his lifetime's work at the university. Piaget developed his theory of how knowledge is acquired, which he called "genetic epistemology", based on his observations of children. His first books were about thinking and language in pre-school and early school-age children: *The language and thought of the child* (1923) and *Judgement and reasoning in the child* (1924). These were widely influential and much to his surprise were acclaimed the world over (see the panel on page 17).

In 1923, Piaget married Valentine Chatenay and in collaboration they studied the development from birth of their own three children, Jacqueline, Lucienne, and Laurent. These observations on the origins of thought and language in infancy formed the basis for three of Piaget's most influential books: *The origins of intelligence in children* (1936/1952), which describes how intelligence progressively arises in the baby's repetitive activities; *The construction of reality in the child* (1937/1954), which describes how elementary concepts of space, time, causes, and physical objects arise in development; and *Play, dreams and imitation in childhood* (1945/1951), which describes the beginnings of fantasy and symbolism in infancy. In this trilogy he outlined the theory that the precursors of thinking and language lie in the elementary actions, perceptions, and imitations of babies.

Many other influential books were to follow, especially those that had an impact on educational theory and practice in mathematics and science teaching, such as *The child's conception of number* (1941/1952 with A. Szeminska) and *The child's conception of geometry* (1948/1960 with B. Inhelder and A. Szeminska).

In some of his later works, Piaget outlined his theory of the relation between the acquisition of knowledge as a biological process and evolution (e.g. *Biology and knowledge*, 1971). Piaget is sometimes unjustly accused of recapitulationism (see p. 7) because he tried to draw parallels between evolution and developmental theory. His key theoretical idea

# Brief biography of Jean Piaget (1896–1980)

Jean Piaget was born on 9 August 1896 at Neuchatel, in Switzerland. In a very long and scholarly life he wrote more than 75 books and literally hundreds of scientific papers in which he elaborated his theory of cognitive development in children. His father was a university professor of mediaeval history who taught him the value of painstaking work. Unfortunately, his mother suffered poor mental health and her main influence was to lead him "to prefer the study of normalcy and the workings of the intellect to that of the tricks of the unconscious". Although he showed a passing interest in studying psychopathology, he devoted his research to the study of normal intellectual development.

While still a child, Piaget became interested in natural history and at the age of 11 years, in 1907, he published his first paper "On sighting an albino sparrow". The curator of the local natural history museum was so impressed with this precocious affinity for natural history that Piaget became his part-time and unpaid assistant! On Saturday afternoons he collected and catalogued the molluscs of the Swiss lakes, becoming especially interested in the way that their shapes varied with the depth of water where they lay. At university he studied biology and philosophy and in 1918 he was awarded a doctorate for his work on the special adaptations evolved by the molluscs in the shallow waters of the Swiss lakes.

Perhaps influenced by his mother's poor mental condition, Piaget then went to Zurich where he worked as an experimental psychologist with the famous psychoanalyst C.G. Jung and assisted in the psychiatric clinic. These experiences were to be influential in helping to combine the rigour of the laboratory experimental method with the more informal interviewing techniques typical of psychiatry, which were to feature strongly in his early studies of children's thinking.

The most influential event in Piaget's own development occurred in 1919 when he was invited to work in Binet's laboratory in Paris, deriving the age norms for items on the Binet–Simon intelligence tests of Parisian school children (see p. 8). The test included many simple items which measured children's ability at logical reasoning and Piaget became fascinated by the systematic nature of children's errors. Problems that seem totally simple to an adult, such as the syllogism: "John is taller than Mary and Mary is taller than Jane. Who is the tallest?", were not solved by the child until 11 or 12 years of age. This led Piaget to the theory that logical thinking develops slowly, and his background in biology soon led him to conceive of intellectual development as a gradual, stage-like evolution. He was particularly interested in how children acquire scientific knowledge, an aspect of advanced cultures. The slow accumulation of scientific knowledge over the centuries was conceived by Piaget as reflecting the human's progressive understanding of reality.

Fig. 2.1    Jean Piaget, circa 1978. From J.J. Ducret (1990) *Jean Piaget: Biographie et Parcours Intellectuel*, published by Editions Delachaux et Niestlé, Lausanne.

was that human knowledge can be considered as if it were a biological "organ" of the mind. Acquiring knowledge can be thought of as an evolutionary process in the sense that knowledge is adaptive. It consists of a relation between the individual and the environment (or, more specifically, between the knower and the known). Just as organs, such as the liver and the heart, ensure an adaptive equilibrium between organism and environment in the metabolism of air and food, so the process of acquiring knowledge can be thought of as one of equilibration, as the knower slowly arrives at more adequate descriptions, explanations, and predictions about reality.

Piaget argues that how children acquire knowledge, particularly scientific ideas, may show important parallels with the historic progress of science, but there is no suggestion that the sequence of stages in acquiring knowledge recapitulates the history of ideas (for an extensive discussion of recapitulationism and Piagetian theory, see Butterworth, Rutkowska, & Scaife, 1985).

Piaget's technical vocabulary, which he adopted from James Mark Baldwin (see pp. 9–10), is biological. For example, the assimilation of information by the structures of the mind is seen as analogous to the assimilation of food as nutrition for the body. Equilibrium is achieved through accommodation, as the organism adapts to, or incorporates the effects of, the environment. The notion of equilibration is also based on the idea of achieving a natural balance between the individual and the world, just as there is a balance of the forces that sustain life in nature.

Piaget's model of development is of a self-regulating interaction between the child and the physical and social environment, which gives rise to new forms of knowledge. His theory is analogous to the formation by natural selection of new species in evolution, where new forms of life arise from pre-existing ones under the influence of pressures from the environment. In evolution, only those species that can adapt to the new environment survive. By analogy, new forms of knowledge arise in development because they are better adapted to the demands of the environment than the forms they replace. The main stages described in his theory are listed in the panel on page 19. Each of these stages will be discussed in detail later in the book.

**Piaget's key biological ideas about development.** A key biological idea in Piaget's theory is that intellectual development can be thought of as an evolutionary process. Later stages succeed earlier stages because they are more adaptive, that is, more adequate to the demands of reality. Piaget argued that the acquisition of knowledge proceeds in a manner analogous to the evolution of species. He was much influenced

## Piaget's four main stages of intellectual development

Piaget described four major stages of development (each with sub-stages): the *sensori-motor*, the *pre-operational*, the *concrete operational*, and the *formal operational* stages of intellectual development extending from infancy to adulthood. The ages associated with each stage are averages and may vary considerably from child to child and from culture to culture but they occur in an invariant order. Piaget believed that stages I, II, and III are universal, whereas he thought stage IV to be characteristic of some adult thinking only in advanced, technological societies.

Mental operations begin in development as elementary actions, which can be integrated with other actions, and which form part of an organised network. With development, actions are internalised (represented) to give rise to organised mental operations which have the important properties of reversibility (i.e. thought can return to its starting point) and logical necessity (i.e. conclusions necessarily follow from the logical basis of their premises). The main stages of development in Piaget's theory are:

I   *The sensori-motor stage:* From birth to about 2 years. The child comes to know the world in terms of the physical activities he or she can perform. The stage ends with the acquisition of thought and language.

II   *The pre-operational stage:* From 2 years to about 7 years. So-called because, according to Piaget, the pre-school child has yet to acquire fully logical thinking.

III   *The concrete operational stage:* From 7 to about 12 years. Typical of the primary school age child who can think logically about "concrete" problems in the "here and now". With the acquisition of concrete operations, thought becomes reversible and the child understands the intrinsic necessity of deductions about the concrete properties of things.

IV   *The formal operational stage:* A form of thought acquired by adolescents in Western society who can think about abstract or hypothetical problems, especially in the realm of scientific reasoning, proceeding by systematic deductions from hypotheses.

by the evolutionary biologist C.H. Waddington (1957) and he adopted his concept of the "epigenetic landscape" as a metaphor for the developmental process.

Figure 2.2, overleaf, is a diagram of the epigenetic landscape. The ball represents the developing organism, while the layout of the hills and valleys, along which the ball may roll, represents possible pathways for development. The landscape imposes constraints on the movements of the rolling ball as it progresses downhill. For example, in the event of some environmental perturbation that could knock the ball off course, a deeper valley would be more difficult to leave than a shallower one.

The diagram attempts to schematise the fact that there exist natural pathways which development might take, and these are differentially susceptible to environmental influences. The constraint on development is known technically as *canalisation*. Canalisation is what ensures that certain aspects of development, such as having two arms and two legs, are nearly universal. Even so, perturbations may operate at choice points to alter even seemingly inevitable aspects of development, as people are

Fig. 2.2 The epigenetic landscape (after Waddington, 1957).

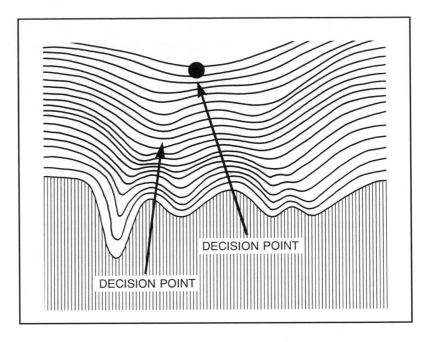

sometimes born without arms or legs when the developmental process goes wrong.

The location of junctions between the valleys in the epigenetic landscape model can represent critical points in development, where further development may take one of several forms, depending on environmental factors that obtain at the time. The transition points between adjoining valleys can also represent movement between stages. The slope of the valleys can represent the rate of the developmental process, with shallow valleys representing a relatively steady state and steep valleys at choice points representing rapid change and transition from one mode of organisation to another. At such transitions, crucial environmental influences may have consequences, but the same events would have no consequences at other points in the epigenetic landscape. Finally, the landscape metaphor illustrates the important developmental principle that the same endpoint might be reached by different routes. The principle of "equifinality" explains how development may be slower or quicker in different individuals because it takes different developmental routes.

Piaget's ideas on the development of thinking have had the most profound influence in twentieth-century developmental psychology. Some idea of his impact can be gained from the fact that his work is cited by others more frequently than that of any other psychologist apart from Sigmund Freud. His description of the developing mental powers of the child has inspired many followers and much constructive criticism with which we will become more closely acquainted in subsequent chapters. Even though he died in 1980, work in the Piagetian tradition continues and there is little doubt that Piaget's theory will exercise great influence for years to come. (For a more extensive account of Piaget's influence on psychology, biology, philosophy, and cybernetics, see M. Boden, 1979.)

## Lev Semeonovich Vygotsky

Piaget was mainly concerned to explain the development of intelligence and reasoning in humans from biological roots. Vygotsky, by contrast, was most concerned to show how culture influences the course of development. Culture is used as a broad term to describe the customs of a particular people at a particular time and their collective intellectual, material, scientific, and artistic achievements over historical time.

As his Marxist philosophy required (see the panel on page 22), Vygotsky was particularly concerned to identify the historical and social aspects of human behaviour that render human nature unique. For Vygotsky, speech pre-eminently has the role of carrying culture: language both stores and carries the historical stock of social experience and it is a "tool" of thought. People also differ from animals because they use tools to create artifacts which change the conditions of life. Culture is constituted both symbolically, in language, and materially, in the environment and objects created by humans.

One of the main differences between Piaget and Vygotsky concerns their views on the relationship between language and thought. Vygotsky placed much greater emphasis than Piaget on the formative role of culture on development, as it is transmitted both through social interaction and speech. Consequently, Vygotsky saw a much closer link between the acquisition of language and the development of thinking, and he also gave much greater prominence to the importance of social interaction in development, especially as it influenced language and thought.

Vygotsky's ideas were in fact rooted in Western psychology. He had read James Mark Baldwin's theory of development (which was available in French and had been translated into Russian in 1911) and, like many educated Russians, he was able to read French and so was acquainted with Binet's ideas about intelligence and Piaget's writings on language and thought in the child.

In some respects, then, Vygotsky's intellectual heritage was similar to Piaget's. However, Vygotsky was formulating his ideas during the revolutionary period in Russia, when great emphasis was placed on the way in which the social organisation channels human potential. It is not surprising that Vygotsky emphasised the influence that culture and social

## Brief biography of Lev Semeonovich Vygotsky (1896–1934)

Lev S. Vygotsky, a Jewish Russian developmental psychologist, was born in the same year as Piaget. Although less well known than Piaget, because he died at the early age of 38 before his work became available in the West, he too has had great influence. Little is known of his early days except that he was the second of eight children, his father was a bank official, and that Vygotsky's home was at Gomel, a small town about 400 miles south-west of Moscow (Kozulin, 1990; Valsiner, 1988).

Vygotsky studied literature and cultural history at Moscow University where he graduated in 1917, the same year as the October Soviet Revolution. From 1917 he taught literature and psychology at the teacher training college in Gomel. He founded a literary journal, and carried out literary research that was eventually published in his book, *The psychology of art* (Vygotsky, 1971). He was also working on ideas in psychology and presented a paper on the relation between Pavlovian conditioned reflexes and consciousness at the Psycho-Neurological Congress in Leningrad in 1924. As a result of the impression these ideas made on his fellow psychologists, Vygotsky was invited to join the Institute of Psychology in Moscow in the same year.

In line with the prevailing Marxist theory of the time, Vygotsky saw culture and social organisation, and the historical forces that shape society, as having an important influence on the development of the child's mind. Paradoxically, Vygotsky's revolutionary work fell foul of Stalinism and his writings were suppressed in Russia. His early death from tuberculosis meant that he did not become well known, outside a close circle of students and col-leagues, until the early 1960s when his major book *Thought and language* was first translated into English (a second, much revised, edition was published in 1986).

The contemporary American developmental psychologist, *J.S. Bruner* (born 1916), was particularly influential in introducing Vygotsky's work to Western scholars. Bruner's own work offers a synthesis of many features of Piagetian and Vygotskian psychology (Bruner, Olver, & Greenfield 1966).

Fig. 2.3   Lev Vygotsky.

organisation has on the development of the child's mind. These ideas can be seen very clearly in Vygotsky's theory of the *zone of proximal development*.

## Vygotsky's theory of the zone of proximal development (ZPD).

A key theoretical idea of Vygotsky concerns the zone of proximal development or ZPD. This may be defined as the difference between what a child can achieve unaided in problem solving and what can be achieved with the help of adults or with the peer group. A simple example is the difference between how an 18-month-old child might attempt to stack a set of beakers when there is no older person there to assist and how he or she might attempt the same task with the assistance of an adult or older child. Vygotsky's important contribution was to point out that the child's own knowledge develops through experience of adults guiding the child towards a more sophisticated solution to a task. In the case of the beaker play, for example, the adult might guide the child towards a systematic selection of beakers on the basis of size.

As we noted earlier, Vygotsky argued that there is a close link between language and thought. Initially, language—and the complex mental processes that go hand-in-hand with language—is only available to adults. The earliest thought of the child is pre-verbal. Thus, when adults carefully explain something difficult to a young child, they give the child access to intellectual processes that are normally based on language. In this way, social relationships provide the child's initial contact with language-based intellectual processes and the context in which the child can learn to internalise these same processes which, with further development, will later operate autonomously as verbal thought.

Vygotsky called this pattern of development, in which intellectual processes move from being external (i.e. social) to internal, "the general, genetic law of cultural development". He describes it as follows:

> All the basic forms of the adult's verbal social interaction with the child later become mental functions … Any function in the child's cultural development appears twice, or on two planes. First it appears on the social plane and then on the psychological plane. First it appears between people, as an interpsychological category and then within the child, as an intrapsychological category. This is equally true with regard to voluntary attention, logical memory, the formation of concepts and the development of volition. (Vygotsky, 1988, p. 73)

Play is also related to the concept of the ZPD. Although play functions in the absence of explicit instructions from the adult, it may make use of culturally provided artifacts to support it (toys) and it often involves trying out culturally defined roles (teacher, mother, father, doctor, bus driver). Vygotsky (1976, p. 552) says: "In play the child functions above his average age, above his usual everyday behaviour, in play he is head high above himself". The zone of proximal development, therefore, measures the "leading edge" of the developmental process, where teaching, instruction, and the peer group may exercise their greatest effect.

## John Bowlby

Whereas Piaget's and Vygotsky's theories had mainly addressed the child's intellectual development, John Bowlby was primarily concerned with emotional development. His theory, although an eclectic mixture of ideas from various developmental disciplines, was ultimately based in the Freudian psychoanalytic tradition (see the panel on page 25). Bowlby was a child psychoanalyst whose main professional concern was with factors giving rise to psychopathology. His theory offers a critical synthesis of evidence from modern research in psychology and biology with some of the more traditional psychoanalytic concerns about development.

**John Bowlby's theory of attachment.** A key idea in Bowlby's theory is that the mother provides a secure base from which the developing infant can explore the world and periodically return in safety. The emotional attachment of the baby to the mother normally provides the infant with a sense of safety and security. The evolutionary function of such attachment behaviour is thought to be to protect the child from predators, and the further implications are that emotionally secure bonds between individuals have basic survival value in the short term and contribute to the reproductive success of the species in the long term.

Bowlby was much influenced by the work of Harlow (Harlow, McGaugh, & Thompson, 1971) who tested the psychoanalytic theory that the infant becomes attached to the mother because she satisfies the child's basic needs, such as hunger and thirst. In psychoanalytic theory these are known as primary drives, which constitute fundamental psychological motives. The assumption that the child learns to love the mother because she satisfies these basic needs has been nicknamed the "cupboard love" theory. Harlow pointed out that mothers not only provide food, they also provide comfort and warmth. Harlow studied the effects of maternal deprivation on infant rhesus monkeys reared in social isolation. They grew up to be severely incapacitated in their social relationships and ultimately they became very poor, incapable parents.

Harlow tested the primary drive theory in a study in which he gave baby rhesus monkeys the choice of clinging to a comfortable cloth-covered support which did not dispense food or to an uncomfortable wire support which dispensed milk. The monkeys would feed on the wire support but immediately returned to cling to the preferred cloth-covered support, which suggested that contact comfort was more important than simply being provided with food.

## Brief biography of John Bowlby (1907–1990)

John Bowlby was born in London in 1907. He was the fourth of six children of a distinguished family. His mother, May Mostyn, married a successful London surgeon, Major-General Sir Anthony Bowlby, who eventually become Royal Surgeon to King Edward VII and King George V. John Bowlby followed his father into medicine and gained a first-class honours degree in pre-clinical sciences and psychology at Cambridge University (1929). Before going on to finish his medical studies, he worked in a school for maladjusted children where he became convinced that some of the problems of the severely disturbed, anti-social young people might be explained as the result of faulty relationships between parents and children. He was particularly interested in disturbed adolescents, who seemed incapable of giving or receiving affection, a deficiency that he thought to be a consequence of prolonged lack of affection in early childhood. He subsequently trained as a psychoanalyst and qualified in medicine and psychiatry at the University of London in the early 1930s.

Bowlby became a child psychoanalyst and worked during the 1930s at the London Child Guidance Clinic. He was sympathetic to the analytic approach but rather critical of some of its more unscientific aspects. He developed a unique synthesis of method and theory drawn from the traditions of Freudian psychoanalysis, from observation and recording of natural history, from field studies of behaviour in the natural environment (especially the work of Lorenz and Tinbergen in ethology), from comparative studies of attachment in non-human primates (especially the work of Harlow in the USA and Hinde in Britain), and from cognitive developmental psychology.

The lynchpin of his theory was the attempt to explain the formation of the earliest attachment bonds between infant and mother along ethological principles reformulated in human terms. His original concern was to explain the consequences of severe disruption of the attachment bond between mother and child for personality development. His theory placed less emphasis on the traditional Freudian account of infantile sexuality, with its oral, anal, and phallic stages in the formation of personality (see the Table on p. 29). Instead, he argued for a primary emotional bond between the infant and the mother which is unrelated to infantile sexuality (see Holmes, 1993, for a sympathetic account of Bowlby's life and work).

Fig. 2.4   John Bowlby © The Guardian, 119 Farringdon Road, London, England. Photographer: Martin Argles.

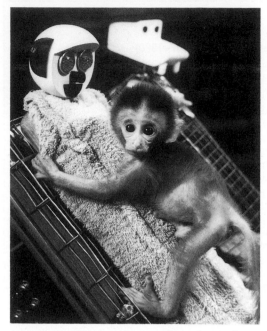

In further tests Harlow showed that, given the choice of a comfortable cloth-covered support that dispensed milk and an identical one that did not, the monkeys preferred the support that dispensed milk. However, during the first 20 days the infant monkeys actually preferred a heated wire support to a comfortable but cold cloth support, which suggests that warmth was also a factor. Thereafter, they preferred the cloth support, even though it did not provide food. These results led Harlow to argue that the Freudian "cupboard love" theory of attachment was inadequate. Instead, Harlow argued that a multifactorial theory of attachment in rhesus monkeys is required, which includes such species-specific factors as the desire in monkeys to cling, as well as the more general factors of contact comfort and motherly warmth.

Fig. 2.5 Contact comfort in the rhesus monkey. Photograph courtesy of Harlow Primate Laboratory, University of Wisconsin.

In monkeys, the mother initially provides basic "organic affection", and attachment develops as the mother meets the physical and emotional needs of the infant. This, in turn, provides a sense of safety and security as the infant monkey becomes more mobile and ready for autonomy. The monkey's curiosity about the external environment has as its counterpart the sense of emotional security which provides the necessary courage for exploration.

According to Harlow, the longer-term importance of the love of the mother for her offspring and, reciprocally, the attachment of the infant monkey to the mother, is that it establishes a sense of basic trust which is preparatory for peer (age-related) social relationships. These emotional relationships, in turn, lay the groundwork for heterosexual relationships and for eventual satisfactory parenting in a long-term cycle of species reproduction.

Bowlby applied some of Harlow's ideas to human development. He argued that the first attachment bond in humans is analogous to that in rhesus monkeys but it is based on species-specific human behaviours. In human infants clinging is poorly developed, so crying and smiling serve the purpose of eliciting maternal caretaking in the early months. As the child becomes more autonomous, the quality of attachment of the infant to the parent is an important factor in regulating the child's willingness to explore. The emotionally secure child uses the mother as a base, to which the child can periodically return as he or she discovers novelty in the surroundings, while keeping the mother in "eyeshot" (see pp. 107–110 for more on the details of the formation of human attachment bonds).

A secure attachment relationship is thought to lead the child into a range of psychologically healthy developmental pathways. Bowlby argued that insecure patterns of attachment contribute to the formation of a neurotic personality because they take the child down psychologically unhealthy developmental pathways. That is, either the malformation or the forcible disruption of attachment bonds may progressively give rise to personality problems and mental ill-health. One example, for which some evidence exists, concerns the relationship between disruption of attachment in young girls and the onset of depression in adulthood. Girls whose mothers had died before their twelfth birthday were found to be at much increased risk of severe depression as adults (Brown & Harris, 1980). It is important to note, however, that such an outcome of disrupted attachment is not inevitable. Large-scale epidemeological studies which have explored the role of family experiences as antecedents of depression and anxiety disorders in later life show that many factors can lessen the long-term effects of even severe disruption, as when a parent dies. These include good relationships with grandparents, success in school, making a good supportive marriage, and being of resilient personality (Holmes, 1993).

An early, practical application of Bowlby's ideas arose in the changes he effected in the hospitalisation of young children. As a result of his work on prolonged maternal separation not understood by the child, mothers from the 1950s were allowed to remain in hospital with their young children. A very great deal of research is now devoted to studying the formation and elaboration of patterns of attachment between parents and children in cultures as diverse as the United States, Britain, and Japan.

## Stage theories and transitions in development

Modern psychology has accumulated a great deal of knowledge about human development, starting even before birth. One of the fundamental questions that has been addressed concerns whether the course of development is best understood as a continuous process of change or whether there are sharp discontinuities, or stages, in the organisation of behaviour. Piaget introduced the concept of stages in his theory of cognitive development (see the panel on Piaget on p. 19).

The concept of a stage has a rather specific usage. It is intended to convey the fact that there is a change in the quality or characteristics of the individual that has arisen as a function of development. The American psychologist, John Flavell (1993), has suggested the following criteria for a stage in development:

1. Stages are distinguished by qualitative changes. It is not a matter of simply being able to do more of something but it also involves doing it differently. For instance, babies usually move around first by crawling (or bottom-shuffling) and only later by walking. These are qualitatively different types of locomotion and therefore this aspect of motor development has at least one of the characteristics of a developmental stage.
2. The transition from one stage to another is marked by simultaneous changes in a great many of the other aspects of a child's behaviour. For example, when children first learn to speak, which involves understanding the symbolic value of words, they also behave as if objects have symbolic properties in their play, when they pretend that a brick is a car, or a doll is a person. That is, there is a widespread effect of acquiring the capacity to treat the world in terms of symbol systems.
3. Stage transitions are typically rapid. A good example is the adolescent growth spurt where a child may, in a few months, gain several inches in height and weight. Similar, rapid reorganisations can be observed in other areas, as when the child acquires language and there is an exponential increase in the number of words learned once the first 20 or so words have been acquired (although many stages are actually involved).

As we have said, the major modern stage theory of development is due to Jean Piaget, but it should be noted that other stage theories were also put forward by Freud (who spoke for example of the oral, anal, and phallic stages of infancy and the Oedipal stage of early childhood) and by Vygotsky. Each of these authors was influenced by the evolutionary implications of Darwin's theory, which accounts for the resemblance between them. The Table opposite gives a comparison of the stages proposed by Piaget, Vygotsky, and Freud.

Although not all psychologists would agree with the specific details of any one of these stage theories, there is reasonable agreement that human development actually comprises a mixture of continuous and discontinuous changes, as in the epigenetic landscape diagram (Figure 2.2) where development proceeds along one valley (continuous change) until it trans-

### Comparison of major stages of different theorists
### (Adapted from Cole & Cole, 1993)

| Folk Wisdom | Piaget | Freud [a] | Vygotsky |
|---|---|---|---|
| Infancy<br>0–2 years | Sensori-motor | Oral<br>Anal<br>Phallic | Affiliation |
| Early childhood<br>2–7 years | Pre-operational | Oedipal | Play |
| Middle childhood<br>7–12 years | Concrete<br>operational | Latency | Learning |
| Adolescence<br>12–19 years | Formal<br>operational | Genital activity | Peer |
| Adulthood<br>19–55 years | Formal<br>operational | | Work |
| Early old age<br>55–70 | | | Theorising |
| Late old age<br>70+ | | | |

[a]Bowlby did not subscribe strictly to the Freudian stage theory. He denied that there is a strict linear succession of stages in development and adopted instead a stage theory based on Waddington's epigenetic landscape. On this account, several lines of development are possible, the outcome depending on the particular organism–environment interaction (see Figure 2.2). Other developmental theorists such as Erik Erikson have also based their accounts broadly on Freudian theory. Erikson extended his theory to development through the lifespan. His theory is summarised on p. 237.

fers to a new valley at a choice point (discontinuous change). Transitions in development result in changes in the organisation of the developing child, while retaining some continuity with previous stages.

In the case of the adult, we are often more concerned with the ways in which discontinuous changes, for example from employment to unemployment, generate individual development. Although such experiences may result in a regularly reported sequence of emotional experiences, there is less agreement that these are really developmental stages which fulfil the criteria listed earlier (see also Chapter 13). Sometimes psychologists use the idea of stages too loosely, merely to describe a sequence or succession of behaviours, and this need not imply any qualitative reorganisation of constituent processes.

# Methods of study in developmental psychology

Before concluding this chapter, it will be useful to say a little about the methods that have been adopted to study development. Development takes place as a process over time; it is influenced by many factors including nutrition, parenting, schooling, and biological growth. It is not possible to study all the factors that influence development at the same time and so it has been necessary to design research methods which allow sources of error in observation to be controlled.

Methods of observation include simple diary records, of which Darwin's study is an early example (see p. 6), observations made in natural settings as in studies of children's language development made in the home (see pp. 124–129) and laboratory studies of spontaneous behaviour as, for example, when play is observed under standardised conditions using an identical environment containing identical toys . The most formal method is to make systematic experiments as, for example, when objects are hidden under different conditions to assess the search skills of babies (see pp. 92–100).

In order to observe the process of development it is necessary to make comparisons between people at different ages, and this raises methodological complications because people differ along so many dimensions. The solution to these problems has been to sample the population very carefully in order to make controlled comparisons between selected groups. Developmental research is also constrained by time. Where developmental changes occur rapidly, as in infancy for example, it is economical to carry out *longitudinal* studies in which the same child is studied on successive occasions. However, where long-term developmental relations

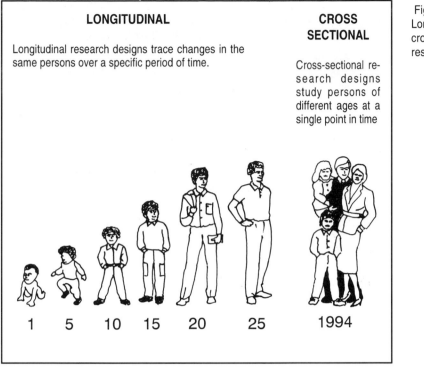

**LONGITUDINAL**

Longitudinal research designs trace changes in the same persons over a specific period of time.

**CROSS SECTIONAL**

Cross-sectional research designs study persons of different ages at a single point in time

1  5  10  15  20  25  1994

Fig. 2.6
Longitudinal and cross-sectional research designs.

are of interest, it may only be feasible to carry out *cross-sectional studies* where groups of children of different ages are compared to obtain an understanding of the typical characteristics of children at any given age. The panel on pages 32–33 summarises the main characteristics of longitudinal and cross-sectional research methods in developmental psychology.

## Conclusion and summary

Modern theory in developmental psychology is based on biological and social insights from evolution, from embryology, from our understanding of processes of physical growth, from social, linguistic, and cultural processes. As a scientific discipline, one of its major concerns is with the origins of knowledge and the contributions of self-initiated and social factors to cognitive growth. We have seen that evolutionary ideas permeate the discipline and inform almost all theories of development.

Much contemporary research is based on, or is a reaction to, Piaget's, Vygotsky's, and Bowlby's theories. Their ideas will be evaluated in greater detail in subsequent chapters which will review contemporary findings

# A note about research design and methodology

Over the last 100 years two different kinds of research design have emerged which, in inter-relation, fulfil the demands of scientific investigation. In a *longitudinal design* the developmental psychologist collects information about the same person at different ages. Thus, if the behaviour of children at 5, 6, and 7 years is to be compared, the same children would be tested when they were 5, 6, and 7 years old. Obviously, this method may require a prolonged commitment of the researcher if changes occurring over several years are to be studied, but a major advantage is that differences among individuals can be taken into account.

A number of the studies that we discuss in this book adopt a longitudinal design. For example, Chapter 7 summarises a study by Bates, Bretherton, and Snyder (1988), of early language development. Bates et al. studied children from the time they were 10 months old until they were just over 2 years old. Their main interest was to look at the relationship between very early language ability and later ability. They found that there were important consistencies between children's language in the first year of life and their language several months later. They also found some important inconsistencies. For example, children's understanding of words before their first birthday was highly predictive of how well they could understand language at 16 months. However, early comprehension was not predictive of how well children were talking at 20 months. Analysis of change within the individual is essential where there is large individual variation in development, as in the case of language.

In other cases, however, it is possible to assume that children will show a high degree of similarity in their development. Here it is appropriate to use a *cross-sectional* design comparing two or more different groups of people who are of different ages. Unlike the longitudinal design, each group of people is seen at only one age. Thus, if a researcher wished to study development between 5 and 7 years, three different groups of children would be selected who were 5, 6, and 7 years old respectively.

A cross-sectional design has the advantage that studies can be carried out much more quickly, to reveal the general way in which behaviour and ability changes with age, and they are often used when a wide age-range is to be compared. However, cross-sectional designs will not always reveal as much about individual differences in development.

Because they are less time-consuming to carry out, the majority of studies in developmental psychology employ cross-sectional designs. One such study, which was carried out by Hughes and reported by Donaldson (1978), is described on pp.169–172. This experiment was concerned with the developing ability of children between the ages of 3.5 to 5 years to understand what another person can see from a particular viewpoint. In order to test this, a group of children was selected so as to span the age range. They were all given the same task which required them to play a game in which they had to hide a boy doll out of sight of a policeman doll. The hiding game was played with a model which could be varied in complexity so that it was increasingly difficult to tell whether the policeman could see the boy.

The results showed that the youngest children could almost always tell whether the policeman could see the doll providing that the layout of the model was very simple. However, as the task was made more difficult by increasing the complexity of the model, the younger children became less accurate. The oldest children in the study could perform accurately even with the most complex layout.

In a cross-sectional design, it is very important that the children who are compared differ only in age and not in any other respect that might affect the outcome of the experiment. For example, it is generally important that the children at the different age levels have similar levels of ability. Sometimes researchers use *intelligence tests* (see pp. 214–221) to select children of similar ability levels for

(continued)

## A note about research design and methodology (continued)

the different age groups. Other factors that may be relevant include gender (male or female), socio-economic status of parents, birth order (only child, first born, second born, etc.), handedness (left- or right-handed) and whether children live in an urban area or in the country. Of course, not all of these factors will be relevant in every study. It will depend on what aspect of development is being investigated.

Some factors about the selection of subjects are also of concern in longitudinal designs. In both cross-sectional and longitudinal research designs it is essential to allow for effects of the *cohort* being studied. A cohort is a group of people whose development has occurred under similar social, historical conditions.

People born in the same era may share environments that are not held in common with people born in a different era, and the long-term effects of such environmental differences may confound our investigations. For example, nutritional standards have changed significantly over the last 50 years in western Europe and the quality and quantity of food available to children born in 1940 were significantly different to that available in 1990. This, in turn, may have repercussions for many aspects of physical and mental development, such as the time of onset of adolescence and subsequent changes in behaviour and cognition, or on the ways in which we age. Educational practices have also changed and these, too, have had an important influence on people's ability.

In Chapter 13, we discuss a study by Schaie (1990) that illustrates the importance of cohort effects. Schaie was interested in whether people's mathematical and reasoning abilities had changed over time. He tested a large sample of adults born between 1889 and 1959 and found that reasoning skills had consistently increased: adults born in the 1950s had the best reasoning skills and adults born in the 1890s had the worst. However, the pattern for mathematical ability was not one of simple improvement with time. There was an increase in number skills among adults born between 1889 and 1910 followed by a period of stability until 1924.

Between 1924 and 1959, however, there was a consistent decline in ability. These findings are important for studying the effects of ageing because they show that intellectual functioning is not only a function of age but also of the year in which someone was born.

In addition to the choice between a longitudinal and cross-sectional research design, developmental psychologists also have a variety of different methods of data collection available to them. Many studies continue to use *observation* of naturalistic behaviour. In recent years, the opportunity for observation has been greatly extended by the use of videotaping which allows behaviour to be analysed in much greater detail. Videotaping also allows the same segment of behaviour to be viewed over and over again to check on the accuracy of observation. Other methods of studying development are through *experiments* and the use of *clinical methods*, such as interviews and standardised tests. Research based on all these approaches will be described throughout this book.

The choice of research design and method of data collection will depend on the aims of the research. A combination of longitudinal and cross-sectional research designs, using observational, clinical and experimental methods, is characteristic of the best of modern work. When combined with *training methods* where, for example, a carefully controlled comparison is made between matched groups who receive different training experiences, it is possible to arrive at causal hypotheses about factors influencing development.

For instance, it has been shown that pre-school children who receive both training in rhyming sounds and experience with letters of the alphabet progress faster in learning to read than comparison groups of children who experienced comparable but different training. This suggests that the combined experience of rhyming and letters of the alphabet assists the child in learning how written letter groups relate to sounds when learning to read (Bryant, 1991; see pp. 206–207 for more details).

on cognitive, social, and applied aspects of developmental psychology. Each of these theories shares the assumption that development occurs in stages, although they differ in their main focus. Piaget's theory is most concerned with the mechanisms of intellectual development and the acquisition of knowledge, whereas Vygotsky's main contribution was to our understanding of the way in which culture influences development, through language and the social and material structure of society. Bowlby was an eclectic thinker who drew on Freudian theory and many other sources in biology, psychology, and ethology to propound an original theory of interpersonal relationships and socio-emotional development.

As in other branches of psychology, there are important methodological constraints which operate in developmental psychology to ensure that research meets the standards of good science. There are different kinds of research design and a variety of different ways of gathering data according to the question that a particular researcher is addressing. These various theoretical and methodological approaches will be explored throughout the remainder of this book.

## Further reading

Boden, M. (1979). *Piaget*. Glasgow: Collins Fontana.
Holmes, J. (1993). *John Bowlby and attachment theory*. London: Routledge.
Kozulin, A. (1990). *Vygotsky's psychology*. Hemel Hempstead: Harvester.
Piaget, J. & Inhelder, B. (1969). *The psychology of the child*. London: Routledge & Kegan Paul.

PART 2

Infancy

# Pre-natal development 3

**M**ost textbook accounts of early development begin with the abilities of the newborn baby, perhaps because, until recently, development before birth has been so difficult to observe. However, in recent years the invention of specialised techniques has made possible a number of fascinating studies of pre-natal development which offer a much more detailed picture of the origins of the developmental process. We will begin this chapter with a general description of the pre-natal period.

Pre-natal development is traditionally divided into the germinal stage (from conception to implantation of the fertilised egg in the uterine wall at about 2 weeks); the embryonic stage (from 2 weeks to 7 weeks when the major organs and limbs are formed) and the fetal stage (from 8 weeks to birth). Figure 3.1 summarises the main stages of prenatal development and Figure 3.2 shows the sensitive periods when the developing embryo is particularly susceptible to teratogens (foreign substances). These risk factors reveal in their own way that pre-natal development depends on the interaction of the developing fetus with the environment, as the epigenetic landscape model would predict (see Figure 2.2). The concept of developmental stages is also readily apparent in pre-natal development where there are clear distinctions between the various forms of the developing embryo and fetus.

## Pre-natal development

Human gestation takes 40 weeks between conception and birth. As we noted earlier, the pre-natal period has traditionally been divided into three sub-stages:

**The germinal stage: From conception to 10 days.** The first two weeks after conception is primarily a period in which the fertilised egg (ovum) undergoes repeated division into identical copies. This stage ends when the fertilised ovum becomes implanted in the uterus. From then on, the cells begin to differentiate and take on specialised functions with the formation of the basic structures of the living organism.

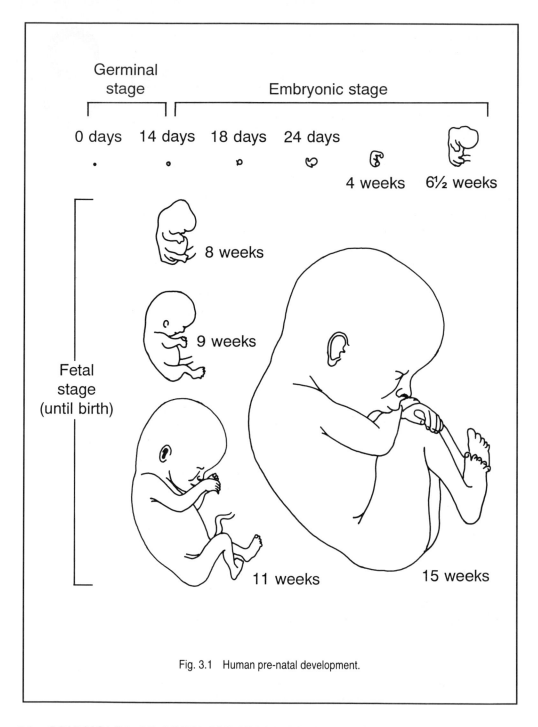

Fig. 3.1  Human pre-natal development.

**The embryonic stage: From 10 days to 7 weeks.**    During the embryonic stage, the embryo starts to take shape and various organs and cells take on specialised functions, as cells differentiate and begin to acquire different roles in the biological organisation. There is rapid differentiation of the fertilised egg, with the formation of limbs, fingers, and major sensory organs. By 8 weeks, the embryo is about 1 inch long, limb buds have appeared, and eyes and eyelids have begun to form.

The embryonic period is the danger period for German measles (rubella). Babies are at risk of being born blind and brain damaged if the virus is contracted during the first month (up to 47% of babies), the second month (22% of babies) or third month of pregnancy (7% of babies). Girls in Western societies are often immunised against rubella during adolescence to avoid problems caused by catching the disease when they reach reproductive age.

The importance of the pre-natal environment for the normal development of the embryo is vividly illustrated by the thalidomide tragedy. In the 1970s, pregnant women who had taken the drug thalidomide during early pregnancy, to alleviate morning sickness, gave birth to infants with various malformations. The site of malformation depended on the exact time after conception that the drug crossed the placenta to the developing embryo. At different points in development, the same dose of thalidomide resulted in different deformities, either to the legs, arms, or ears (see Figure 3.2).

One lesson from the thalidomide tragedy and the effects of rubella is that the interacting systems of the mother's intra-uterine environment and the developing embryo are extremely finely balanced. Development only seems inevitable when everything goes to plan. It is revealed to be under complex epigenetic control under these unfortunate conditions. Where abnormal environmental (or genetic) conditions obtain, the developing embryo may be forced down abnormal pathways at choice points in the epigenetic landscape, with resulting atypical development (see Figure 2.2).

**3. The fetal stage: From 8 to 38 weeks.**    The fetal stage coincides with major developments of the nervous system. The fetus rapidly takes on distinctively human characteristics so that by 12 weeks it is easily recognisable. By 16 weeks it is 6–7 inches long but it cannot survive outside the mother's body because the lungs are immature. By 23 weeks the fetus has a sleep–wake cycle synchronised with that of the mother.

The fetus continues to develop for the normal gestational term of 40 weeks. Like all biological phenomena there is natural variation in the time

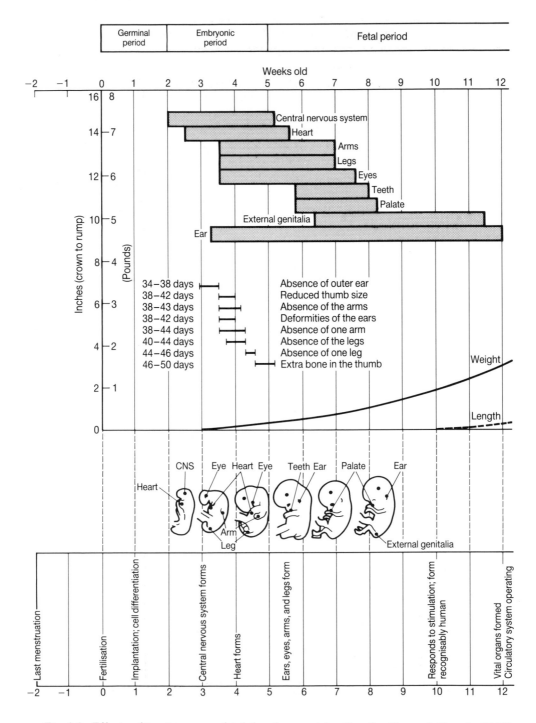

Fig. 3.2  Effects of teratogens on fetal development (partly after Saxen & Rapola, 1969).

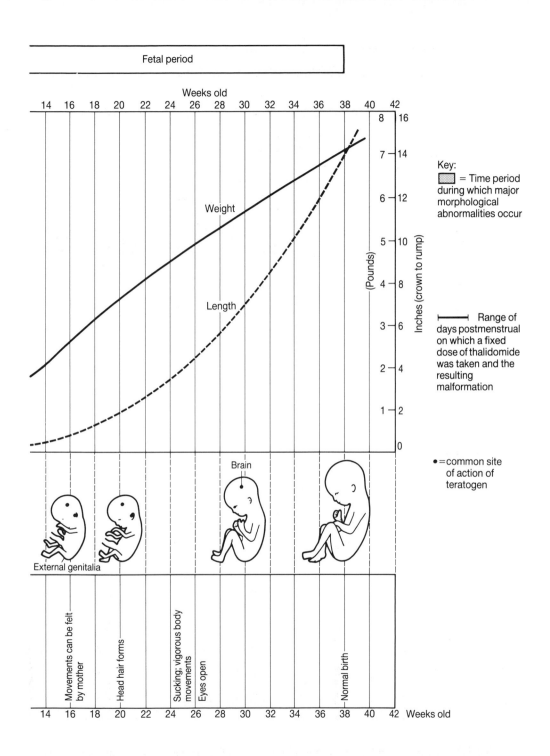

of onset of birth and in the duration of the birth process itself. For a first-born child, a natural labour may last as long as 13–14 hours.

Prematurity used to be defined as birth before 266 days, but some babies who are born early are of normal weight and health. Nowadays, fairly complicated measures of size in relation to date of conception are used and a birth weight of less than 2500 grammes (5.5 pounds) is used to define prematurity.

The normal baby at birth, around 40 weeks, weighs about 7 pounds and is about 21 inches long. The head, which has grown fastest *in utero*, is disproportionately larger than the body (see Figure 3.3). The head and neck make up about 30% of the total body volume compared with 15% at 6 years and only 10% in adults. It is worth remembering that the changing proportions of the body pose particular problems in gaining motor control—a point to which we will return in Chapter 5. Changes in body proportions also illustrate the epigenetic principle that different parts of the whole child may develop at different rates. *In utero*, the head grows fastest but, later in development, the proportions of the body change as hands and feet, shoulders, trunk, arms and legs have separate growth spurts (Sinclair, 1978).

In Western societies, where babies are usually born in hospital, the newborn is assessed for birth condition using simple standardised meas-

Fig. 3.3
Changes in body proportion with age. Adapted from Sinclair (1978).

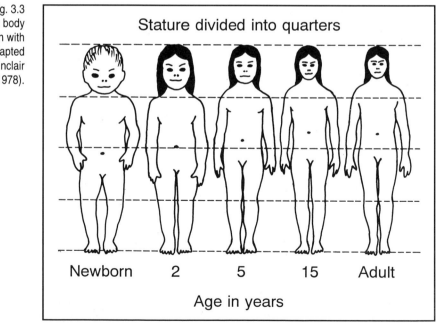

Stature divided into quarters

Newborn    2    5    15    Adult

Age in years

ures of physical well being, such as the *Apgar scale*, which gives a score based on measures such as skin colour, heart rate, muscle tone, and respiratory effort. Recently, more psychological tests, such as the *Brazleton scale*, have been devised to measure variables like ease of calming the newborn, irritability, and other temperamental characteristics. Characteristic reflexes, such as sucking, the rooting reflex (where the baby will turn towards stimulation of the cheek), and the stepping reflex (where the baby makes alternating movements of the legs when held with the feet touching a surface) may also be measured. These innate reflexes are culturally universal (Eibl-Eibesfeldt, 1989).

# Behaviour as a factor in prenatal development

Until recently, it was not possible to study the behaviour of the normally developing fetus except under very unusual circumstances. As a consequence, not very much was known about fetal behaviour before birth. Some of the most detailed and fascinating accounts have become available in recent years from developmental biologists and developmental neurologists. These reveal that the fetus is constantly active. The novel thesis being pursued by current investigators is that the continuous activity of fetuses may feedback into the growth process and give rise to the innate behaviours that can be observed in the newborn. Some of these innate behaviours may, in turn, be related to subsequent developments.

## Behaviour in the fetus

The developmental biologist M. Hofer (1981) has emphasised the importance of behaviour in pre-natal development. In a graphic phrase, he has described the transition from "cell to psyche" as "telling the story of development from a pair of cells to an infant that has a mind of its own". Hofer argues that interesting behavioural phenomena are to be observed as early as the fertilisation of the ovum by the sperm (see panel overleaf). Hofer stated that if humans could observe development from the moment that the fertilised egg is implanted in the uterine wall, we would have a different conception of our nature. Because basic aspects of intra-uterine development have been so long hidden from view, we have only recently become aware of some of its fundamental principles.

The very first detectable movements of the embryo are the heartbeats. The embryo is only 3 weeks old and ¼ of an inch long. This "behaviour" of heart beating occurs before there is any nervous system at all! The heartbeat is really a biochemical phenomenon, as muscle tissues "beat"

## Fertilisation of the ovum

Characteristics of the female fallopian tube (where the ovum is released) can influence which sperm eventually fertilises the egg. Female hormones from the ovary have a regulatory action on sperm transport. The sperm, too, have individual characteristics such as different swimming speeds. Hofer suggested that sperm must have some kind of navigational equipment, because they swim upstream even against a constant current. Hydraulic considerations may also need to be taken into account, as the sperm swim in schools, rather like fish. These are intriguing suggestions about the behaviours of the gametes, of which little is yet known, but they do bring home the important insight that sperm and ova are individual, single-celled organisms, each holding half the genetic material (haploid organisms) needed for human development.

Only about 0.1 of 1% of 350 million sperm actually get as far as the fallopian tube where the ovum is. A sperm penetrates the egg, the "swimming" tail breaks off, and the nuclei of sperm and egg combine their genetic material to form a single organism with the full complement of genes. Recent evidence reviewed by Hofer suggests that, after fertilisation, the female immune system coats the remaining sperm in the uterus with an antibody that renders them incapable of fertilisation. Thus, numerous factors exercise a selective effect on which sperm actually fertilises the egg.

when placed in saline solution. Soon, a regular rhythm is established and, by 5 weeks , the whole embryo is dominated by the rhythm of the heart.

The fact that activity is intrinsic to the developing embryo gives a clue to the cause of development. As Piaget once said, the basic motive for any living system is to function; being alive involves maintaining the integrity of the living system, however simple, through the vital processes which maintain life. The organism, even at its most elementary stage of development, exists under the dynamic conditions of energy exchange with the surroundings that will eventually generate the sequence of transformations in its own functioning. Piaget called this process—giving rise to a directed trajectory of development—"homeorhesis" (by comparison to "homeostasis", where self-regulation serves to maintain a steady state of the system).

Only after the heart starts beating does the nervous system begin to form. Hooker, in the 1930s, observed fetuses 1 inch long, aged 8 weeks. He showed that light stimulation of the fetus, with a hair, in the area of the mouth, led to mouth opening. Stimulation also tended to produce movements of the limbs and trunk. By 16 weeks, the fetal response to external touch is localised to the area of contact.

These early studies presupposed fetal responses to be the result of reflexes to external stimulation. Little was known about spontaneous fetal movement patterns. Although pregnant women often note feeling fetal movements at about 16 weeks gestation, they are only aware of the most gross movements. In fact, depending on the measuring technique, up to 20,000 movements per day can be recorded in the fetus of less than 16 weeks gestational age.

The advent of real-time ultrasonic scanning in the 1970s has offered a safe means of imaging fetal movements *in utero*. Using this technique, ultra high-frequency sound (outside the audible range) is transmitted into the pregnant woman's abdomen. The echoes of the sound are picked up electronically and converted to a visual image which provides a view of the fetus as it moves. Skilled observers can interpret these images to obtain information about fetal behaviours. Figure 3.4 shows an ultrasound picture of a fetus.

## Fetal movement patterns

De Vries, Visser, and Prechtl (1984) have described 15 different movement patterns in the 15-week fetus. They have observed fetal breathing movements, where the amniotic fluid is regularly inhaled and exhaled, stretching movements and turning movements. Later in fetal development, they observed thumb-sucking. Under the relatively weightless conditions of the fetal environment, these movement patterns are well coordinated.

### Spontaneous fetal movement patterns

The advent of real-time ultrasonic scanning has enabled, for the first time, detailed observation of the behaviour of the fetus in the natural environment. Ultrasound (sound at frequencies well above the normal range of human hearing) is harmlessly transmitted through the abdomen of the pregnant woman. The sound is reflected from the fetus (and other internal structures in the mother) and these "echoes" are turned into moving pictures by a computer. This allows the spontaneous behaviour of the fetus to be observed. The technique has revealed a wide variety of patterns of movement, many of which are similar to the behaviour that will be observed later in post-natal life. The developing pattern of fetal movements is summarised in the panel overleaf. (These observations are summarised from De Vries et al., 1984, pp. 50-53.)

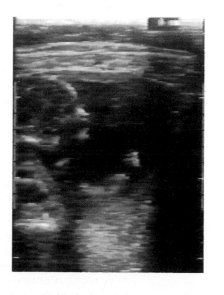

Fig. 3.4 (right)  Ultrasound image of a fetus at 15 weeks.

## Developing movement patterns in the fetus

| Week | | Week | |
|---|---|---|---|
| 7 | **Just discernible movements** — Between 7 and 8.5 weeks a small and slow shifting of the fetal contours can be seen. Small size of the fetus (about 2 cm) and limit of resolution of scanning equipment restricts detailed analysis. | 10 | **Hand–face contact** — Hand slowly touches face and fingers frequently extend and flex. |
| 8 | **Startle** — A quick generalised movement, lasting about 1 second, always initiated in the limbs and sometimes spreading to neck and trunk. | 10 | **Rotation of fetus** — The fetus can rapidly change position by a complex rotation either of the head in relation to the trunk (somersault type of movement) or by alternating stepping movements of the legs which result in rotation around the hips. |
| 8 | **General movements** — The whole body moves but no distinctive pattern or sequence of body parts can be observed. These movements may cause the fetus to shift in position. The movements are graceful in character. | 10– 11 | **Stretch and yawn** — This pattern of behaviour strongly resembles the species-typical yawning pattern, with elevation and rotation of the arms and prolonged wide opening of jaws followed by rapid closure of the mouth. |
| 9 | **Hiccup** — Jerky contraction and abrupt displacement of the diaphragm, lasting about 1 second and occurring in rapid succession. | 12 | **Finger movements** — The fingers can move independently of each other. |
| 10 | **Breathing movements** — Fetal breathing movements obviously do not involve inhalation of air. A regular pattern of movement of diaphragm, thorax, and abdomen can be observed, sometimes in combination with jaw opening and swallowing of amniotic fluid. | 14 | **Rotation of the hand** — The hand moves at the wrist, independently of movement of the fingers. |
| | | 16 | **Global extension** — Feet and head thrust against opposite uterine walls. |
| 9 | **Isolated arm or leg movements** — Rapid or slow extension and flexion movements of the arm or leg, can be accompanied by rotation of the limb without involvement of other body parts | 18 | **Eye movements** — Well-controlled, endogenously generated, lateral scanning movements of the eyes can be observed, although the fetus cannot be seeing anything as there is insufficient light in the womb. |
| 9– 10 | **Retroflexion, anteroflexion and rotation of the head** — The head is slowly displaced backwards, sometimes with jaw opening and tongue movements, or the head may rotate from side to side around the midline. Forward displacement of the head may be accompanied by hand–face contact when sucking may be observed. | 24 | **Thumb-sucking** — The hand is brought to the mouth and repetitive jaw movements can be observed. |

Some of the behaviours show a pre-adaptive organisation that will be essential for post-natal life, of which fetal breathing movements may be an example.

At about 17 or 18 weeks, the amount of fetal activity drops and a stage transition occurs which lasts to the 24th week. It has been suggested that this relatively quiescent period coincides with the formation of the higher regions of the brain which will modulate the behaviours previously controlled by mid-brain centres. After the 24th week, finer degrees of movement control are observed, including expressive facial movements. Fetal activity resumes, in the increasingly cramped living quarters, and is now subject to sleep–wake cycles. A 40-minute cycle of activity can be observed, which is endogenously generated and continues after birth, and a 96-minute cycle, which disappears after birth and which is linked to the mother's sleep cycle. By 30 weeks gestational age, rapid eye movement sleep (REM) can be observed in the fetus. This is a phase in the sleep–wake cycle which, in adults, is associated with dreaming but which, in the fetus, is more likely to be related to the cycles of biochemical activity of the brain. At 32 weeks, about 70–80% of the time is spent in REM sleep, associated with the fetal "breathing" movements mentioned earlier.

The first postural reflex, to be observed at 28 weeks, is the tonic neck reflex (TNR). In this movement pattern the arm and leg, on the side to which the head is turned, extend and the opposite arm and leg are flexed. This "fencer posture" continues to the 8th post-natal month and it is thought to have the effect, once the baby is born, of bringing the baby's hand into the visual field. The grasp reflex is also present by 28 weeks.

The spontaneous movement patterns of the fetus may serve not only to exercise the developing system but also to provide the system with feedback. Some evidence comes from a condition known as *fetal alcohol syndrome*, in which the babies of alcoholic mothers suffer from malformed joints. Among other symptoms, the articulation of the limbs is abnormal and this is thought to arise because the alcohol passing across the placenta anaesthetises the fetus. This prevents the normal patterns of movements which aid the growing joints to take their correct shape. Experiments in chicks have shown that as little as 2 days of restricted leg movements during the sensitive period for formation of the joints is sufficient to result in abnormalities. Another possible function of pre-natal activity is that it provides a high level of input to the developing ears, eyes, and other sensory receptors. The cutaneous (skin), taste, and olfactory (smell) receptors, the vestibular and auditory systems are all functional by the 24th gestational week. The visual system is functional by the 26th week. Finally, the continuous rotation and "crawling" movements of the young fetus may prevent adhesion to the uterine wall.

The implication is that fetal behaviour contributes to normal development—it is not simply a question of automatic maturation, nor is the fetus simply a reflexive responder. Spontaneous movement, graceful and complexly patterned, is generated by the fetus. De Vries et al. (1984) list a number of observed movement patterns (see panel on page 46).

## Continuity from pre- to post-natal life

The interesting question is whether there is any relation between pre-natal movement patterns and post-natal behaviour. The transition from womb to world involves the possibility of new types of action in which the extent of movement, the additional weight of one's own body, and the possibility of using vision to control activity did not exist before. It is very likely that there is a continuous relationship between some fetal movement patterns and later forms of behaviour, across the transition brought about by birth.

For example, De Vries et al. describe a stretch and yawn pattern at 10 weeks fetal age. With such an obvious and universal behaviour we are tempted to suppose continuity in the organisation of yawning and stretching movements throughout the lifespan:

> A complex motor pattern, always at a slow speed, consists of forceful extension of the back, retroflexion of the head, external rotation and elevation of the arms. The yawn is similar to the yawn observed after birth, prolonged wide opening of the jaws followed by quick closure, often with retroflexion of the head and sometimes elevation of the arms. (De Vries et al., 1984, p. 53)

Other fetal behaviours are less obviously related to later ones but it is nevertheless worth considering the possibility that species-typical and universal patterns of action may have inbuilt biological roots. Among the fetal movement patterns that are of interest is one in which the fetus rotates in the womb by making regular crawling movements. Prechtl describes the rotation of the fetus at 10 weeks as follows:

> Rotation occurs around the saggital or transverse axis, complete change of position around the transverse axis is achieved by complex general movement, including alternating leg movements. Total change in position can be achieved in as little as two seconds but may take longer. (De Vries et al., 1984 p. 53)

The question is whether this fetal rotation is related to later patterns of locomotion of crawling and walking. It has been known for some time that newborn babies will make the so-called "stepping reflex". If the newborn baby is supported in an upright posture, so that there is some pressure on the sole of the foot, this will elicit a cyclic stepping movement, as the legs alternate in walking movements. Such motor patterns have generally been considered to be reflexes, which disappear as the baby matures.

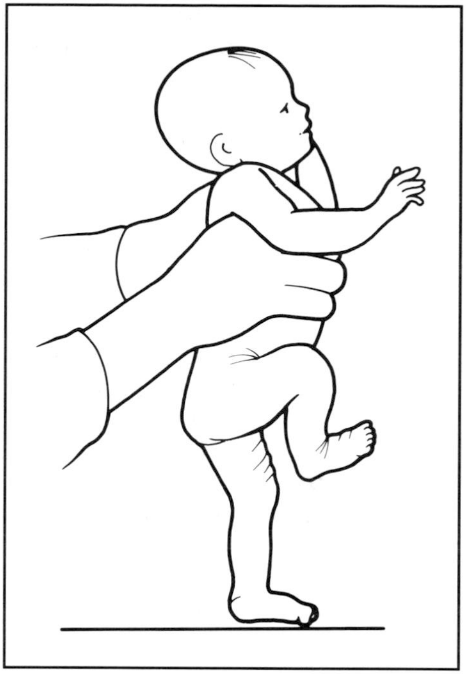

A variety of explanations have been put forward for the disappearance of the stepping reflex. For example, it has been argued that development of the cerebral cortex (the outer layer of the brain) results in the inhibition of these motor patterns. An important recent insight has been that babies put on weight so quickly after birth, especially in the upper legs where fat is deposited, that the legs become too heavy for the infant to lift. This fat deposit acts as insulation because the baby's ability to regulate its own temperature is still underdeveloped. The reflexive stepping movement actually re-emerges when the baby is held so that the legs are under water and their weight is thereby reduced.

Fig. 3.5
Stepping reflex in a newborn baby.

Thelen (1984) has argued that the disappearance of stepping is illusory, and that there is a relationship between stepping and later crawling and walking. She suggests that the patterning of walking movements is innate but that babies must gain sufficient strength to support their own weight before upright locomotion becomes possible. So, the argument here is that there may be continuity between the stepping movements observed as the fetus rotates in the womb, the crawling movements of the 6-month-old baby, and the later typical alternating walking movements of upright locomotion.

Of course, there may also be a discontinuity between neonatal stepping movements and walking at the end of the first year. Other aspects of development are also proceeding in parallel during the first year. In particular, babies are developing sophisticated intentions and some theorists have argued that humans walk when they do, typically at the end of the first year of life, because the general change in intellectual development enables the baby to use the motor system as a means to an end. That is, babies walk when they do in order to fulfil their intentions to explore. The behaviour of walking, typically seen at the end of the first year, emerges perhaps as a combination of an innate motor pattern, which is continuous with the behaviour seen in the womb, and intellectual processes that arise later in development and which bring walking under voluntary control.

# The sensory capacities of the neonate

In the final part of this chapter, we will consider the basic sensory capabilities of the newborn. In technical terminology the newborn is known as a *neonate*. The first 10 days after birth is the neonatal period. (The reader seeking further information will find that Bremner, 1994, offers an extensive overview of perception in the newborn.)

## Vision

Relative to adult standards, vision in the newborn is very poor. However, we need to beware of falling into the trap of supposing that it is therefore inadequate for the infant's purposes. Various specialised measures of visual functioning show that the finest spatial detail that a newborn can see is very much less than an adult, but it is perfectly adequate for the large social objects, such as faces, that the very young infant will frequently encounter. Neonates can discriminate between stationary black and white stripes 1/8th of an inch wide and a uniform grey surface. By 3 months, the stripes can be as narrow as 1/64th of an inch wide. Moving the cards, so that the stripes attract visual following movements, gives a finer measure of visual discrimination.

At birth, the lens of the eye, which brings the visual image to a sharp focus at the retina by a series of muscles that change its shape, is not yet fully functional. This means that the eyes of the neonate have a fixed focal length. Only objects that are 21cm from the eyes of the newborn will be perceived in sharp focus. The fixed focal length arises because, until the infant is about 3 months old, the lens does not accommodate by changing the curvature of its surface in order to bring objects at different distances into focus.

Interestingly enough, the fixed focal length of 21cm coincides with the average distance of the mother's face from the baby, when the infant is held in the mother's arms. So, even though distant objects will be blurred, important social objects can be seen from birth. Furthermore, because the

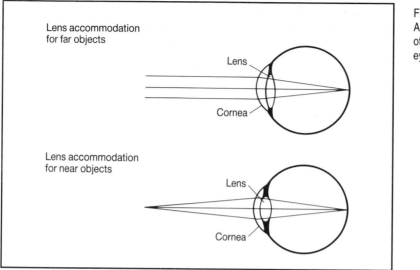

Fig. 3.6
Accommodation
of the lens of the
eye.

Lens accommodation
for far objects

Lens

Cornea

Lens accommodation
for near objects

Lens

Cornea

eye is functioning at a fixed focus, the depth of field (i.e. the range over which an object can move without the retinal image becoming blurred) may well be sufficient to keep track of large moving objects, with the important limitations on perception being set by the inexperience of the visual system of the brain.

It is also known that babies younger than 4 months of age see in colour as do normal (non-colour blind) adults. Bornstein, Kessen, and Weiskopf (1976) showed that babies divide the physical spectrum of light into the four main colour categories: blue, green, yellow, and red. Babies respond to transitions across the boundaries between colours as a change in the stimulus. Thus, at wavelengths between 480 and 510nm (nanometres), where adults perceive the colour as changing from blue to green, infants will also respond as though there are two different colours. (This change is shown using an habituation paradigm described in the panel on p. 64.) However, a change of the same magnitude within a colour category, for example from 480 to 450nm, is treated by the infant as another instance of the colour blue in an habituation test. Thus, long before the beginning of language or any formal tuition, babies group the visible wavelengths of light into categories of colour much like those of adults in many different cultures. Such findings of universal colour categories in early perception have important implications, for they suggest that structures available at the level of perception may have primacy in the processes of cognitive development.

## Sensitive periods and
## early experience in visual development

Stereoscopic vision depends on the fact that the eyes, being horizontally separated, each receive a slightly different image. The corresponding points of the image on each eye are slightly further apart for near objects than for far ones and the brain makes use of this retinal disparity to read depth from the fused images of the two eyes.

Although there is depth perception by other means, stereoscopic binocular vision—particularly useful for depth perception in near space—does not start to develop until about 13 weeks. This may be a function of poor control over the convergence of the eyes, because when we focus both eyes on the same object, the eyes must converge differen-

Fig. 3.7
Stereoscopic
vision.

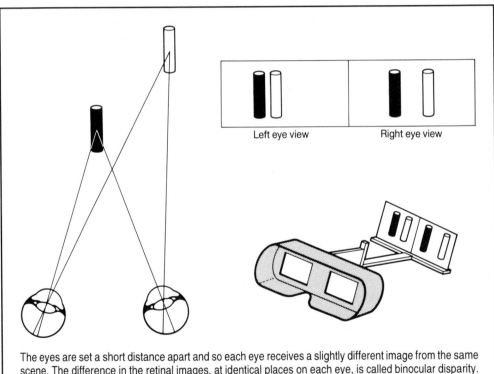

The eyes are set a short distance apart and so each eye receives a slightly different image from the same scene. The difference in the retinal images, at identical places on each eye, is called binocular disparity. The brain makes use of these slight differences as one means to register spatial depth. This is the principle of the stereoscope, where photographs taken from slightly different angles, corresponding to the position of each eye, appear to the viewer to fuse as a single three-dimensional image.

tially according to the distance of the object. Changes in the axes of alignment of the eyes in the early weeks of life and "tuning" the visual cortex of the brain, so that the neural cells responsible for binocular vision receive the same information from both eyes, may be responsible for stereoscopic vision.

Quite extensive research on binocular vision indicates very strongly that binocular aspects of visual functioning depend on early visual experience during a "sensitive" period. The concept of a sensitive period is derived from ethology; it designates a period of susceptibility for a particular kind of learning. It is related to the concept of plasticity, which may be defined as the capacity of the nervous system to undergo transformations as a result of experience. The period of maximum sensitivity is up to 2 years and declines thereafter. There are important implications for the treatment of squint, where the axes of the eyes are not parallel (this condition is also known as *strabismus*).

In a child with a squint, the binocular cells in the visual nervous system do not receive the same input from equivalent regions of the two eyes. For this reason it is important to realign the squinting eye by surgery if vision is not to be adversely affected. Children who have received corrective surgery after the sensitive period of 2 years do not regain stereopsis, whereas infants who had strabismus corrected during the sensitive period show some evidence of regaining binocular vision (see Aslin, 1985, for an extended discussion).

## Control of eye movements

Newborn infant eye movements are very similar to those of adults in their dynamics. Successive shifts of visual fixation from object to object are known as *saccades*. Smooth tracking movements of the eyes develop at about 2 months, whereas younger infants follow moving objects by making a series of saccadic jumps in their eye movements (further information about newborn infant vision is available in Atkinson & Braddick, 1989). Infants make eye movements both *in utero* and in the dark, which shows that the scanning pattern must be internally generated and not simply a reaction to incident visual stimulation. The newborn is born prepared to explore the visual environment.

Haith (1980) has suggested that the looking patterns of the newborn infant may be governed by the following four rules:

1. If awake and alert and light not too bright, open eyes.
2. If in darkness, maintain a controlled detailed search.
3. If in light with no form, search for edges by relatively broad, jerky sweeps of the (visual) field.

4. If an edge is found, terminate the broad scan and stay in the general vicinity of the edge.

Newborns are particularly prone to picking out the external edges of visual objects, although they will shift their gaze to the interior of the object if it has internal movement. So, babies are scanning for salient features of objects. They do not simply search at random even though their ability to scan improves over the first 3 months.

## Hearing

The auditory system begins to function well before birth. Physically, the inner ear has grown to its adult size by the 20th gestational week, and the middle ear, with its complex structure of bones and membranes, is functional by the 37th week of pregnancy, although it continues to change shape and size into adulthood. The shape of the external ear is adult-like by the 20th gestational week, although it will continue to grow in size until the child is about 9 years old (Rubel, 1985).

Infants are attentive to sounds from before birth but because the middle ear of the fetus is filled with amniotic fluid, the conduction of sound will be quite different than post-natally. The fetus will only be able to hear loud external sounds that are transmitted through the mother's abdominal wall and which penetrate a fairly high level of background noise. Mothers report feeling their babies startle to such loud sounds at about 32 weeks gestational age. The mother's speech, transmitted downwards through the diaphragm, is the most likely source of sound to be heard by the baby. Most perceptible are the patterns of onset and offset at the higher frequencies that are not masked by the mother's heart beat and the rushing noise of her blood circulation.

Recent studies have shown that newborns can distinguish their mother's voice from the voice of another female, which suggests that aspects of the mother's voice may become familiar to the child *in utero*. De Casper and Fifer (1980) carried out an ingenious study to demonstrate this. Mothers read aloud during the last trimester of their pregnancy from a story book so that the same story was "heard" by the fetus many times. Then, on the first day after birth, babies listened with earphones to either the mother's voice or that of a stranger reading the same story. As they listened they sucked on a dummy and they learned to adjust their pattern of sucking in order to hear their mother's voice rather than the stranger's. It therefore seems very likely that this preference for the mother's voice has its origins pre-natally.

Newborn babies generally prefer voices in the female range (average frequency 260 cycles per second) to the male range (on average one octave lower at 130 cycles per second). Adults and children use a higher-pitched tone of voice when they talk to babies, as if this is a particularly effective way of speech "getting through" (Snow, 1977).

## Smell and taste

Newborns show aversion to a sour taste just as do adults. They will pucker up their lips and show a "disgusted" expression. They can also discriminate sweetness in liquids and show contented emotional expressions. Newborn babies show a similar range of "disgusted" or contented expressions when presented with smells that are unpleasant (rotten eggs) or pleasant (a milky smell, honey, chocolate; Steiner, 1979). The babies in this study were tested in the first few hours of life, before they had been fed, so they had had no oral experience of food.

Neonates recognise the smell of their own mother's breast milk within the first 6 days of life. MacFarlane (1975) placed a pad, which the mothers had previously worn to catch seeping breast milk, on one side of the infant's head and a pad from another nursing mother on the other side. The babies turned their heads towards the side of the mother's pad. They preferred the familiar smell, which they must have learned rapidly to recognise in the first few days of life. Even very young infants show that they are not simply passively bombarded by stimulation but they actively seek out what to attend to.

# Cultural aspects of childbirth

So far there has been little mention of the cultural contribution to procreation and childbirth. However, a moment's thought reveals that there are significant cultural variations that surround even the universal biological aspects of pre-natal development. For example, the voluntary alteration of normal patterns of reproduction, through family planning, varies widely from society to society.

Fogel (1991) points out that, in countries with high population growth rates, such as India, the population would double every 25 years without family planning. India passed a law in 1970 (which was repealed in 1977) requiring sterilisation of all parents of two or more children who wished to continue to receive social welfare payments. China, too, has checked its rate of population growth by restricting families to one child per family. There are, however, other societies that forbid contraception on religious grounds and where families of seven children may be common. In advanced technological societies, couples who would otherwise remain childless through infertility, may now have children through artificial insemination and even by surrogate parenting. Personal and cultural values are clearly an important aspect of the process of reproduction.

Similarly, there are great cultural variations in the practices that surround birth itself. In advanced technological societies, drugs may be used to relieve pain, and most births take place under sterile conditions in hospitals. In other societies, pain relief may come through the use of music in labour, as among Laotians, or by applying heat to the abdomen of the mother, as in the Comanche tribe of North America (Fogel, 1991). There are also cultural variations in the position for giving birth, from sitting in special birthing stools, to kneeling, to lying with support to the back.

Fogel (1991) reports that in traditional Japanese society there are a number of community rituals surrounding pregnancy and birth. From the fifth month of pregnancy, women wear a special belt beneath the kimono which symbolises the child's tie to the community. After birth, the umbilical cord is dried and saved in an ornamental box to remind the mother and child of their close original physical bond. On the day of birth and on the third and seventh days of life, feasts are celebrated among the relatives to ensure good health for the baby, and a naming ceremony is performed on the seventh day. This example shows clearly how the biological and cultural aspects of childbirth are intimately linked. These examples also show the mutual dependence of biology and culture in the processes of reproduction and birth. Biology and culture function as mutually embedded systems, with both having an important part to play in the very origins of development.

## Conclusion and summary

This chapter has considered the general question of the origins and nature of human development from conception to birth. The Piagetian model of the "epigenetic landscape", in which development is conceived as a process of transformation occurring over time, has been used to illustrate the main stages and transitions in pre-natal development. The reader may ask whether development is a process of continuous change or a series of discontinuous transitions from one type of organisation to another.

Most contemporary theorists would argue that a full understanding of the process of development requires both continuous and discontinuous aspects of developmental change to be taken into account. The recent exciting information from pre-natal development gives us some idea about the initial state of the developing system. In the case of walking, we find evidence in the fetus for locomotor patterns that are analogous to crawling and walking, which will not be fully developed until several months later. Do babies learn to walk simply by maturation or do motor abilities emerge by the incorporation and reorganisation of already existing systems? The question of motor development will be considered in Chapter 5.

Birth marks a transition to a new environment, one that will offer new opportunities, especially for vision and action but, again, we must expect continuities as well as discontinuities with the earlier stages of development. As far as the development of perception is concerned, the evidence suggests that all the basic sensory systems are functional from birth or before. This is not to say that the process of perception is fully developed. On the contrary, much development is still to come. However, even newborns will show preferences in what they attend to in vision, hearing, taste, and smell. This implies that they are not passive recipients of stimulation, nor are they simply captured by sensory stimulation. The same questions about continuity and discontinuity need to be asked. If the neonate has the ability for basic perception of reality, how does this initial state enter into the subsequent course of development? The next chapter will consider perceptual development in infancy.

Finally, even where development seems at first glance to be biologically determined, there are cultural factors at work. There are variations in reproductive practices, from culture to culture, which influence the probability of fertilisation. There are variations in the process of giving birth and in the ways in which different societies welcome the newborn. In its origins, human development is simultaneously biologically and culturally determined.

## Further reading

Hofer, M. (1981). *The roots of human behaviour*. San Francisco: Freeman.

# 4 Perceptual development in infancy

The newborn baby (or neonate) was for a very long time thought to be little more than a reflexive organism, helpless, motorically immature, and capable of seeing or hearing very little. The nineteenth-century philosopher and psychologist William James famously described the world of the newborn as a "buzzing, blooming confusion, where the infant is seized by eyes, ears, nose and entrails all at once". This vivid phrase conveys an image of a passive infant, inundated by meaningless sensations, with little awareness of self or external reality.

Although there were periods of active study of infants in the late nineteenth and early twentieth centuries (see Chapters 1 and 2), there has never before been such a prolonged and intensive preoccupation with basic human development as in the contemporary study of babies. One of the major achievements in developmental psychology of recent years has been to show that William James' preconception of the perceptual world of the newborn was mistaken. The infant is much more competent in perception than had been assumed.

## Presuppositions

The nature of early visual perception has a long and contentious history, which is very much a function of how we understand visual perception of space to be possible. The paradox is that the two-dimensional surface of the eye, the retina, on which visual images of the world are projected, lacks the third dimension and yet we perceive the world as three-dimensional and extended in space. Philosophers have long puzzled over this paradox and they have suggested that our experience of visual space must be derived from the sense of touch and from our motor activities. The philosophical background is summarised in the panel on page 59.

It has been assumed by many theorists that "touch tutors vision"—that is, babies have to learn to see by correlating touch with vision during the early months of life. The assumption has been that, even though the visual system is functional at birth, the visual sensations received by the baby are initially meaningless. As Morss (1990) has recently pointed out, this

## Philosophers' assumptions about space perception

There is a long-standing philosophical tradition, apparent both in the French philosophy of Jean Jacques Rousseau and in Bishop Berkeley's eighteenth-century English philosophy, that visual sensations cannot yield knowledge of reality, except in relation to sensations of movement and touch. William Molyneux posed a question to the philosopher John Locke (1690) whether a blind man, who can recognise a sphere and a cube by touch, could with sight restored immediately see the difference between these shapes. Locke thought that the blind man with sight restored would not be able to recognise these objects by vision alone until he had gained some experience of simultaneously touching and seeing the objects in order to establish a correlation between the senses.

Berkeley (1709) argued that we learn about visual space by association between "clues" from different sensory and motor systems. For example, the retinal image contains "clues" for depth such as the occlusion of far objects by near ones. As the viewpoint of the observer changes relative to objects at different distances, those that are further away in the field of view appear to pass behind those that are nearer to the observer. Thus, occlusion of an object arising from a change in one's own viewpoint can be used as a clue to the relative distance of the object from the observer.

Other "clues" occur in the motor system, such as the differential convergence of the eyes when focusing on objects at different distances, or the effort involved in locomotion from one place to another. On Berkeley's theory, vision obtains information for solidity of objects through touch (he said we know a stone is solid because we can kick it) and about the third dimension as a result of locomotion through space.

The theoretical implication that Berkeley's philosophy carries into developmental psychology is that seeing the world appropriately would require rather extensive experience of touching things and of moving about in the world.

basic assumption about infant perception leaves the newborn a "prisoner of the senses". Even if perception is functional at birth (see Chapter 3), if the senses are not connected then the baby's experience would not be of reality as adults know it; it could only be a world of meaningless sensations. This is why James argued that early experience would be a buzzing, blooming confusion.

The effect of importing these assumptions into developmental psychology is that it is necessary to explain how the infant can organise experience in order to progress beyond such chaotic beginnings in understanding the visual world.

# Piaget's theory of perception

Piaget shared the starting assumption that "touch tutors vision" in early development. He suggested that the visual world of the newborn is two-dimensional and lacking in depth. Perception of shape and size develops only slowly during the first 6 months of life. Piaget assumed that the senses are initially separate and become coordinated through the child's own activities. In the first 3 months, seeing and hearing become coordinated but remain separate from touching and looking. Then, between 3 and 6 months, these two coordinations form a new, multisensory coordination which incorporates touch, vision, and hearing. Only when this has happened does the infant become capable of knowing that the same physical object can simultaneously give rise to tactile, visual, and auditory sensations.

Piaget (1954) argued that the baby gradually comes to know about the properties of objects through his or her own activities. A very important aspect of his theory concerns the acquisition of the "object concept". The object concept is defined by Piaget as a belief that physical objects are :

> Permanent, substantial, external to the self and firm in existence even though they do not directly affect perception and ... to conceive of them as retaining their identity whatever the changes in position. (Piaget, 1954, pp. 5 and 7)

Piaget described a series of six stages in the development of the object concept whereby this knowledge slowly gives structure to the baby's early perception. We will return to his observations on the object concept in Chapter 6 when we consider how babies learn to search for hidden objects. For the moment, we should simply note that Piaget's theory of early perception assumes very limited perceptual abilities indeed in the first 6 months of life.

## Gibson's alternative

A radical alternative to the traditional view of visual perception that was adopted by Piaget was developed by James Gibson (1904-1979) see Gibson, 1966. He argued that perception should be considered as an active process of seeking after information, with no one sense being more important than any other. Thus, seeing a stone provides just as good information about its presence as kicking it.

According to Gibson, the different senses are "tuned" to different ranges of the available energy impinging on them, but they are able to yield equivalent information. Hearing depends on mechanical transmission of patterned sound, touch depends on mechanical transmission of object properties through the skin, seeing depends on radiant transmission of the patterned light reflected from complexly structured surfaces, while taste and smell depend on patterned chemical transmission.

Gibson stressed that space is not empty, but full of textured objects and surfaces. He argued that perception of visual space occurs because terrestrial space is filled with structures that are perceived in relation to the surfaces of the earth. These textured surfaces reflect light to the eye and the pattern of texture is preserved in the image that falls on the retina, the light-sensitive surface of the eye. The relative distance of objects from the observer is preserved in the retinal image because the pattern or texture of the retinal image becomes more fine-grained as the distance from the observer increases. These patterns of texture are called *texture gradients* (see the panel below).

## Texture gradients

The relative density of a textured surface varies systematically with its distance from the observer. Imagine, for example, the pebbles on a beach receding into the distance: they appear more densely packed the further away they are. As the beach is formed of pebbles packed at nearly identical density, the gradient of change in texture as the distance from the observer increases provides the eye with direct information about the structure and distance of visual space. Figure 4.1 illustrates how gradients of texture, reflected from the environment and preserved in the retinal array, can specify three-dimensional relationships in space.

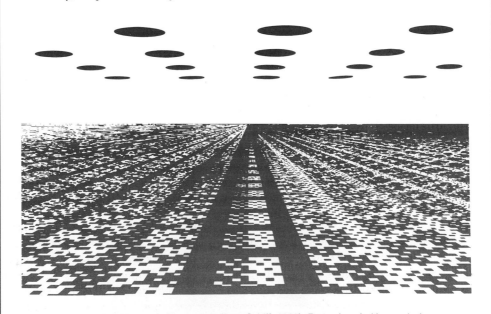

Fig. 4.1 Depth specified by texture (from Schiff, 1986). Reproduced with permission.

While each of the senses has specialised functions, such as visual perception of colour or cutaneous perception of temperature, there is also information common to different senses, such as rhythmic patterns that can be perceived by eye or ear. Furthermore, the information to which perceptual systems are attuned is especially relevant for the control of action. The implication of Gibson's theory is that perceptual systems have evolved to put the infant in direct contact with the real world from the outset. The theoretical implication is that babies may be able visually to perceive the world before they can act upon it.

The data from studies of perception in infancy not only tell us about infant perception but also enable us to choose between rival theories as to the status of perception in early development. If young babies can perceive the shape and size of an object, this would imply that they visually perceive the real world of objects from the outset, without any need for prolonged learning by correlating vision with hearing, touch, and the muscular senses. If babies can inter-relate information obtained through different senses, before they have extensive capabilities for movement, then it allows them a prolonged period of learning through the distance senses (vision and audition) before having precise control over action.

## Perception of complex object properties in early infancy

In recent years, a variety of novel techniques for testing infants' perception of objects have been developed (see panel on p. 64). These techniques have enabled researchers to demonstrate that young babies have a more precocious ability to perceive objects than had previously been recognised.

Objects exist in time and space; they have particular material attributes— they may be hard or soft, rigid or elastic, animate or inanimate; they may produce sounds or be silent; they have a particular size and shape. The question that has concerned developmental psychologists is whether babies are able to perceive these attributes directly or whether they have to undergo prolonged learning in order to perceive. Of course, babies will still need to learn about the particular properties that are characteristic of the objects they encounter, but the question we are asking here is whether babies need to learn how to perceive, or whether they may already be equipped to use perception to learn about the world.

### Size and shape constancy

As was illustrated in the panel on p. 59, following the philosophical assumptions prevalent in the earlier part of this century, it was natural for

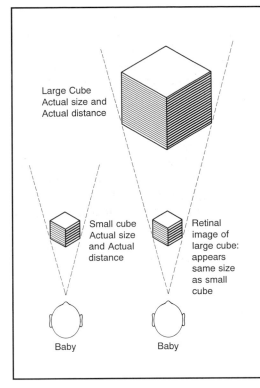

Fig. 4.2 Bower's demonstration of size constancy in babies. A static retinal image is ambiguous with respect to the true size of an object. For example, when viewed from different distances, two cubes of different sizes may actually project a retinal image of the same size. Bower (1966) showed that babies of 3 months nevertheless perceive the size (and shape) of a cube as constant, despite changes in the viewing distance. He suggests that size (and shape) constancy in babies makes use of dynamic changes in the retinal image arising from the baby's own eye and head movements. Eye movements induce lateral movement in the retinal image, relative to the rest of the spatial field, which covary with the distance of the object from the observer. This information is known as motion parallax. Such changes in the dynamic aspects of the retinal image may be sufficient for the baby to perceive that relative size (and shape) remain constant despite changes in the distance (and projected shape) of the cube. This example highlights the importance of dynamic information for infant perception.

Labels in figure:

Large Cube Actual size and Actual distance

Small cube Actual size and Actual distance

Retinal image of large cube: appears same size as small cube

Baby

Baby

Piaget to suppose that babies first have to learn to coordinate touch with vision in order to perceive things as having solid, substantial properties. Then, having learned to grasp the object, the baby can twist and turn it, move it further away and nearer in the field of view. By coordinating vision and touch, babies gradually make the discovery that visual objects are solid. According to this view, babies would not begin to learn about visual constancies until they could reach for and grasp things with their hands, normally at about 5 months.

The first demonstration that size and shape constancy is possible before this age was made by Bower (1966) in 3-month-old babies. His finding has been replicated in newborns by Slater and Morrison (1985) using the *habituation method* (Slater, 1989, reviews many studies based on this method; see the panel overleaf). The infants were first familiarised with a square presented in different orientations. Then, during the first post-familiarisation trial, a trapezoidal shape was paired with the square. Babies preferred to look at the novel trapezoid than at the familiar square. A square undergoing rotation projects a trapezoidal retinal image during

## Methods of studying perception in babies

Even young babies show spontaneous visual preference, preferring to look at one thing rather than another. This means that it is possible to study what the infant chooses to look at. The pioneer of the visual preference method was Robert Fantz (1965). The infant, who may be lying down, or who can be specially supported, is presented with a pair of visual targets, one to the left and the other to the right of the midline. The investigator notes the direction of the baby's first eye movement and the total amount of time that the infant fixates the target. On succeeding trials, the targets are alternated from left to right, so that any bias a baby may have for looking to one side or the other cancels out. Figure 4.3 illustrates Fantz's method.

In the early studies using the preference technique, babies were presented with simple choices between patterned or plain two-dimensional targets. It was established that babies prefer to look at patterns rather than plain surfaces. In one variation, a face-like mask was compared with a bullseye pattern and it was found that newborns showed a preference for the face-like stimulus (see Figure 6.8). Similar methods were used to demonstrate that babies discriminate different colours, and to measure their visual acuity. Visual acuity is a measure of how fine is the detail that the eye can discriminate. This is shown for babies by their preference for finer and finer graded black and white stripes over a uniformly grey surface.

A variation of the Fantz technique involves presenting babies with the same stimuli repeatedly. This is called the *habituation method*, because it involves accustoming the baby to the visual object, so that it becomes progressively less interesting. Then, once the infant's attention has declined to some criterion value (usually 50% of the time spent fixating the target on the first trial), a new object is presented and any recovery of interest by the baby is measured. Providing that babies do not naturally prefer one stimulus over another, this method creates the potential for discriminating between a familiar stimulus and a new one, once again revealing what the baby perceives. Furthermore, the success of this method also implies that the baby remembers something of the stimulus, because the procedure relies on the test material becoming increasingly familiar. Many contemporary studies of infant perception use variations of the visual preference and habituation methods to tease out what babies may be capable of perceiving.

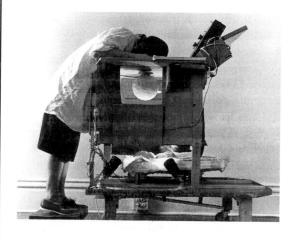

Fig. 4.3   Fantz's visual preference technique. Photograph courtesy of David Linton © Scientific American.

part of its movement, which implies that babies discriminate a trapezoid from a square as real-world objects. If the newborn baby perceives real objects, then he or she is not a "prisoner of sensation" but is actually in a position to learn about things in the real world through the distal senses.

In recent years, many new findings about the relations between sensory systems in early perception have come to light. Recent research has focused on the relations between the senses—on how vision may specify tactile properties of things, and on how audition and vision are inter-related in the very young baby.

## Intersensory perception:
## Vision and touch

Piaget considered that extensive touching, grasping, and looking at objects was necessary for gradually putting together knowledge about object properties. One source of evidence against Piaget's theory came from infants born without arms or legs following the thalidomide tragedy (see Chapter 3). These babies often showed normal intellectual development, despite the fact that they lacked the opportunity for extensive physical interaction with objects (DeCarie, 1969). In particular, they lacked the opportunity to hold things and look at them simultaneously, a condition that Piaget considered essential to tutor the visual system about the solidity of objects.

Other evidence against the Piagetian theory that "touch tutors vision" came from ingenious experiments which demonstrated that infants are capable of picking up visual information that an object is about to collide with them. Bower, Broughton, and Moore (1970) made objects move rapidly towards the faces of young infants. The infants, aged 6 to 21 days, rotated their heads upward and pulled away from the "looming" object . Looming is characterised by rapid expansion of the retinal image, as the object approaches, and this specifies an imminent collision.

Controlled studies by Ball and Tronick (1971), using a shadow cast by an object illuminated with polarised light, showed that the response is specific to the object "approaching" the infant on a collision course. In this study, the baby wore polarising goggles which produced an image of a three-dimensional object whose shadow is seen to be located as far in front of the screen as the object casting the shadow is behind it. Objects approaching on either side of the axis of sight merely elicit visual tracking. However, objects that approached directly along the axis of sight—and so looked as though they would collide with the baby—produced rapid head movement as in the study by Bower et al.

In another study, Bower (1971) also suggested that babies perceived a "virtual object" as solid. The virtual object was produced by projecting a

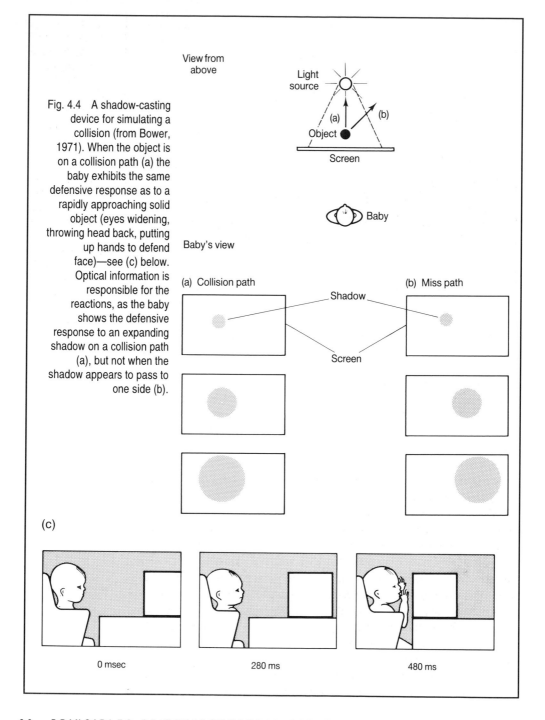

Fig. 4.4 A shadow-casting device for simulating a collision (from Bower, 1971). When the object is on a collision path (a) the baby exhibits the same defensive response as to a rapidly approaching solid object (eyes widening, throwing head back, putting up hands to defend face)—see (c) below. Optical information is responsible for the reactions, as the baby shows the defensive response to an expanding shadow on a collision path (a), but not when the shadow appears to pass to one side (b).

View from above

Light source

Object

Screen

(a)

(b)

Baby

Baby's view

(a) Collision path

(b) Miss path

Shadow

Screen

(c)

0 msec

280 ms

480 ms

polarised light shadow of a stationary cube which infants viewed using polarising goggles. They were surprised when their hand passed through the object as they swiped at it.

These early studies were the first to suggest that very young babies may perceive that objects are solid before they have had extensive experience of touching things. Other studies have demonstrated that very young babies may also extract basic visual information about objects that they have touched but not seen. This problem relates to the question Molyneux posed to Locke (discussed in the panel on p. 59) concerning whether objects known by tactile exploration only would subsequently be recognised visually.

Meltzoff and Borton (1979) tested babies aged 29 days in a task where they were given a pacifier of a particular shape to suck. Some babies received a smooth dummy, others received a knobbly dummy; however, in both cases, the dummy was placed in the baby's mouth without being seen by the baby (see Figure 4.6). The baby actively explored the dummy with lips and tongue. Then large-scale models of both dummies (measuring 6.4cm across) were placed to the left and right of the baby's visual field. Babies preferred to fixate the shape that they had explored orally. They looked at the model that was the same shape as the dummy they had been sucking for approximately 70% of their total visual fixation time.

The Meltzoff and Borton experiment shows that active oral exploration conveys something to the baby of what the object looks like. Of course,

Fig. 4.6
Dummies used in
the Meltzoff and
Borton 1979
study.

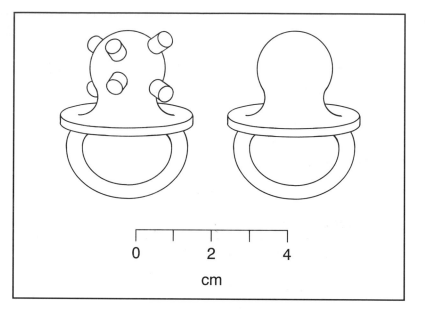

this could be as simple as "knobbly" versus "smooth", but the important point is that tactile exploration through oral touch is linked to vision even at 1 month of age. The data suggest that infants can recognise the equivalence of information picked up by different sensory modalities. As Meltzoff has suggested, had Molyneux framed his question with respect to babies, instead of the sight-restored blind adult, philosophy and psychology might have had a different history.

In recent years Baillargeon (1991) has systematically measured infants' perception of physical objects. Her studies involve repeated presentation of a visual display using the habituation method (see the panel on p. 64). Changes in looking patterns, when a new object or event is presented, reveal which combinations of physical events babies perceive as possible or impossible. Babies often show renewed interest in a familiar display when an impossible event happens while they are watching.

In one study of infants' perception of substance, the principle that a solid object cannot move through the space occupied by another object was violated (Baillargeon, 1991). One example concerns babies of 3.5 months. A screen, in the form of a drawbridge, seen end-on by the infant, was rotated repeatedly in a 180° arc (see Figure 4.7). Once the infant was habituated to this display, a large box was placed behind the screen and the infant was shown one of two test events. In one event, the physically possible case, the screen stopped rotating when it was obstructed by the

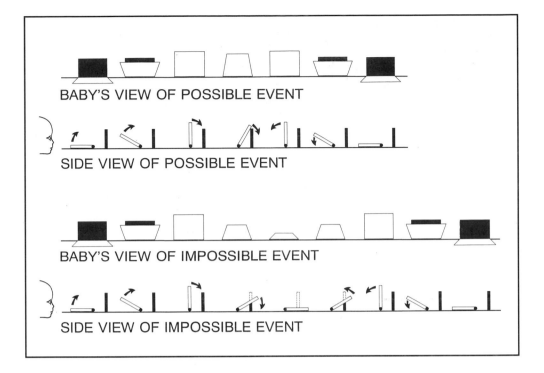

BABY'S VIEW OF POSSIBLE EVENT

SIDE VIEW OF POSSIBLE EVENT

BABY'S VIEW OF IMPOSSIBLE EVENT

SIDE VIEW OF IMPOSSIBLE EVENT

box. In a second, impossible event, the screen continued to rotate through a full 180°, as if the box were no longer behind it. Babies looked longer at the impossible event than at the possible event. This suggests that infants perceived the continued existence of the hidden box and that they also perceived that the screen should not rotate through it.

In subsequent experiments, Baillargeon (1991) went on to demonstrate that by 6.5 months babies not only understand that the screen should stop when there is a box behind it, but also that the screen will stop at different positions depending on the height of the box, or depending on whether the object behind the screen can be compressed or not. That is, the baby appropriately perceives occlusion and the possible physical interactions between rigid and elastic objects, and finds it unusual (to say the least) when the experimenter presents visual events that violate basic physical laws.

In summary, contemporary research suggests that vision and touch function as correlated modalities from the outset. The infant does not require extensive tactile experience to perceive basic properties of substance. These findings lend support to the views of Gibson, rather than Piaget, about the nature of perception in early infancy.

Fig. 4.7 The drawbridge study of Baillargeon. Adapted from Baillargeon, Spelke, & Wasserman (1985).

## Intersensory perception: Auditory–visual coordination

Wertheimer (1961) was one of the first to ask whether there may be innate relationships between the senses. Immediately his daughter was born, when she was only 8 minutes old, he made a random series of soft "clicking" noises to her left and right ear. He noticed that her eyes moved towards the sound on 18 out of the 24 occasions of testing (and away from the sound on 6 trials).

Statistically speaking, the baby looked to the sound significantly more often than would have been expected by chance. If the infant was unaware of the spatial direction of the sound, then we would expect half her eye movements to be towards and half away from the sound (i.e. 12 towards and 12 away). Wertheimer therefore concluded that there is an innate coordination between seeing and hearing, such that when the baby hears a sound, the eyes will be reoriented as if to discover the visual object at its source.

These results have subsequently been replicated and clarified by several investigators. Butterworth and Castillo (1976) found that newborn babies made sound-contingent eye movements, but that the neonates looked away from the source, presumably because it was too loud. In another study by Castillo and Butterworth (1981), newborn babies were shown identical pairs of red dots on the left or right of the field of view. These were either at the same place as the sound source or opposite the sound source. Babies looked more frequently at the dot that was on the same side as the sound source.

This study showed that newborns would look to a distinctive visual feature of the environment for the source of a sound, even when the sound actually came from the other location that was not visually marked. This example of "visual capture" corresponds to the phenomenon an adult experiences at the cinema, where the sound is attributed to the figures on the screen, even though the sound actually emerges from loudspeakers at the side of the hall. This suggests that vision and audition interact in sound localisation from birth, with vision assisting audition to localise sounds.

In a rather convincing study by Muir and Field (1979), two rattles were set into identical motion on either side of the baby. Only one of the rattles made a sound, because the granules had been removed from inside the other rattle. Newborn babies preferred to look towards the sounding rattle. This again suggests that auditory and visual systems of the neonate function as mutually supportive and coordinated systems from birth.

Coordinations between the auditory and visual systems are not, however, fixed and unchanging. In fact, there is a rather complex development over the first 5 months. Much evidence suggests that the innate coordination lasts for the first 2 months, and then eye movements to sound become increasingly difficult to elicit until 5 months, when the coordination re-emerges. U-shaped functions, where an ability is present, then apparently absent, and then returns (but in a more highly developed form), are rather common in early development. Development is not simply a linear increase in an ability; it involves reorganisation of constituent subsystems to give rise to new abilities.

As was mentioned earlier (see pp. 54–55), infants recognise their mother's voice soon after birth and there is also evidence for an early olfactory preference for the mother. Could there also be an early visual preference for the mother? Bushnell, Sai, and Mullin (1989) tested this hypothesis in a very carefully controlled study of 5-day-old babies. Each baby was seated facing a large white screen into which had been cut, at head height, two apertures separated by 12cm on either side of the infant's midline. The mother and a female stranger, of similar hair length and hair colour, were seated behind the screen so that their heads were visible through the apertures. The screen itself was liberally sprayed with an air freshener to eliminate any olfactory clues, and the mother and stranger exchanged seats from trial to trial to eliminate any possible side bias of the infant's looking. The mothers were silent during the experiment.

The infant was supported upright, at 30cm from the screen, and an observer measured the duration of the baby's fixation to either face over the 20 seconds following the appearance of the two faces. It was found that the neonates preferred to look at their own mother approximately 61% of the time. This preference was eliminated when mother and stranger wore identical wigs, which suggests that something about the mother's hairline may be distinctive for visual recognition of the mother in the very early days.

This research begins to demonstrate the possibility of a developmental progression. Could an innate coordination between hearing and seeing help the baby discover rapidly what his or her mother looks like? Pre-natal familiarity with the mother's voice, coupled with an innate tendency to look where a sound is heard, may be sufficient for the baby to learn rapidly the distinctive aspects of the mother's appearance. Further research would be needed to test this hypothesis; for example, it would be relatively easy to establish whether newborns prefer to look at a video-recording of their mother when she is speaking rather than when the same video-recording is silent.

Within a few months there is definite evidence that babies remember the sound of their mother's and father's voices. In one study by Spelke and Owsley (1979), babies heard a tape-recording of their mother's voice played over a loudspeaker placed exactly between their mother and father. The parents sat without talking or moving their mouths, so there was no information in visual synchrony with the sound. Babies from 3 months looked towards their mother when they heard their mother's voice and towards their father when their father's voice was played. This suggests that correlated aspects of auditory and visual information, characteristic of each parent, must be remembered by 3 months. Even though there need not be a very precise auditory–visual memory, the infant is nevertheless acquiring some familiarity with the sound and sight of the caregiver.

Kuhl and Meltzoff (1982) examined another aspect of auditory–visual coordination in 4-month-old babies who were presented with two video-recorded faces of strangers to the left and right of the midline. One face was shown repeating the vowel "i", while the other repeated the vowel "a". However, the baby heard only one soundtrack, to correspond with one of the visually presented sounds. Babies preferred to look at the face that corresponded with the soundtrack. This suggests that the babies must detect a correspondence between the auditory and visual information for the vowel sound. This ability might be very useful in acquiring language, because it means that visual and auditory information for speech are to some extent overlapping (or redundant). An elementary level of lip-reading may also help the young infant to produce appropriate speech sounds, as well as to perceive them. Further evidence in support of this hypothesis comes from difficulties that blind children have in learning to produce certain sounds (Mills 1987).

Meltzoff and Moore (1977) demonstrated that perception of movements may facilitate their production. These investigators showed that newborns can imitate tongue protrusion, mouth opening, and lip-pursing movements. It is worth noting that imitation of tongue protrusion has been observed in newborn infants in cultures as diverse as North America, Switzerland, Sweden, and a nomadic tribe in Nepal (Reissland,1988).

Vinter (1986) replicated and extended these results. She showed that newborns can also imitate sequences of finger movements. The ability to imitate was demonstrated only when babies actually saw the action being carried out by the adult; they did not imitate if only a stationary model was observed. For example, tongue protrusion occurred on seeing the tongue actually in motion, not if the baby only saw the protruded tongue in its final stationary position. The implication is that newborns depend on the dynamics of the perceived event in order to imitate it.

As in many other newborn behaviours, a U-shaped developmental function was found with imitation of hand movements disappearing at about 7 weeks and tongue and mouth imitation disappearing at about 3

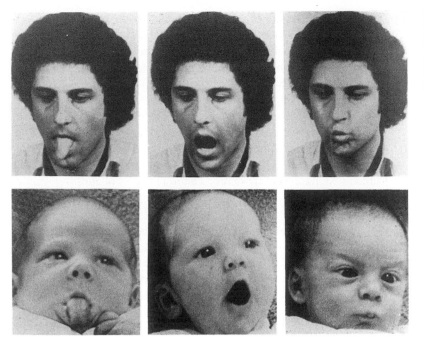

Fig. 4.8 Innate imitation in babies. Meltzoff et al, 1977. Copyright 1977 the AAAS.

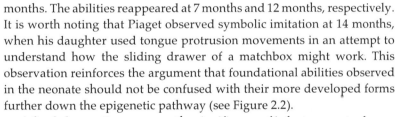

months. The abilities reappeared at 7 months and 12 months, respectively. It is worth noting that Piaget observed symbolic imitation at 14 months, when his daughter used tongue protrusion movements in an attempt to understand how the sliding drawer of a matchbox might work. This observation reinforces the argument that foundational abilities observed in the neonate should not be confused with their more developed forms further down the epigenetic pathway (see Figure 2.2).

A final observation concerns the significance of infant perceptual competence for acquiring speech and language. Obviously, auditory–visual perception is particularly useful for perceiving the communicative actions of another person. Babies learn to communicate through speech in a very few months, and one important problem for developmental psychology is to explain how this achievement is possible. Spelke and Cortelyou (1981) suggest that there are three aspects of auditory–visual coordination that may contribute:

1.  Young infants are able to locate a person when they hear a voice. There is a basic, innate spatial coordination between vision and hearing such that the auditory system will seek out a visual object to help locate the sound. At the most basic level, this need not

entail any innate link between faces and voices (but it might simply be that a link has not yet been demonstrated).

2. By 4 months babies are able to determine whether a person they can see speaking is the source of the voice, by perception of the synchrony between the face and the voice (as in the Kuhl and Meltzoff study).

3. Also by 4 months there is evidence that infants begin to have specific expectations about which face goes with which voice, at least in the case of the highly familiar mother and father.

## Speech perception

Babies appear to be well-equipped to recognise speech in the sense that they have an innate or very early learned ability to recognise speech sounds (or *phonemes*). Different languages have different phonemes and a phonemic distinction in one language may not occur in another language, even one that is closely related. There appears to be a critical period for setting the boundaries of phonemes and once they have been set in one way as a child, it is very difficult as an adult to master a different set of phonemes that draws distinctions in a way that is incompatible with the first language. For example, /r/ and /l/ are different phonemes in English, but not in Japanese, which is why Japanese people who learn English as adults have great difficulty in hearing the difference between the two.

Babies very rapidly learn the phonemes of the language that they hear. Indeed, they have no difficulty in learning the phonemes for two or more different languages if they are being reared in a multilingual family. Eimas, Siqueland, Jusczyk, and Vogorito (1971) demonstrated the remarkable ability of the young infant to distinguish between phonemes. They used a sucking paradigm in which babies sucked on a dummy that was wired up to a tape-recorder. Sucking on the dummy allowed the baby to hear particular sounds.

Having established a baseline of sucking for each baby, Eimas et al. then played the babies a single sound /pa/. At first the babies increased their rate of sucking in order to hear this unfamiliar sound. Then, as the babies became familiar with the new sound, their sucking rate settled back to the baseline. Once the babies were familiar with /pa/, a new sound was played, which was similar. For half the babies the new sound was a different phoneme, /ba/. The other babies heard a sound that was also physically different from the original /pa/ but did not cross the phoneme boundary. The babies in the first group, who heard /ba/, started to suck rapidly again in order to hear the new sound, but babies in the second group did not increase their rate of sucking, suggesting that the "new" sound did not appear to differ from the original one.

The ability to hear the difference between phonemes is not restricted at birth to the language that the child hears at home. Japanese babies can hear the difference between /l/ and /r/ even though monolingual Japanese adults find this difference very difficult to detect. But the language that the baby hears soon starts to have an influence because, by about 8 months, babies begin to show a marked decrease in their ability to distinguish between phonemes that are not present in the language that they hear around them.

Werker and Tees (1984) compared three groups of babies growing up in monolingual English, Hindi (Indian), and Salish (North American Indian) communities. They found that, a few weeks after birth, babies who had heard only English could distinguish equally well between phonemes in each of the three languages. However, by 8 months, these babies began to show a decreasing ability to discriminate between pairs of phonemes that were specific to Hindi or Salish. When Werker and Tees tested 1-year-old infants, they found that the babies who had heard only English were 100% accurate in distinguishing between English phonemes but were unable to discriminate phonemes that were specific to the other two languages. However, 1-year-old babies who had heard only Salish were 100% accurate with Salish phonemes and babies who had heard only Hindi were 100% accurate with Hindi phonemes.

The ability to make phoneme distinctions is not uniquely human, as chinchillas can also discriminate between synthetic phonemes (Kuhl & Miller, 1978). This suggests that this ability has developed from some more basic auditory perceptual ability. However, there is no evidence that animals show the selective learning that is demonstrated by infants for whom phonemic contrasts take on communicative significance.

We will take up the question of language acquisition again once we have considered the perceptual and cognitive abilities of young babies in the months before speech is acquired.

## Conclusion and summary

This chapter has reviewed the contemporary literature on perception in young babies based on the philosophical and historical preconceptions which have informed theories of cognitive development in infancy. We examined Piaget's theory that action gives structure to perception, and an alternative account, based on Gibson, which stresses the informative value of perception. Simple methods of studying infant perception, based on the spontaneous and learned preferences of babies, reveal that they do indeed perceive complex object properties, such as size and shape constancy, solidity, and permanence early in development, before they have had the opportunity to construct these properties through their own activities. Babies also show important abilities to imitate, which may be implicated in the acquisition of speech and which also imply that they may recognise other people as importantly similar to themselves. The implication is that complex perceptual systems are part of our evolutionary heritage.

Although it does not appear to be necessary to learn how to perceive, what will be perceived does, of course, vary from culture to culture depending on the characteristics of the environment. Research also shows how contemporary developmental psychology is moving into a new post-Piagetian phase, in which the results of detailed studies lead to revisions of grand theories. Nowadays, more circumscribed descriptions of development based firmly in empirical data are the norm. The results of contemporary investigations do not always support all the presuppositions made early in the twentieth century by Piaget, and the consequence is that his theory needs some revision to take into account the new information. In particular, the new research raises questions about the role of perception in intellectual development, because perceptual systems are functional from the beginning. This issue will be taken up again in Chapters 6, 7, and 8. Contemporary research nevertheless vindicates Piaget's broader theoretical framework in relation to evolutionary biology. The more that is learned about perception in very young infants, the more the contribution of evolution to the origins of human development must be acknowledged.

## Further reading

Bremner, J.G. (1994). *Infancy*, 2nd edn. Oxford: Blackwell.

Gibson, E.J. & Spelke, E.S. (1983) The development of perception. In J.H. Flavell & E.M. Markman (Eds.), *Cognitive development. Vol III Handbook of Child Psychology* (pp. 1–76). Chichester: John Wiley.

Mehler, J. & Dupoux, E. (1994). *What infants know*. Oxford: Blackwell.

# The development of motor skills in infancy

# 5

**A**lthough babies are born with a variety of coordinations between the sensory and motor systems, they still need to acquire *skilled* control over their actions. Much development in the first year of life is concerned with gaining skilled control over the body.

Even the newborn baby has some well-coordinated actions. When sucking, the newborn baby rapidly acquires very skilled control over the pressure and vacuum produced by the mouth in obtaining milk. As skilled sucking is essential for survival, it is not surprising that babies soon become very good at it. So good, in fact, that the sucking response can be used as an indicator of their abilities in other domains. Kalnins and Bruner (1974) showed that babies of 3 months could be trained to suck with a particular pattern of bursts on a dummy that had been coupled to a film projector, in order to keep the projected film in focus! In other domains, however, such as reaching to grasp something or in acquiring independent locomotion, only the most basic elements of visual–motor coordination can be observed at birth and the acquisition of skilled control takes many months.

Much development in the first year is concerned with gaining mastery over the body: for the baby the body presents a problem in gaining skilled control. Not the least problem is to gain control over the head. The head occupies by far the largest proportion of the total body-length and weight at birth. Changes in body proportions that accompany growth will eventually reduce the proportionate size of the head and increase the proportionate size of the legs. This simple change, which begins during the first year of life, will help the baby gain control over the head, then the head and trunk, and finally the legs as the upright head, sitting, and standing postures are acquired. These changes in body proportions will also help to lower the baby's centre of gravity and contribute to gaining balance when the baby is learning to walk.

# General features of motor development

It is understandable that the early theorists, such as Gesell (see pp. 13–14), supposed that the well-known motor milestones, whereby the baby gains progressive control over the head, the head and chest, sitting, standing, crawling, and walking, are a consequence of maturation. The progression is so universal, and seems so inevitable, that it appears to be the automatic consequence of biological growth.

## Motor development in the first two years

| Months | Behaviour |
|--------|-----------|
| 1 | Lifts chin when prone; holds head erect for a few seconds |
| 2 | Lifts head when prone |
| 3 | Rolls from side to back |
| 4 | Lifts head and chest when prone; holds head erect |
| 5 | Rolls from side to side |
| 6 | Sits with slight support |
| 7 | Can roll from back to stomach; stepping reactions |
| 8 | Tries vigorously to crawl; sits alone for short time |
| 9 | Can turn around when left on floor; makes some progress crawling |
| 10 | Stands when held up |
| 11 | Pulls self up by holding onto furniture |
| 12 | Crawls on hands and knees; sidesteps around furniture |
| 13 | Stands alone |
| 14 | Walks alone |
| 15 | Climbs stairs |
| 16 | Trots about well |
| 17 | Climbs on a low chair, stoops |
| 18 | Can walk backwards |
| 19 | Climbs stairs up and down |
| 20 | Jumps, runs |

Adapted from Griffiths (1954).

The Table opposite is taken from Griffiths' (1954) scale of the motor abilities of babies. It shows month by month the motor development to be expected in the average child. There are major achievements in gaining control over posture and in acquiring independent locomotion. These are not stages of development because there is variation in the order of motor milestones from baby to baby. For instance, some babies learn to walk without ever passing through a crawling "stage", whereas others do learn to crawl before they learn to walk. Nevertheless, the Table serves very well to illustrate the wide range of motor skills the infant will master between the earliest attempts of the neonate to lift his or her heavy head from the pillow to the running, jumping, and climbing activities of the toddler. Other major achievements occur in gaining control of the hands for reaching and grasping, as well as in their use for locomotion when crawling. Each of these activities can be understood as an aspect of the development of motor skill.

We now know that there is nothing inevitable about the maturation of these motor skills. On the contrary, the mastery of each skill contributes to the acquisition of others. To illustrate these processes, some of the factors involved in the development of locomotion, in the acquisition of visually guided reaching and grasping, and the visual control of balance in babies will now be discussed.

## Locomotion

In the weeks and months after birth the baby progressively gains motor control in a typical sequence which was first described by McGraw (1943). Babies lift their heads first, then they become able to raise head and chest, then they will lift head and trunk by raising themselves on arms and

Fig. 5.1 Some early motor milestones (after McGraw, 1943).

hands, and eventually they raise themselves on all four limbs. By 9 months babies usually crawl, although some babies get around by bottom shuffling. Soon they will pull themselves to stand upright and, by 12 months, most babies take their first steps in walking.

Many theorists assumed a purely maturational basis for such skills, but it soon became apparent that cultural factors enter into motor development. Dennis and Dennis (1940) studied the Hopi Indians of New Mexico who, at that time, were only partly Westernised. It was traditional to strap an infant securely to a cradle board which the mother carried on her back (Figure 5.2) while engaged in her work. The cradle board limited the opportunity of the infant to engage in unrestricted motor activity. Despite this, the traditionally reared Hopi babies learned to walk at the same age as the Westernised Hopi (who were not strapped to cradle boards). At first sight, it seemed that the restriction of the opportunity to practise movements did not affect the age of walking. However, on closer examination, it emerged that the babies were not strapped to the boards for more than five hours a day, and so it cannot be assumed that locomotor practice was totally unimportant.

Fig. 5.2 Native American cradle restricting infant's movements. From S. Eastman in *Schoolcraft's Indian Tribes (4)*, 1856. Photo courtesy Mary Evans Picture Library.

Dennis and Najarian (1957) studied severely deprived infants in an orphanage in Teheran. They found that children as old as 2 years had still not acquired even the most elementary motor skills of sitting or standing. They attributed the delay to the almost total lack of social stimulation in the orphanage. This finding nicely illustrates Vygotsky's point that the social structure enters into development at the zone of proximal development (see pp. 22–23). When the baby is learning to walk, the "scaffolding" of the social environment, as Bruner called it, usually passes unobserved, except under special circumstances. However, it is easy to see the social contribution when the child takes his or her first faltering steps with the protection and support of the parent.

As was noted earlier (see pp. 48–50), there may be continuity between the newborn stepping reflex and later crawling and walking movements. Zelaso, Zelaso, and Kolb (1972) showed that practising the stepping reflex prevented it from disappearing in development, and this resulted in marginally earlier walking than in a control group who did not practise the stepping movements. There is also evidence from some African tribes, such as the Kipsigi of Nigeria who help their babies to practise various postures, that postural control of sitting can be accelerated by up to five weeks (Super, 1976). Such cultural practices accelerate motor development, but it is not yet clear whether this is because they provide specific experiences or because they more generally improve muscle tone and build up strength so that the babies can support their own weight earlier.

Why do babies generally walk towards the end of the first year? Thelen (1984) suggests that babies walk when they have sufficient strength to support their own weight. Her argument depends on bodily constraints that prevent walking, such as the weight of the head and limbs and the position of the centre of gravity. Zelaso (1984), on the other hand, stresses the instrumental uses of walking. Walking is a means to an end and it generally develops with other intentional actions. Zelaso's argument stresses the role of cognitive development in allowing the infant to plan sequences of complex activities.

In fact, both arguments may be partially correct. On the one hand, the basic pattern of movements of walking cannot depend on intellectual development, because the fetal studies suggest it may be innate. On the other hand, walking can serve complex purposes and intellectual development may give babies a reason to use their motor abilities for exploration and mobility.

## Gaining control of posture

Acquiring independent locomotion depends on maintaining the dynamic stability of the body in its progression through space. Walking can be considered as "controlled falling", in the sense that the child must constantly counteract the effects of gravity in a repetitive cycle of activity to produce forward progression. A necessary condition to gain such dynamic control is first to master the static posture of the body. The infant makes major achievements in gaining control over postures such as balancing the head, sitting, and standing. Each of these skills is normally achieved with the help of vision, as is illustrated by the severe delay in locomotion in the congenitally blind baby (Fraiberg, 1974). The panel overleaf shows how the dynamic flow of visual texture at the eye, which normally accompanies body sway, is used to gain control of postures and assists in learning locomotion.

In fact, the optic flow pattern is involved in gaining postural control long before there is independent locomotion. Butterworth and Cicchetti (1982) showed that babies who have recently learned to sit unsupported also depend on the flow of visual information at the eye to gain control over the seated posture. They would sway markedly when seated in the moving room under conditions of misleading visual feedback. The earliest posture tested was in a study by Pope (1984), who showed that 2-month-old babies, who are just learning to balance the head, also depend on the visual flow pattern to maintain head control. These babies were so young

## Optic flow patterns and control of posture

It has been shown that babies rely on stable visual surroundings to help them gain balance. An infant who has just learned to sit or to stand will lose balance if seated in a visual environment that moves. This was first shown by Lee and Aronson (1974). They tested infants who had recently begun to stand unsupported in a "moving room", a small enclosure comprising three walls and a ceiling suspended just above the floor. The baby stands inside the room which is then moved slowly towards (or away from) the infant, thus producing a flow of visual information at the eye which would occur if the baby were really swaying backwards (or forwards).

Babies compensated for a non-existent sway by moving in the direction opposite to the apparent direction of instability specified by the misleading visual motion of the room. Thus if the front wall was moved towards them, babies leaned backwards which, in turn, caused them to lose balance. This involuntary compensation reveals that babies normally use the flow of visual information contingent on their movement as continuous feedback to maintain their balance.

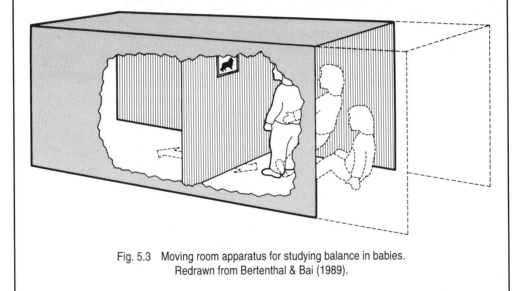

Fig. 5.3  Moving room apparatus for studying balance in babies.
Redrawn from Bertenthal & Bai (1989).

that they had to be supported in the sitting position in the moving room. When the room was moved around them, they made compensatory movements of the head, consistent with the misleading visual information. The visual system, vestibular system (a sensory system in the ear that detects movement of the head), and kinaesthetic mechanisms involved in maintaining balance are closely intertwined from the outset and help the infants gain mastery over their own bodies.

In summary, contemporary research suggests that visual feedback helps the baby to stabilise the succession of postures observed in the typical "motor milestones". Skilled control is acquired on the basis of the rather precise feedback offered by vision. Once the baby has acquired a stable posture of the head and trunk, this paves the way for rapid development of reaching and grasping. Control of the hand and arm involves bringing the hand to a position specified by the eye. Aiming the arm movement needs a stable launching "platform", hence postural stability is one of the conditions contributing to the development of reaching. So, gaining postural control helps in mastering the skills of eye and hand.

# Reaching and grasping

Let us begin with a definition: *A motor skill is an organised sequence of goal-directed activity which is guided or corrected by feedback.* Visual perception has a particularly important part to play in the control of action because it provides feedback about the success of actions and enables errors to be corrected. This section will review recent evidence on the origins and development of visually guided reaching and grasping, skills that have a prolonged period of development.

Piaget (1952) thought that hand movements and vision are initially independent. He noticed that 3-month-old babies spend a lot of time looking at their own hands and he argued that this period of "hand regard" enables the infant to acquire visual control of the hand. His theory was supported by some extensive investigations made by White, Castle, and Held (1964), who noted that the onset of reaching could be slightly accelerated by equipping the baby with brightly coloured mittens. However, Bower (1982) found that congenitally blind infants also seem to go through a period of "hand regard" where their unseeing eyes follow the hand as it moves, although no visual feedback can occur. Thus, it appears that the mechanisms controlling eye tracking and hand movement may already be coupled and this linkage is not established by visual feedback. Blind infants are delayed in reaching and grasping, despite the link between eye and hand, because they cannot see a target for which reaching may be aimed. In fact, Fraiberg (1974) suggests that reaching in the blind depends on substituting audition for vision, with blind babies eventually reaching for objects they can hear.

This type of evidence led Bruner and Koslowski (1972) to argue that learning skilled reaching consists of gaining voluntary control over a pre-established coordination of eye and hand. They noted that 2-month-old babies, when presented with an object in the visual field, made grasping movements with their hands but failed to extend their arms towards the object. At other times, they extended their arms but failed to grasp. Bruner and Koslowski suggested that the infant's problem lies in ordering the constituent actions into the appropriate goal-directed sequence. That is, part of becoming skilled is to establish the correct serial order between acts to fulfil the goal of reaching and grasping the object.

Contemporary research tends to favour the view that basic eye–hand coordination is innate. Bower (1982) and Von Hofsten (1983) have independently demonstrated that newborns will attempt to make gross "swiping" movements of the hand and arm in the vicinity of an attractive object that is suspended within reach, in the baby's field of view. Babies will swipe rather ineffectively at the interesting object with only occasional contact, and although these movements are goal-directed they do not result in the baby grasping the object. These swiping movements are called "visually elicited" reaching, because they seem to be pre-programmed or ballistic movements that are triggered by the sight of the interesting object.

As the baby's aim gets better, contacts become more frequent and by about 4 months, the baby sometimes succeeds in grasping the object after contacting it. That is, reaching is visually elicited and the action of grasping is triggered by touching the object. As the actions of visually elicited reaching and tactually elicited grasping become coordinated, the baby increasingly becomes able to anticipate the arrival of the hand at the object. By about 5 months the so-called "top level reach" emerges, where both reaching and grasping are coming under visual guidance. The action of reaching is guided and the fingers close onto the object as contact occurs.

The detailed observations of reaching in babies are important because they show once again that the amount of preadaptive structure available in early development is greater than traditional theories would suppose. However, the baby only slowly gains the skills required to put the co-ordination to use. Contemporary theorists of motor development emphasise the extent to which such processes are self-organising. Development begins from preadapted systems which become inter-coordinated into more complex systems, themselves stable within certain dynamic limits. Reaching behaviour, as one example of this general process, becomes more stable and less likely to be perturbed by unexpected events as it becomes more skilled. Ineffective behaviours drop out of the repertoire, as the effective ones are selected and integrated to form a new level of self-organisation (Thelen, 1989).

In fact, developments in the grips of babies can be observed well into the second year of life, as the infant first becomes able to grasp objects and then gains finer and finer control over the fingers (see Figure 5.4). Babies first grasp by pressing all the fingers against the object in the palm of the hand. These palm grips give way to more precise finger grips, so that by the end of the first year, the baby is able to pick up rather small objects in

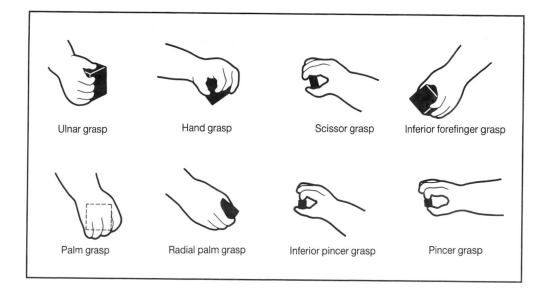

| | | | |
|---|---|---|---|
| Ulnar grasp | Hand grasp | Scissor grasp | Inferior forefinger grasp |
| Palm grasp | Radial palm grasp | Inferior pincer grasp | Pincer grasp |

a "pincer grip" between the very end of the index finger and the extreme tip of the thumb. This precision grip is species-specific to humans. It involves full opposition of the fingers and thumb, so that they may be brought into contact for very skilled tool use, as for example in later development when sewing or writing.

Fig. 5.4   Range of hand grips in the first year of life (after Verweij, 1988).

Reaching and grasping continue to develop in a variety of ways during the first year of life. For example, once reaching and grasping has been mastered, the baby must learn to coordinate the actions of the two hands with each other. Bruner (1974 ) showed that 6-month-old babies will reach and grasp a proffered object but, if they are then offered a second object, they drop the first one because they only have sufficient control over the action pattern to cope with one object at a time.

From about 6 months, the baby begins to get the idea of transferring the object from one hand to another but, if a third object is then offered, the baby will drop the second one. It is not until 8–9 months that the baby develops a storage routine. Now, the third and subsequent objects are deposited in a safe place following transfer from hand to hand. This sequence illustrates nicely how the action of visually guided reaching must be coordinated with memory to expand the range of application of the motor skill. The coordination of memory with reaching and grasping is known as "hierarchical integration". The complementary use of the two hands also depends in part on the handedness of the baby (see the panel overleaf). Complex skills are important in many aspects of early cognitive development, as will become apparent in Chapter 6.

## The origins of handedness

Research on the development of the skilled control of reaching is informative about the origins of handedness. Approximately 88% of British adults are right-handed and the remainder are left-handed. It is clear that spontaneous hand preferences can be modified through training, as has been the case, at various times in history and in different cultures, when left-handedness has been suppressed and children have been taught to use their right hand. However, hand preferences are not simply a matter of learning. It is now thought that handedness can be predicted from the spontaneous preference of the infant to lie with the head and arm to the right (or left) in the tonic neck reflex posture which can be observed in the fetus to about 8 months post-natally.

Figure 5.5 (below from Gesell et al., 1949) shows a newborn infant with a spontaneous left-facing preference and another with a spontaneous right-facing preference. If the theory is correct, then one baby should have grown up left-handed and the other right-handed (Butterworth & Hopkins 1993). Consistent hand preferences begin to be noticeable by about 8 months and they can certainly be observed by the middle of the second year of life (Ramsay, 1980).

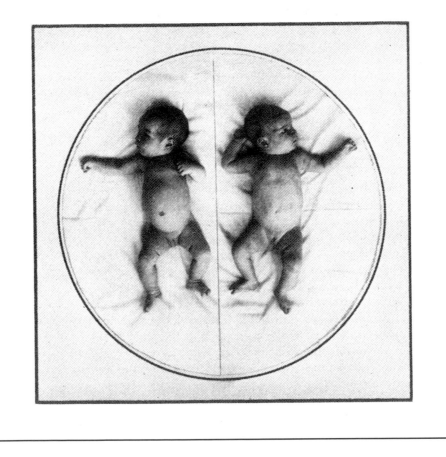

# Conclusion and summary

The view that motor development is simply a function of automatic maturation has been examined and found to be lacking. Contemporary research on motor development would not view the locomotor milestones as the inevitable consequence of maturation. On the contrary, the epigenetic model outlined in Chapter 2 (see Figure 2.2) is highly relevant. There is now rather strong evidence that some of the repetitive , rhythmic motor pattern observed in crawling and walking may be continuous from fetal movements observed *in utero* to the walking movements of the toddler. On the other hand, crawling is not an inevitable sub-stage before walking. Some babies never crawl before they walk, others get about by shuffling along on their bottom; there are alternative pathways to the final upright posture.

Gaining skilled control over this action pattern, as with many other skills, requires not only physical strength but also sensitivity to various kinds of feedback. Gaining control of head, trunk, and legs is assisted by the visual flow pattern (visual proprioception) contingent on body movement. Good control over static balance is a prerequisite for control of dynamic balance, as in walking or running. There are cultural variations in motor development and there is reason to suppose that social support may assist the infant at important moments in the mastery of walking.

Static balance is also a prerequisite for the emergence of visually guided reaching. Here again, an innate coordination becomes modified by feedback, so that by the fifth month, the visually elicited reach of the newborn has become the visually guided reach. Further development enables the infant to gain control over the wide variety of grips of which the human hand is capable. Hierarchical integration of reaching with memory enables reaching to be used in later skills, such as searching for hidden objects. The developing combination of action with cognition forms the topic of the next chapter.

## Further reading

Bruner, J.S. (1974). The organisation of early skilled action. In M.P.M. Richards (Ed.), *The integration of a child into a social world*. Cambridge: Cambridge University Press.

Gallahue, D.L. (1982). *Understanding motor development in children*. Chichester: John Wiley.

# 6 Origins of knowledge

Fig. 6.1 Piaget's hierarchical theory of sensori-motor development.

**P**iaget's general theory was reviewed in Chapter 2 (see pp. 15–21). His theory of cognitive development aimed to explain the development of knowledge in humans, arguing that knowledge originates in the sensori-motor activities of the baby. Piaget stated that infants construct knowledge about the environment through their own actions. He believed that the infant's perception is inadequate to provide information about the world and he argued that perception is given structure by patterns of activity. However, as we saw in Chapter 4, it is difficult to

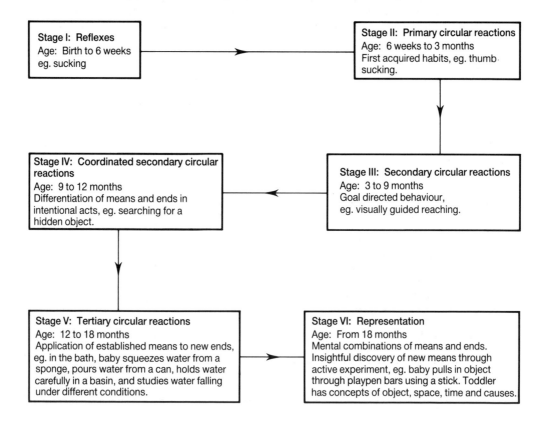

Stage I: Reflexes
Age: Birth to 6 weeks
eg. sucking

Stage II: Primary circular reactions
Age: 6 weeks to 3 months
First acquired habits, eg. thumb sucking.

Stage IV: Coordinated secondary circular reactions
Age: 9 to 12 months
Differentiation of means and ends in intentional acts, eg. searching for a hidden object.

Stage III: Secondary circular reactions
Age: 3 to 9 months
Goal directed behaviour, eg. visually guided reaching.

Stage V: Tertiary circular reactions
Age: 12 to 18 months
Application of established means to new ends, eg. in the bath, baby squeezes water from a sponge, pours water from a can, holds water carefully in a basin, and studies water falling under different conditions.

Stage VI: Representation
Age: From 18 months
Mental combinations of means and ends. Insightful discovery of new means through active experiment, eg. baby pulls in object through playpen bars using a stick. Toddler has concepts of object, space, time and causes.

# Piaget's theory of sensori-motor development

Piaget wished to explain how knowledge is acquired from the earliest beginnings. He argued that knowledge is constructed through the motor activities which link the baby to reality and which give rise to regular sensory consequences. Piaget called infancy the stage of sensori-motor development.

## Sub-stage I: Reflexes

The initial connection of the infant with the environment is elementary and through simple reflexes. The reflexes, although preadapted for rather specific stimuli, are soon applied to a wide variety of new objects. For example, the sucking reflex evolved for feeding but it is soon applied to many things, including the baby's own hand. In Piaget's terminology, the reflex assimilates new objects and in turn accommodates to the new properties of objects encountered. This means that the baby sucks its own hand, and even though this does not provide any food, new information about the hand is discovered through sucking. Thus, sucking has allowed assimilation of information about the hand and, in turn, sucking has been changed or accommodated to allow for exploration of non-food objects.

## Sub-stage II: Primary circular reactions

Once the reflex has become coordinated with another action pattern, it is called a primary circular reaction. This terminology is taken from James Mark Baldwin, who first described these repetitive patterns of activity in babies (see pp. 9–10). A circular reaction is purposeful and not simply reflexive. It has a goal that, once reached, terminates the action and sets in motion a new cycle of activity. For example, the baby may bring its hand to its mouth, touch its mouth and then remove it. The mouth is the goal of the cycle of activity which can be repeated over and over again.

The sub-stage of primary circular reactions lasts from approximately 6 weeks to 4 months. The baby repeats activities for the simple pleasure of doing so and, in the course of the actions, discovers its own body: eyes that can see, ears that can hear, arms that can reach. The baby discovers that objects can simultaneously be looked at and listened to, or that they can be simultaneously touched and felt. These aspects of self-awareness are constructed in the course of activity and as a result of assimilation and accommodation to real things.

## Sub-stage III: Secondary circular reactions

In the next sub-stage, from 4 to 8 months, the primary circular reactions become coordinated with each other. That is, there is a hierarchical integration of the action patterns so far developed. The infant's interest also shifts from repeating actions for their own sake to studying the consequences of the actions. The baby may initially note some accidental consequence of a movement but will then repeat the movement to make the interesting event happen again, as for example when the baby kicks and the hood of the pram moves. As in the previous sub-stages, the circular reactions are terminated by the achievement of the goal.

## Sub-stage IV: Coordinated secondary circular reactions

When secondary circular reactions become hierarchically integrated among themselves, they are known as coordinated secondary circular reactions. This sub-stage lasts from 9 to 12 months. The baby is now able to organise sequences of actions as a means to an end, and is no longer restricted to dealing with the consequences of only one action at a time. For example, the baby can coordinate the action of reaching and grasping a cloth covering an object with a subsequent action of reaching and grasping the object thus revealed. The action pattern is not only terminated (a feedback process) by reaching the goal, as in earlier sub-stages, but it is also goal-directed, because a remote goal is specified from the outset (a feedforward process) and a sequence of coordinated actions is produced.

(continued)

### Sub-stage V: Tertiary circular reactions

The next main change is that infants can deliberately vary their patterns of activity in an effort at trial and error experimentation. They are not concerned simply to make an interesting event last longer but to vary the event itself in order to arrive at a better understanding. A typical behaviour is throwing things out of the pram, which allows the baby both to investigate object trajectories and discover something of gravity as well as the limits of its parents' patience with the game!

### Sub-stage VI: Representation

Infancy ends with the capacity for representation. Piaget uses the word in a specific sense to mean presenting reality to oneself mentally, hence re-presenting reality. Evidence for representation includes deferred imitation, pretend play, and the beginnings of language. Symbolic representation arises as a consequence of the ability to represent reality. Symbols are arbitrarily related to their referents; the symbol stands for an object and serves to represent it. Symbols arise in play, when one object "stands for" another, and also in language, where speech and gestures serve to represent objects.

Representation marks the end of the sensori-motor period. Now the baby can not only act directly on reality but also becomes able to plan actions in relation to imagined realities. The acquisition of the "symbolic function", as Piaget called it, marks a qualitative change to a new stage of development in which symbol systems will play a major part in the development of thinking .

sustain this aspect of his argument in the light of contemporary evidence on perception in young babies. Piaget does, however, offer a systematic classification of the changing patterns of activity in infancy into six sensori-motor sub-stages which may be useful in evaluating the evidence for and against his theory. Figure 6.1 and the panel on pp. 89–90 summarise the six sub-stages of the sensori-motor period.

This chapter describes Piaget's theory of the development of knowledge about physical objects. Of particular interest is the baby's perception and knowledge of object permanence, the principle that objects exist independently of our direct experience of them. Piaget's own observations will first be reviewed in some detail to illustrate the rather subtle argument he pursues. This is followed by a review of some contemporary evidence which is incompatible with Piaget's theoretical assumptions concerning the relationship between the baby's actions and perception of reality. An attempt is made to reconcile these conflicting views.

## Piaget's theory

The infant occupies a social world as well as the physical world. Piaget's description of cognitive development in babies is less concerned with their understanding of persons than with physical reality. Later in this chapter the infant's knowledge of persons is reviewed and this, in turn, sets the stage for an examination of the formation of specific emotional attachments in infancy as described by Bowlby.

A great deal of research has been carried out in the previous quarter century on the infant's understanding of the physical properties of objects. As adults, we know that when one object is occluded by another, so that one of the objects passes from sight, the hidden object continues to exist and to retain its physical, spatial, and temporal properties. Furthermore, the movements of the object and its transformations are subject to regular physical laws and can therefore be predicted. For example, we know when we see a bird fly behind a tree that it is the same bird that comes into view further along its flight path, once the tree no longer obscures the view. A shorthand way of expressing this knowledge is to say that we have the "object concept"—we know that objects are possessed of constant size, shape, and identity, and that things are substantial and permanent.

According to Piaget, the object concept stands at the foundations of thought. He called it the "first invariant" of thinking. Piaget assumed that direct perception of these object properties does not occur and that this understanding must be built up, or constructed, by the infant through the successive coordinations of sensori-motor activity (see pp. 59–60). The general series of coordinations of circular reactions which are said to underlie intellectual development in infancy is reviewed in the panel on pp. 89–90. Each of these sub-stages of development supports a particular level of knowledge about objects, as revealed by the infant's ability to search and find things that have been hidden from view.

Piaget was of the opinion that, until the child is about 18 months old, appearances and disappearances are not understood as the movements of single objects in space. His evidence came from infants' failure to search manually for hidden objects before 9 months. Indeed, he argued that for the young baby the object is a "mere image", lacking permanence, substance, and identity (Piaget, 1954). In Piagetian terminology, the infant does not conserve the object across time and space. Piaget's observations of his own three babies were first published in 1937. They were made by observing the baby or by carrying out simple experiments.

Piaget proposed that six sub-stages could be observed in the development of the baby's understanding of object disappearance, each governed by the general level of sensori-motor organisation appropriate to that sub-stage. The ages are approximate but the sub-stages are said by Piaget to be universal and always to occur in the same order (see the panel on pp. 92–95). The panel presents some of Piaget's own observations, which describe how the baby slowly constructs reality by exploratory actions. The reader may wish to relate the specific observations summarised in this panel to the general summary of sub-stages in the panel on pp. 89–90.

## Six sub-stages in the development of the object concept

### Sub-stage I: Reflex action (0–1.5 months)

Infants do not search for an object that disappears. Instead, they simply repeat the reflex or stare at the place from which an object disappears. Piaget argued that these actions do not require an understanding of object permanence. Rather, the child simply repeats the action pattern that is effective in locating the nipple, or stares at the place of disappearance:

> Lacking prehension, the child could search with his eyes, change his perspective etc. But that is precisely what he does not know how to do, for the vanished object is not yet for him a permanent object which has been moved; it is a mere image which re-enters the void as soon as it vanishes, and emerges from it for no objective reason. (Piaget, 1954, p. 11)

### Sub-stage II: Primary circular reaction (1.5–4 months)

Repetition of reflex actions slowly leads to a new level of coordination (called a primary circular reaction) as the baby explores the objects in the environment. These primary circular reactions are most simply conceived of as habits, and through them the baby first discovers the properties of its own body discovering eyes, arms, hands, and feet in the course of acting on objects. Objects also offer particular types of resistance to actions and so the baby must modify the action pattern (accommodate them) to take these object properties into account, but the baby is still not aware that objects exist independently of the habitual pattern of activity.

### Sub-stage III: Secondary circular reactions (4–8 months)

A new level of coordination is achieved at about 4 months as the primary circular reactions become mutually assimilated and the baby gains simultaneous control over different sensori-motor subsystems. This level of coordination is called a secondary circular reaction. The baby makes discoveries by accident and then repeats the activity as if to find out what caused the particular event of interest. The focus of action shifts to external objects as the baby repetitively explores objects in the environment. Typical actions are repetitive kicking or hand movements, rattle shaking, exploration of bed clothes. Repetition implies a kind of recognition through action and the beginnings of memory, but the baby still lacks awareness of object permanence outside the patterns of activity themselves.

Piaget's observation of Laurent at 5 months and 24 days illustrates this sub-stage:

> Laurent's reaction to falling objects still seems to be non-existent: he does not follow with his eyes any of the objects which I drop in front of him. At 0.5 26 on the other hand, Laurent searches in front of him for a paper ball which I drop above his coverlet. He immediately looks at the coverlet after the third attempt but only in front of him, that is where he has just grasped the ball. When I drop the object outside the bassinet Laurent does not look for it (except around my empty hand while it remains in the air). (Piaget, 1954, p. 14)

Piaget says that a greater degree of permanence is attributed to vanished images, as the baby will look for things that fall and will retrieve a partially hidden object, but permanence remains exclusively connected with the action in progress:

> The child's universe is still only a totality of pictures emerging from nothingness at the moment of the action, to return to nothingness when the action is finished. (Piaget, 1954, p. 43).

Piaget argues that the primary reason for failure to search is because the baby does not understand that the hidden object continues to exist. Figure 6.2 illustrates the baby's problem in searching for a hidden object.

(continued)

## Six sub-stages in the development of the object concept (continued)

Fig. 6.2 (Adapted from Bower, 1982).

Baby retrieves a visible object

Baby searches for and retrieves a partially hidden object

But …

Baby is unable to search for a fully hidden object

### Sub-stage IV: Coordinated secondary circular reactions (9–12 months)

The essential advance of this sub-stage is that the infant, for the first time, becomes able to coordinate means and ends. Babies can now remove covers and search for a hidden object because they can separate the action (the means) from the object to which it is applied (the ends).

Piaget's observation of Laurent at 8 months 29 days illustrates means–ends coordination:

> Laurent plays with a tin box. I take it from him and place it under his pillow; whereas four days previously the child did not react in similar circumstances, this time he grasps the pillow and perceives the box of

which he immediately takes possession … At 9 months and 20 days he searches for a little duck under his pillow, under a spread cloth etc. The behaviour pattern has now been acquired and is accompanied by a growing interest. (Piaget, 1954, p. 45)

Nevertheless, object permanence is still not fully acquired as babies make curious errors when they first become able to search. These errors are variously known as "stage IV" errors, "perseverative" errors or "A not B" errors. An object is hidden at a point A; the child searches for it and finds it. Next the object is placed at a new position B, and it is

(continued)

## Six sub-stages in the development of the object concept (continued)

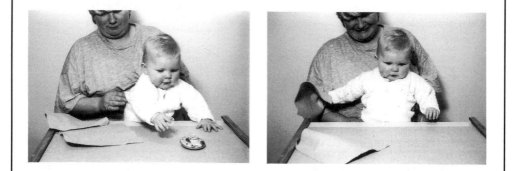

Fig. 6.3    Baby of 9 months making a perseverative error. Photographs courtesy Dr Peter Willatts.

covered while the baby watches. The baby searches for it at the original position A, even though it has just been seen to disappear at B.

Perseverative errors demonstrate that the baby perceives the object to be an extension of action. According to Piaget, the baby has learned a pragmatic procedure for making vanished objects reappear. The baby does not understand that objects are unique and therefore can only be in one place at one time. Instead, the baby is under the impression that its own actions made the object reappear.

### Sub-stage V: Tertiary circular reactions (12–18 months)

The essential progress over the previous stage is that the baby will actively experiment to discover new means to an end in problem solving. By a process of trial and error, the baby discovers that to find the hidden object that has been moved from A to B , one should search where the object was last seen, not where it was first found. Even so, the object is still not completely independent of action. The fact that the object remains known through action is revealed by a repetition of the stage IV error at stage V, when the baby has to imagine the movements of the object between A and B.

This is demonstrated by Piaget's observation on his daughter Jacqueline at 1 year 6 months. She has been playing with a potato, putting it in and out of a box:

> Jacqueline is sitting on a green rug and playing with a potato which interests her very much ... I then take the potato and put it into the box while Jacqueline watches. Then I place the box under the rug and turn it upside down thus leaving the object hidden by the rug ... and I bring out the empty box. ... she searches for the object in the box, looks at the rug etc. but it does not occur to her to raise the rug in order to find the potato underneath. (Piaget, 1954, p. 68)

Piaget argues that babies at stage V understand object permanence only to the extent that they can keep track of the movements of a visible object.

(continued)

# Alternatives to Piaget's theory

As we have repeatedly stressed, Piaget's theory rests heavily on the assumption that perception is insufficient to inform the developing child about the physical world. We should remember that he was writing in 1935 and did not have modern technology to aid him in observing very young babies. He was delighted to learn about newborn imitation and other evidence of infant perceptual competence before he died, and so it seems that contemporary criticisms of his theory should certainly be seen as constructive.

According to Piaget, infants fail to search for a hidden object because they do not perceive that it continues to exist once it disappears. As the object is not permanent, the infant has nothing to search for. If Piaget's interpretation of search failure is correct, then the physical universe of the infant must be very different to that of the adult. However, we have already seen that the weight of the evidence suggests that Piaget's assumptions about infant perception were just too parsimonious to explain modern findings.

Bower (1971) was one of the first to show that infants may perceive the continued existence of objects. He showed that 3-month-old babies were

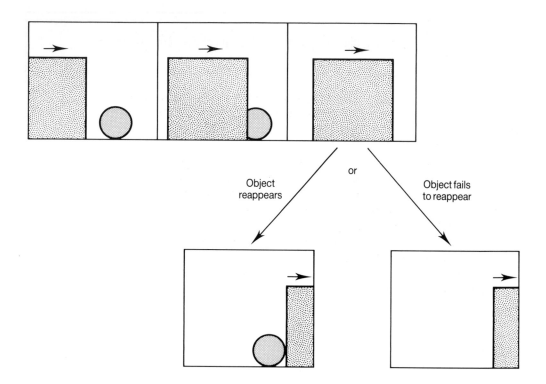

Fig. 6.4 Out of
sight is not out of
mind.

"surprised", as indicated by changes in their heart rate, when an object that
had been seen to pass behind a screen failed to reappear when the screen
moved on (see Figure 6.4).

In another experiment, Bower presented babies with an object that was
made to disappear instantaneously, as if "annihilated", by using a series
of mirrors which could be rapidly moved so that the reflected image of
the object suddenly could no longer be seen. Babies who had been trained
to suck on a nipple in the presence of the object stopped sucking, as if the
conditioned stimulus no longer existed. Another test was carried out by
switching the lights off before the baby could reach for the attractive
object. Several investigators have independently demonstrated that babies who will not search under a cloth for a hidden object, will reach for
an object made invisible by turning off the illumination, even after quite
extensive delays (Bower, 1982; Hood & Willatts, 1986). Thus, out of sight
is not out of mind, as the simple theory of object permanence in babies
might propose.

Bower's argument, which is based on the work of the Belgian psychologist Michotte (1881-1965), is that continued existence and annihilation of
objects are specified quite differently under the particular conditions

where an object undergoes a transition from "in sight" to "out of sight". An object that moves behind a screen is only temporarily occluded. That a permanent object has only temporarily disappeared is specified in the dynamic transitions in the retinal image. When an object moves behind another, the way texture in the occluded object is deleted (wiped) by the texture of the occluding object, specifies that one object is simply moving behind another. In the case of impermanence, when an object is annihilated it either "implodes" so that all its texture disappears without deletion, or it slowly loses texture around the edges (and is replaced by the textured ground) as it disappears. An example would be a puddle evaporating. Bower's argument is that babies' perceptual systems are capable of picking up this distinction between temporary occlusion and annihilation. When the lights are turned off, we perceive the light as going "out of existence" and not the objects it was illuminating. Reciprocally, when a light is turned on in a darkened room, the objects are perceived as pre-existing before the light illuminates them (see Thines, Costall, & Butterworth, 1990, for a full account of Michotte's theory).

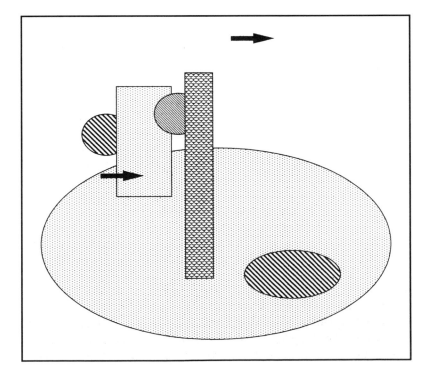

Fig. 6.5 Texture deletion and accretion in dynamic visual arrays.

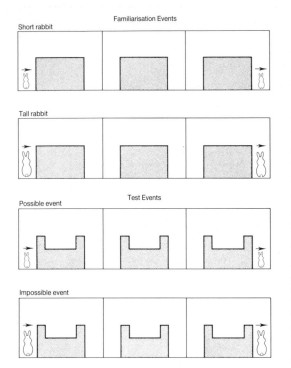

**Familiarisation Events**

Short rabbit

Tall rabbit

**Test Events**

Possible event

Impossible event

Fig. 6.6
Occlusion of a
moving object
(Baillargeon,
1991).

In a recent series of experiments, Baillargeon (1991) studied the ability of 5.5-month-old infants to comprehend occlusion. Two groups of babies first saw several repetitions in which either a tall rabbit or a short rabbit moved behind one edge of a horizontal screen to reappear at the far end. Then a central portion of the screen was removed and a test sequence was shown to both groups of babies, where the tall or short rabbit disappeared and reappeared without becoming visible in the intervening window (see Figure 6.6). Babies attended longer to the impossible event (i.e. where the tall rabbit failed to appear in the window) than to the possible event (i.e. where the short rabbit would have remained occluded beneath the window). This shows that babies perceive not only that the rabbit continues to exist but that it retains its physical size when occluded. For good measure, Baillargeon has replicated this experiment with babies of 3.5 months, using tall and short carrots, and obtained essentially the same results!

If babies are able to perceive that hidden objects continue to exist, we might ask why they are unable to search manually before about 8 months. Piaget's observations on failures in manual search have been replicated on many occasions, so we need to ask: why do babies fail to search if they perceive object permanence? The important issue is not when such physical information becomes available to the infant but why does it take so long before babies can use the information to get their hands on hidden objects? Why is there this disjunction between perceiving the physical properties of objects and using the information to retrieve them?

As the babies' problems with permanence do not seem to lie in perception, we need another explanation of the phenomena Piaget observed. One possibility is that the problem may lie in the infant's ability to remember.

## Coordination of eye, hand, and memory: Explaining failures and errors in search

We have already noted in our discussion of skilled reaching and grasping that babies have difficulty coordinating actions with memory (see p. 83).

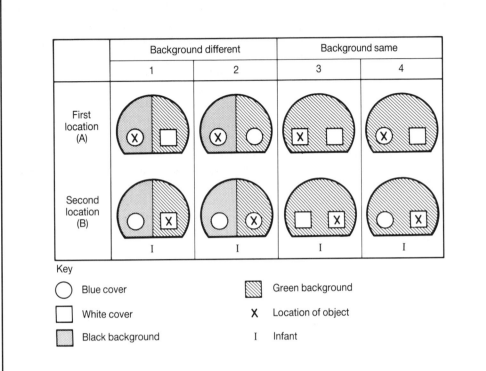

| | Background different | | Background same | |
|---|---|---|---|---|
| | 1 | 2 | 3 | 4 |
| First location (A) | Ⓧ ☐ | Ⓧ ◯ | X ☐ | X ☐ |
| Second location (B) | ◯ Ⓧ | ◯ Ⓧ | ☐ X | ◯ X |
| | I | I | I | I |

Key

◯ Blue cover        ▨ Green background

☐ White cover        X Location of object

▦ Black background      I Infant

Fig. 6.7 Spatial factors determining error in search at Piaget's stage IV. In this version of Piaget's stage IV search task, an object X is hidden on a small table at successive locations to the baby's left and right side. The visual-spatial position of the object is defined relative to the colour of the table surface and relative to the colour of the hiding covers. Babies aged between 8 and 12 months can make use of visual-spatial information to overcome the tendency to make perseverative errors. In fact errors are eliminated in condition 4, where distinctively different covers rest on a continuous background. It is likely that the visual-spatial cues act as landmarks in the small scale space which helps the baby to keep track of the object's movements from A to B. Adapted from Butterworth, Jarrett, & Hicks (1982).

Given a limited ability to hold things in mind, the 9-month-old baby may be able to retrieve hidden objects, but complicating the task may put considerable strain on the baby's ability to hold in mind that he or she had set out to retrieve the object from a particular place. This may explain, at least in part, why babies fail to search or why they make errors.

The stage IV error has been extensively studied and it has been shown that errors are not inevitable, as would be required if the baby truly believes that the object exists only as an extension of his or her action.

Diamond (1988) has shown that a delay of about 3 seconds is necessary between hiding the object and allowing retrieval for babies at 8 months to make the perseverative error of searching at the initial location (A) when the object was seen to disappear at a new place (B). The time needed to generate errors increases by about 2 seconds per month, so that 12-month-old babies only make search errors when the delay exceeds 12 seconds.

There are many other factors that influence the probability of error in babies at stage IV, including the number of alternative locations, whether the object is hidden or simply placed under a transparent container, whether the task is administered in the vertical plane or the horizontal plane, and whether there are distinctive "landmarks" in the field of view.

Errors are not inevitable and can be eliminated where the task is administered in a small-scale space, structured with distinctively different locations at A and B (Butterworth, Jarrett, & Hicks, 1982; see Figure 6.7). This means that babies do not necessarily have problems perceiving the identity of the object at location A with the object subsequently hidden at B. Wellman, Cross, and Bartsch (1987) analysed the results of more than 70 studies of the stage IV error and came to the conclusion that the main factors leading babies in the stage IV age range to make perseverative errors are the delay between hiding the object and allowing the baby to retrieve it, and the number of alternative locations from which the baby must choose.

These results are not entirely compatible with Piaget's theory, because he argued that all infants pass through a stage where they perceive the object as an extension of their own action. At least under some conditions of testing, babies search appropriately for the object hidden at A and B, which implies that they have perceived the object appropriately too. However, there is little doubt that there is a tendency to make errors in visible displacement tasks. It does seem that babies pass through a stage where they are prone to error, as Piaget suggested.

# Reconciliation of Piaget's observations with contemporary data

We examined Piaget's theory that action gives structure to perception in Chapter 4. In the same chapter (see pp. 60–62), an alternative account based on Gibson, which stresses the informative value of perception, was discussed. Simple methods of studying infant perception, based on the spontaneous and learned preferences of babies, reveal that they do indeed perceive complex object properties, such as size and shape constancy, solidity, and permanence early in development before they have had the opportunity to construct these properties through their own activities. This contradicts Piaget's theory, as the infant's perception of reality is not structured by action, as the sensori-motor theory requires.

However, Piaget's observations on babies' typical patterns of action, such as failure to search before stage IV and on errors in search at stage IV, have been generally supported. It seems that if babies perceive reality, the information obtained does not readily help them to find hidden objects. One possible explanation for the baby's difficulty in search might lie in the development of motor skills as was discussed on pp. 83–86. The evidence suggests that babies require many months of practice to master the skills of reaching and grasping a visible object, and that they have difficulties in integrating vision, action, and memory, which could contribute to failures in search. However, babies can reach for an object in the dark; this task does not give the baby the same problem as reaching for an object hidden under a cloth. The demands of both tasks on the infant's memory, at least in terms of time "out of sight", may be quite comparable.

It therefore seems possible that an aspect of Piaget's explanation may still be viable; namely, that babies at stage IV become able to coordinate two sequences of actions, as a means to an end, when they can search for an object hidden behind a cover. The babies must hold the goal in mind (i.e. the object) but first they must reach, grasp, and remove the cover, and then reach, grasp, and possess the object in a hierarchically integrated sequence. The difficulty in searching for a hidden object is analogous to the hierarchical integration of action and memory in dealing with visible, multiple objects, described by Bruner (1974; see p. 85). This difficulty in sequencing actions need not be indicative of failure to perceive permanence and identity. Reaching for an object in the dark does not require the infant to coordinate a sequence of two separate actions, it requires only a single reaching and grasping movement; and babies can carry out this action successfully.

Once search is established, the evidence suggests that although perseverative errors occur, they do not always take the form described by Piaget. It seems unlikely that the baby really experiences the object as an extension of action, as Piaget argued. But his argument here is mainly a consequence of his theory of the status of perception in early development. If infants do perceive reality appropriately, there may still be circumstances where their fragile ability to hold things in mind leads to error and conflict. This happens to absent-minded adults too, but we do not necessarily suppose their whole structure of experience to be different as a consequence.

The status of perception in early cognitive development is a controversial issue from the very outset. We shall see in Chapter 9 that the question of how perception enters into thought and language recurs in contemporary accounts of thinking in young children too.

## Origins of knowledge about persons

It is an interesting question whether a baby's knowledge of persons has different developmental roots than knowledge of physical objects. People are a particular kind of physical object, albeit with social and animate qualities. According to Piaget, the various stages of object permanence apply also to the child's concept of a person, and indeed studies have been carried out in which a baby has to search for his or her mother, who disappears behind a screen (or behind successive screens in an animated version of the stage IV task). Much the same results are obtained as for object search: babies below 8–9 months fail to search for their mother when she hides behind a screen. From 9–12 months they will search at the wrong place for their mother if she hides successively at two locations, A and B. Thus they behave in just the same way as in the manual search task for an inanimate object. There is some evidence that person permanence develops slightly in advance of object permanence but, for the most part, Piagetian tasks yield broadly equivalent results whether the object hidden is a person or a thing (Bell, 1970).

Our earlier discussion of Piaget's search tasks suggested, however, that failures and errors in search may not reflect incomprehension of the principles of permanence and identity. Such problems may rather reflect the difficulty the child has in organising actions on the basis of information recalled from memory. It seems likely that a similar explanation may apply to the baby's developing understanding of persons. That is, early social interactions may be direct and not much influenced by specific memories. Then, as the baby gains sufficient experience with a particular caregiver, typical information about that person may be stored in memory and form the basis for recognition of the adult (certainly by 3 months). Thereafter, the infant may gradually become able to recall information from memory and this will give rise to new social phenomena, such as wariness or fear of strangers, which may indicate that a rather specific memory has formed with respect to familiar adults.

The reason for stating this is that so much information has accumulated about babies' special sensitivity to people that it is difficult to reconcile the new evidence with the view that babies have no awareness of the perma-

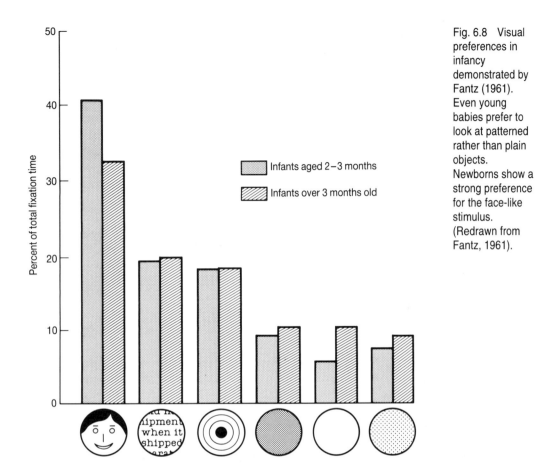

Fig. 6.8 Visual preferences in infancy demonstrated by Fantz (1961). Even young babies prefer to look at patterned rather than plain objects. Newborns show a strong preference for the face-like stimulus. (Redrawn from Fantz, 1961).

Infants aged 2–3 months

Infants over 3 months old

nence and identity of significant persons in their natural environment before 8 or 9 months. For example, early studies of face perception in babies (e.g. Fantz, 1961), suggested that newborn babies prefer to look at a face-like pattern over the same configuration of features randomly arranged. Faces seem to be of special significance, even to the newborn.

Of course, faces are complex, bilaterally symmetrical patterns and some investigators have argued that it is to attribute too much to the baby to suppose that their preference is for faces *per se* and not for some constituent of the facial pattern, such as its symmetry or complexity, or its dynamic animate qualities. Bremner (1994) reviewed the literature on face perception in very young babies and concluded that none of these simpler explanations really accounts for the accumulated experimental data adequately. In fact, most studies have used artificial, two-dimensional pictures of face-like patterns to test babies, and these are not stimuli they are likely to encounter in the natural environment.

In recent years, investigators have turned to the study of real faces, in particular the mother's face, in an attempt to gain greater ecological validity. We have already reviewed evidence which suggests that the focal length of the eye of the newborn is at 21cm, approximately the distance between the mother's face and the infant when held in the natural position for nursing. In addition, we have suggested that the baby recognises his or her mother's voice from birth and that there is an innate coordination between seeing and hearing, such that the baby will look for the visual object at the source of the sound. It does not require a great leap of the imagination to suggest that babies may rapidly learn what their mother looks like from the already acquired knowledge of what she sounds like. We discussed many studies which showed that, by 4 months, babies have quite detailed knowledge of the appearance of the mother's face and voice (see pp. 71–74).

In fact, it seems possible that there is a sensitive period in the hours after birth when the newborn is particularly alert and ready to learn the specific features of his or her mother's face. A recent study by Walton and Bower (1991) showed that babies who were only 7 hours old preferred to look at a coloured image of their mother displayed on a computer screen than at a stranger of similar hair colour. The preference persisted even when the computer was made to reverse the images so that the colour negative of the mother's visual image was displayed. The babies' preference was not for some incidental feature, like hair coloration, but for the face itself. These are exciting findings, difficult to explain, but consistent with our general hypothesis that early learning may depend heavily on the distal senses of audition and vision, with special reference to the social objects to be expected in the natural environment.

In addition to visual recognition of the mother, we have already mentioned that the newborn shows an olfactory preference for the smell of the mother's breast milk. Bremner (1994) also mentions that there is evidence that young babies may recognise the characteristic way in which they are picked up by their mother. It seems most likely therefore that the baby is presented with many sources of information characteristic of the mother and rapidly learns to which person this complex of stimuli is related.

## Smiling and social recognition

Another body of literature, relevant to our understanding of infants' early social relations, exists in the ethological approach to human development. Ethology is the scientific study of behaviour as it occurs under natural conditions (Archer, 1993; Hinde, 1982). Ethologists are concerned with the causes, development, and survival value of naturally occurring behaviour with special reference to the implications for evolutionary biology. Following Darwin's (1872) work on the expression of emotions in humans and animals, ethologists have made a particular contribution in the area of infant non-verbal communication and mother–infant attachment.

Our first example concerns the development of smiling. Smiling in the newborn period was long dismissed as an effect of wind, rather in keeping with the traditional attitude that saw the young infant as an incompetent participant in the social environment. Freedman (1974) went to the trouble to compare the infant's pained facial expression, when actually suffering from wind, with the smile of the newborn. He found many distinct differences between the facial expressions in the two cases, such as the tendency for frown lines in the forehead and red facial colouration when the baby is windy. So newborn smiling is definitely not wind, even though the smile is not obviously directed specifically to people.

It seems most likely that smiling, like other emotional expressions, is one of the species-typical human means of communication, which is at first internally generated and in a sense presupposes an appropriate recipient, whether or not anyone is there to "receive" it. Smiling may be considered as a part of the system that serves to establish a bond between the parent and the child. Furthermore, under normal conditions, the parent will often see the baby smile and sooner or later will perceive it as a social message.

Smiles are not restricted to visual stimuli. By 6 weeks, babies smile to voices, particularly their mother's familiar voice. Nevertheless, the sight of the face becomes a particularly strong stimulus for smiles. It has been argued by Ahrens (1954), an ethologist, that the eyes are a prepotent releaser of smiles. In ethology, a releaser is a specific stimulus responsible for triggering a particular behaviour pattern. Releasing stimuli are simplified configurations which serve in the animal kingdom as minimally sufficient to elicit complex sequences of behaviour in conspecifics (members of the same species). For instance, adult herring gulls regurgitate food for their young when the chick pecks on a red dot on the beak of the adult. The red dot is a sufficient stimulus to release the complex interaction involved in feeding. Ahrens assumed that smiling in babies operates to the configuration of the eyes, as minimal stimuli, in much the same way.

Ahrens found that a pair of red dots painted on a white oval of card was sufficient to elicit smiling. Six dots scattered across the same area of card elicited even more smiling. His ethological approach suggests that smiling in babies is triggered by the eyes as "releasing stimuli". However, congenitally blind babies will smile at the sound of their mother's voice or when touched, although they are often delayed in the development of smiling, so perhaps the eyes are only part of the complex to which the infant responds (Fraiberg, 1974). It seems likely that smiling may at first be endogenously generated but it soon becomes linked to familiar social stimuli and eventually, through social interaction, is most readily elicited by specific people. From about 3 months, smiling is truly social and reciprocal in that the baby's smile is now synchronised with the smiles of the caretaker, much to the gratification of the parents who begin to see their offspring as a lively social companion as a result of this newfound reciprocity. The baby discriminates between familiar and unfamiliar persons, although the infant shows no fear of strangers at this age.

So it can be argued that social smiling, of the kind observed around 3 months, is a measure of the baby's recognition of the familiar adult, contrary to the more parsimonious view that the infant's smile is relatively indiscriminate and not particularly social. Smiling, once established as a reciprocal phenomenon with the parent, is very likely to indicate that the child has a memory, or mental model, of a particular significant person. Even if this is not the case, the multiple sources of information available to the baby about the mother and other familiar people (smell, visual appearance, characteristic manner of interacting, typical intonation patterns) would ensure that the same unique individual is recognised by the baby on each encounter.

## The development of mental models of specific persons

By the age of 8 or 9 months, there is very clear evidence that the baby has built up a memory for specific persons. At this age, babies often show wariness or fear of strangers, a phenomenon that coincides with the beginning of the ability to retrieve information from memory voluntarily. The mental representation tends to be rather rigid. Mothers report that they may inadvertently have frightened their baby by wearing curlers, or when they appear for the first time with their hair concealed by a towel. Fathers who shave off their beard or who finally have a long overdue haircut may also be surprised when this change elicits an anxious or fearful response from their 9-month-old offspring.

In terms of the memory processes involved, the baby becomes capable not only of recognition of the familiar parent but also of recall. Recognition is a memory process that requires the remembered person to be present, as a kind of external stimulus for the memory. Recall is an ability which implies that the infant has, for the first time, spontaneous access to the memory representation of the familiar person. A significant discrepancy between the mental model and a new person elicits fearfulness in the child.

Bowlby (1969) has argued that such an internal working model of the parent figure, constructed from the regularities of everyday social interaction, lies at the foundation of attachment between parent and child.

# The formation of attachment bonds

Attachment may be defined as the ability to form focused, permanent and emotionally meaningful relationships with specific others. Maccoby (1980) has proposed four signs of attachment in babies: (1) from about 8 or 9 months, the baby seeks proximity with the primary caretaker and if separated will periodically return to that person; (2) babies show distress if separated from the caretaker; (3) they are pleased when reunited; and (4) they orient their behaviour by periodically looking to the caretaker as if for approval or reassurance.

Although Bowlby (1969) was very much influenced by psychoanalytic ideas, he actually elaborated his theory of attachment as an alternative to the Freudian view, which had been that attachment of the child to the mother arises through parental gratification of the child's basic needs such as hunger and thirst (the so-called primary needs, see pp. 24–27). Bowlby, by contrast, stressed the security and sense of safety provided by the parent as being at the root of emotional attachment.

Bowlby was particularly influenced by ethological theory, which stressed the importance of imprinting in the formation of attachments in many species of birds. Imprinting is a particularly rapid form of learning in which the specific characteristics of the mother hen are learned in a few hours after hatching by the baby chick. Newly hatched chicks will follow the mother hen and maintain proximity with her. This early experience of following is sufficient for them to learn the specific visual characteristics of the mother (although some of her auditory characteristics may actually have been learned before hatching, just as human infants have pre-natal experience of their mother's voice). The evolutionary significance of rapid imprinting is thought to lie in protection of the offspring from predation. In the longer term, imprinting is also thought to exercise an effect in the selection of partners for mating, who may be chosen to resemble, to some optimal degree, the imprinted parent.

Bowlby was well aware that the specific mechanisms serving early parent–infant relationships are likely to differ between widely separated species, although there may be similarities between closely related primate species. His concern was with the general principle that the formation of parent–offspring relationships is likely to be significant for survival, whatever the species. By comparing different species, it may be possible to discover by analogy how attachment in humans may proceed.

One possibility is that there is a period of rapid learning of the characteristics of the mother through proximity with her, as in the case of imprinting in chicks. In the human case, the difference is that the young infant lacks the motor ability to follow the mother. Instead, Bowlby suggested that signals such as social smiling, crying, and babbling serve to keep the mother in proximity during the early months and this allows the baby to build up a memory of the mother (and father) figure.

Once babies can crawl, they will periodically leave their mother's side and explore a novel environment, returning to the security of the mother from time to time. Exploration using the security of the mother as a base for forays into the environment is a reciprocal aspect of the attachment process. A standardised procedure, known as the strange situation test,

---

### The strange situation test

Over the last few years, a standardised procedure has been developed by Ainsworth and Bell (1970) to measure the quality of attachment between mothers and their infants. The procedure is called the "strange situation" and it involves observing the baby's reactions to a stranger when in the presence of the mother, then when alone with the stranger, and, in a third phase, when reunited with the mother. The test is usually carried out with babies aged about 1 year. Four characteristic patterns of reaction are observed.

*Securely attached* babies are content to explore, while the mother is present, and they react positively to the stranger. However, they become upset when the mother leaves the room and they are left alone with the stranger. On reunion, they seek proximity with the mother, soon calm down and resume their play activities. This group comprises more than two-thirds of babies tested.

Three other groups form a significant minority of babies. *Anxious/avoidant attachment* babies do not particularly seek to be close to their mother when alone with her, nor are they particularly distressed when left alone with the stranger. On being reunited with mother, the baby may not seek proximity to her. Babies who are classed as showing *anxious/resistant attachment* stay close to their

mothers and appear anxious even when with her in the strange situation of testing. They are upset when she leaves the room and are not consolable by the stranger. On reunion, they seek renewed contact with the mother, while actively resisting her efforts to comfort them.

A small group of children have recently been demarcated who are described as *insecure with disorganised attachment*. These children show confused behaviour including "freezing" or stereotyped movements on being reunited with their mother.

These different patterns of attachment have complex causes. They are thought to develop as a response to different styles of mothering, and as a consequence of the temperamental characteristics of the child. For example, mothers who respond rapidly and sensitively to their infants' needs seem more likely to have securely attached babies; neglectful mothers are likely to have infants rated as insecurely attached in strange situation tests. However, the proportion of babies classified as securely or insecurely (anxiously) attached will vary from culture to culture, and the same baby may show different patterns depending on whether parents or siblings accompany the baby in the test.

has been devised by Ainsworth and Bell for measuring attachment, (Ainsworth & Bell, 1970; see the panel opposite).

The onset of independent locomotion, at about 9 months, tends to coincide with other developmental changes, including the beginnings of the ability to recall information from memory. The baby now shows a new wariness or caution in approaching novel objects and often shows fear of strangers. The baby can now recall some aspects of the familiar environment and of attachment figures, and this limits the extent to which the baby ventures into danger. For Bowlby the quality of the maternal relationship is therefore crucial in determining the kind of mental model that the baby develops of the mother, and whether the baby feels secure with her. This in turn influences how the baby takes up opportunities for new learning through exploration.

Babies form attachments not only to their mothers but also to their fathers and to other siblings, especially when their brothers or sisters are involved in infant care, as happens in some societies. Societal values concerning infant upbringing also influence the patterns of attachment observed in strange situation tests. For example, German babies may be socialised for independence, whereas Japanese mothers rarely leave their baby in the care of another person. Consequently, German and Japanese babies are likely to have rather different degrees of experience at being left alone with a stranger and this, naturally, will influence how the infant is classified on Ainsworth's system. It does not mean that Japanese babies are more anxious than German ones. Attachment is a dynamic concept which must be understood in the appropriate socio-cultural context. It should not be thought of as a stereotyped fixed pattern. (For a comprehensive overview of attachment literature, see Bretherton & Waters, 1990.)

The practical importance of attachment research has already been mentioned briefly in Chapter 2 (see pp. 24–27). Hospitalisation and other brief separations of mother and infant are now treated more sensitively than in the past to avoid the distress experienced by babies over 9 months when separated from their parents. Mothers (or fathers) are allowed to stay in hospital with their babies and young children. An important contemporary concern is with provision of day care for the young children of working mothers. Research suggests that brief separations of mother and baby, in an otherwise secure family situation, may not disrupt a healthy attachment bond. On the other hand, insecure attachment and separation where the family is already under stress may result in various "knock on" consequences. For example, in early schooling, the male child may be much less secure and compliant and may affiliate aggressively with other children, while the insecurely attached female child may show marked dependency (Turner, 1991).

Longer-term consequences of disrupted attachment are more difficult to establish and, as the attachment system is rather flexible, they may in any event be reversible. For example, children brought up in orphanages, where there is limited scope for forming specific attachments, nevertheless can become securely attached to their adoptive parents even when adoption is as late as 8 years (Tizard & Hodges, 1978). Theorists nowadays place greater emphasis on the cumulative effects of successive risk factors in making the child vulnerable to disrupted attachment. A British study by Brown and Harris (1980) showed that girls from socially disadvantaged families, whose mothers died before their twelfth birthday, were found to be at risk for psychiatric depression in their early thirties. These women had contracted early, unsatisfactory marriages and the onset of their depression often coincided with further extreme stressors, such as the death of the remaining parent. By contrast, women of similar backgrounds, who had made satisfactory marriages with supportive families and partners, were more resilient under similar conditions of bereavement and less at risk for psychiatric depression. This kind of transactional model (whereby psychological problems may be exacerbated or ameliorated by the sequence of life-events) has been shown to be useful in explaining vulnerability to severe psychiatric illnesses in a wide variety of studies.

## Conclusion and summary

We have reviewed Piaget's theory of the development of object knowledge in infancy. Most modern research has found a similar sequence of stages to those that Piaget outlined in the development of babies' ability to search for a hidden object. However, there is now a great deal of evidence that babies perceive object permanence long before they will search for a hidden object. It could be that infants' perception and understanding of the permanence of objects is well in advance of their ability to put into effect sequences of action in search tasks. This is important because it means that the perceived world would be much more stable and predictable than Piaget had allowed. Furthermore, people are a particular kind of animate, physical object, and again infants' perception of people might be much more stable than had been allowed on the basis of Piaget's theory. When the emotional attachment of the infant to the parent is also considered, it becomes apparent that the baby may already have accumulated a great deal of perceptual experience both of the physical and the social world. When our new-found knowledge of the perceptual abilities of babies is combined with the infant's changing capacity for action, which Piaget documented, it becomes apparent that a great deal of the groundwork for the acquisition of language may have been laid in the perceptual and social experiences of the first few months of life. Pre-verbal communication and the acquisition of speech and language will be one of the major topics of the next chapter.

## Further reading

Archer, J. (1993). *Ethology and human development*. Hemel Hempstead: Harvester.

Bowlby, J. (1969). *Attachment and loss, Vol. 1*. Harmondsworth: Pelican Books.

Butterworth, G.E. (Ed.) (1982). *Infancy and epistemology*. Brighton: Harvester.

PART 3

# Early Childhood

# The emergence of symbols 7

**M**ost people would agree that by the age of 2 the child is no longer a baby. In fact, the typical 2-year-old might well protest if he or she is treated as a baby! The transition from infancy to childhood is gradual and it is difficult to say exactly where infancy ends and childhood begins. The toddler will have learned to walk, he or she will have good comprehension of language and be able to talk, and is very independent by comparison with the infant. These landmarks in physical and intellectual growth might be taken as important indicators of a new developmental stage. However, as was discussed earlier (see pp. 27–30), evidence for a widespread qualitative change in the organisation of behaviour is required before it can be argued that early childhood marks a new stage of development.

There is evidence for qualitative change in physical development from infancy to the pre-school years. Most children will have gained a full set of 20 primary or deciduous teeth by the age of 30 months, which will allow them to cope with a more adult-like diet. Overall physical growth slows down markedly by comparison with the rate of growth in infancy. Between the ages of 2 and 6 years, children gain on average 3 inches in height per year and about 4.5 pounds in weight (Johnston, 1986).

There are also marked changes in body proportions, with the relative growth rate of the head and trunk slowing down, while the growth rate of the arms and legs speeds up. At 2 years, the head is about 25% of the total height of the child, whereas by 5 years, the proportion falls to about 16%. The top-heavy infant starts to acquire proportions that are more adult-like. The changes in the relative proportion of the head are accompanied by major growth spurts in the brain, so that by 3 years of age, the brain has attained approximately 75% of the adult weight. By the age of 6 years, the brain has attained 90% of the adult weight.

Motor development proceeds apace and the child becomes much more skilled in movement as baby-fat is lost. The changes in body proportions have the effect of moving the centre of gravity of the body downwards, and this enables the toddler to perform feats that require strong muscles and good balance, such as running, throwing, and catching. Fine motor skills also improve rapidly, so that between 3 and 5 the child becomes capable of building with bricks, and acquires the fine coordination needed to hold a pencil, to use scissors, to button clothes and tie shoe-laces.

The main evidence for a stage transition between infancy and early childhood comes from Piaget's theory of cognitive development. Piaget argued that the major difference between the sensori-motor stage of infancy and early childhood is in the capacity for representation. Representation may be defined as the ability to think about objects without having to act directly on them. Put simply, representation involves the imagination. Piaget (1951) outlined his theory of the transition from the sensori-motor stage of infancy to representation in early childhood in a book entitled *Play, dreams and imitation in childhood*. An important aspect of the capacity for representation is that the child becomes able both to think and to act symbolically.

Symbols arise when one object, action, or thought is made to stand for another. The relation between a symbol and its referent can be completely arbitrary and a matter of social convention, as is the case in spoken language, or the symbol may resemble what it stands for, as in some cases of children's drawing and in symbolic play. All symbols involve representation, and they require the capacity for mental imagery, but not all representation is symbolic. In some cases, representation may simply be a literal memory for an object, an action, or an event. Nevertheless, the capacity for symbolism and the wide impact of the newly emerging ability constitutes the best evidence for a stage transition in cognitive processes from infancy to early childhood.

Piaget called the period of early childhood the "pre-operational stage". He argued that, although young children can think symbolically, they cannot yet perform the logical "operations" which will transform knowledge into an organised network. The logical aspect of Piaget's theory of development, together with criticisms based on contemporary research, will be dealt with more fully in Chapter 9. Before this, we will concentrate on three interrelated aspects of symbolism in early childhood. This chapter considers the acquisition of language. Chapter 8 covers symbolic play and symbolism in children's drawing. The case of childhood autism, considered as a profound failure in the development of the capacity for symbolic thought, will also be considered in Chapter 8.

## The transition to symbols

One of the most intractable problems in developmental psychology has been to explain how the "symbolic function" arises. Although the temptation is to suppose that there is an all-or-nothing transition from complete lack of representation in infancy to symbolic representation in early childhood, a closer look suggests that there may be developmentally intermediate forms of signification whereby an action or image may stand for another object. One way to understand this transition is to distinguish between the ways in which signs may indicate other things "here and now" in reality and the ways in which signs come to be represented, to take on the status of symbols, in an imagined reality.

A sign may indicate something in the present and this level of signification is accessible to many animals, as when a dog or cat recognises the call to dinner. However, a sign may be used to indicate something that is not physically present in the actual surroundings. As Langer (1969, p. 31) put it, such representational signs "are not announcers of things, they are reminders". Such symbols take the place of things that have been previously directly experienced and so represent reality.

Many theorists follow the Swiss linguist, *Ferdinand de Saussure* (1857–1913), in distinguishing between *signifiers*, which stand for an object , and the *signified* (the object itself). The Table below shows a four-fold matrix which contrasts conventional with non-conventional signifiers and intentional with non-intentional signifiers. These are not absolute distinctions and there is some overlap between the categories. Nevertheless, the

---

### Sign, Index, Gesture and Symbol (after Kaye)

| Signifier | Undifferentiated (Unintentional) | Differentiated (Intentional) |
|---|---|---|
| Conventional | Sign<br>e.g. brake-lights<br>e.g. involuntary "ouch"<br>e.g. iconic sign, photograph, map | Symbol<br>e.g. words<br>e.g. warning traffic triangle |
| Non-conventional | Index<br>e.g. footprints<br>e.g. cry of pain<br>e.g. smoke | Gesture<br>e.g. pointing<br>e.g. threatening fist |

Horizontal and vertical axes show relations between signifier and signified.

classification system may prove useful in understanding the development of symbolism, especially in the ways that young children make use of signifiers in referential communication, in play and in drawing.

To explain the origins of language we need to understand how infants make the transition from non-verbal communication to verbal communication by means of symbols. The Table on p. 117, taken from Kaye (1982), offers a useful classification which shows the several ways in which signifiers can carry shared meaning. The four cells differ in the extent to which the signifier is conventional and intentionally differentiated from the object signified. The left-hand column summarises means of communication that are basically unintentional, whereas the right-hand column is concerned with intentional communication. The upper row is concerned with conventional, socially agreed modes of communication, whereas the lower row deals with non-conventional signifiers. The transition to symbols can be summarised as a double movement, from non-intentional to intentional and from non-conventional to conventional means of communication. Remember that these distinctions are not intended to be absolute; it can be difficult to determine exactly when a behaviour should be considered an intentional communication. Nevertheless, the matrix is useful for distinguishing different aspects of the development of symbolism. It should also be obvious that social processes must play an important part in the acquisition of conventional forms of communication.

The first cell in the matrix consists of *signs*: these are defined as conventional, undifferentiated (hence unintentional) signifiers. A sign, such as the brake-lights coming on in a car, signifies something— that the car is slowing down. It is conventional to fit such lights but the lights do not perform their function intentionally. In the case of the pre-verbal infant some behaviours (e.g. lip smacking when feeding) rapidly become conventions shared with the caretaker. Such signs do not begin with the intention to communicate but they rapidly take on that function as the caretaker reads meaning into them.

The second cell consists of indices: these are defined as undifferentiated (unintentional) and non-conventional signifiers. An *index*, such as smoke from a fire or a footprint left by an animal, is an unintended consequence of some other event. There is a physical connection between the index and that which it signifies, and this is not a matter of social convention. The animal did not intend to leave its footprints, and if the footprints have any meaning, it is again only to the eye of a knowledgeable observer. An action may separately be intentional and also be a signifier, such as when a bird takes flight and this is taken as an index of danger by other animals. However, the bird itself is not intentionally signifying danger. An example from human development might be when the young baby cries from hunger, or when the infant smiles at a moving lampshade. In both cases, the actions carry meaning for a knowledgeable adult but are involuntary indices of the infant's emotional state.

Of course, the same actions may be performed intentionally, by older babies, when they will acquire the status of *gestures*—differentiated (intentional) signifiers. Actions like smiling or crying may be gestures if used intentionally to communicate pleasure or fear. A gesture, such as pointing, which the human infant can comprehend and produce at about 1 year, is an intentional signifier, because it is used to single out an object for another observer. It is universal in normal development and not a matter of social convention. The majority of gestures are not, however, universal and they are a matter of convention. For example, the hand signals that are used by the police to direct traffic, or the head shake that means "no" in Western society, are conventional and have the status of symbols. The important distinction between a gesture and a symbol is that the gesture is differentiated from what is signified but it is not taken as equivalent to the signified object.

The fourth cell of the matrix consists of *symbols*: these are differentiated (intentional), conventional signifiers. Symbols are socially defined and they are taken to be equivalent to the objects and events that they signify, at least with respect to their role in the representation of reality. A *language* is built from a symbolic code that has meaning in a particular cultural context. The language may be spoken, written, or a manual sign language, but in whatever form its elements will be conventionally defined and serve as intentional signifiers.

Some signifiers may simultaneously occupy two cells in the matrix. For example, an *iconic signifier* (iconic because it resembles what is signified), such as a photograph or drawing, may carry meaning at the level of realistic depiction (as an index) but it may also carry a symbolic meaning. Hieroglyphics are an example of logographic symbols which retain an iconic resemblance to their referent. Children's drawings may also serve as indices and as symbols. These levels of signification can be studied developmentally, with some forms emerging before others and sometimes with more than one form of signification being available simultaneously to the child.

## The development of language

Learning language requires the child to learn not only about the meaning of individual symbols—words—but also about the rules by which words can be combined to form phrases and sentences. These combinatorial rules—or *grammar*—are what give language its phenomenal power, because they allow for an infinitely large number of word combinations.

Each language has its own vocabulary and its own grammatical rules, and the child's task is to discover what these are in the language or languages that are used by the adults and older children that the child comes into contact with. Traditional theories of language acquisition have been concerned with the way in which the child attains such linguistic knowledge.

In order to understand some of the key issues in child language research, we will briefly discuss four very different theories—those of Skinner, Chomsky, Piaget, and Bruner.

## Key theories of
## the development of language

*Skinner* worked in the tradition of American Behaviourism and was much influenced by Watson (see pp. 11–14). Skinner's aim was to explain the whole of human and animal learning according to a set of basic principles. In order to do this, he trained laboratory animals such as rats and pigeons to make simple responses such as pushing a lever or pecking at a disk. The training regime used a technique known as "operant conditioning" (see Walker, 1984, for a detailed account), which involves the trainer bringing about the linking of a response to a stimulus through the use of carefully controlled reinforcement. In the case of a rat being trained to press a lever, for example, the lever would be the stimulus, a press of the lever would be the response, and the reinforcement would be food which the rat would receive after pressing the lever.

Skinner claimed in his book, *Verbal behavior* (1957), that children "learn" language through operant conditioning. According to Skinner, children receive reinforcement for uttering certain sounds. The reinforcement is not, however, food or water but parental encouragement and approval. Skinner gives several examples of how the conditioning of children's verbal behaviour might occur:

> In all verbal behavior under stimulus control there are three important events to be taken into account: a stimulus, a response and a reinforcement. These are contingent upon each other... The three term contingency ... is exemplified when, in the presence of a doll, a child frequently achieves some sort of generalised reinforcement by saying "doll". (Skinner, 1957, p. 81)

*Noam Chomsky* wrote a strongly worded and now famous critique of *Verbal behavior* in 1959. He rejected the critical role of reinforcement in children's learning of language and he also criticised Skinner for failing to take account of the central role of syntactic rules in people's knowledge of language. *Syntactic rules* provide information about how words can be ordered to form sentences, and mastery of them is essential for the child who is learning to talk.

Chomsky was perhaps somewhat unfair in claiming that Skinner paid no attention to syntax, as he did make some attempt to explain how speakers could produce novel utterances. However, Skinner's attempt to deal with the mastery of syntactic rules was unconvincing because, as Chomsky argued, there was an inherent problem with the claim that language could be "learned" through operant conditioning. Chomsky pointed out that the essence of knowing a language is acquiring knowledge that gives rise to linguistic productivity, that is, the ability to produce and understand utterances that the speaker has never heard before. Thus, for Skinner, the issue of linguistic productivity was a secondary one, whereas for Chomsky it lay at the heart of accounting for language acquisition.

Learning a language involves the acquisition of a body of knowledge. In Chomsky's view, such knowledge is best described by a set of rules (Chomsky, 1965) or, in more recent accounts (Chomsky, 1986), by a set of principles and parameters. Chomsky drew attention to the fact that, although syntactic rules are complex, almost all children acquire them. Furthermore, this acquisition of rules does not take place as the result of careful "teaching". Parents do not normally instruct their children in how to acquire language. Indeed, how could such instruction occur, given that instruction requires children to have language in the first place! Neither, according to Chomsky, do children receive the careful, repeated, and systematic exposure to language that would be required for operant conditioning to occur.

Chomsky claimed that children acquire language because they possess an innate, language-specific mechanism, which he called a *language acquisition device* (LAD). According to Chomsky, this device is present only in the human brain and it endows human offspring with a unique ability to acquire language. Far from being learned, children develop—or "acquire"—language in much the same way that they grow arms and legs or undergo physical changes at puberty. A programme for the development of language is laid down at birth and, according to Chomsky, only a minimal contribution from the environment is required for it to proceed.

Chomsky's claim that the capacity to acquire language is uniquely human has been tested in a series of studies in which chimpanzees have

## Teaching language to chimpanzees

Over the last 20 years or so there have been a number of studies that have attempted to teach language to chimpanzees. These studies have made use either of sign language as in the case of Washoe (Gardner & Gardner, 1971; 1974) and Nim (Terrace, 1979; 1985), who were trained to produce signs from American Sign Language (ASL), or they have used an artificial language communicated via a keyboard (see Premack, 1986, for a review). The use of sign language or a keyboard is designed to overcome the fact that chimpanzees have only a very limited ability to produce speech sounds.

There has been considerable disagreement about the way the outcome of these studies should be interpreted. Authors such as Fouts (1972) have claimed that chimpanzees show a considerable capacity to use symbols and to combine them into novel but meaningful sequences. On the other hand, Petitto and Seidenberg (see Petitto & Seidenberg, 1979; Seidenberg & Petitto, 1979) have attempted to dismiss the chimpanzee's use of signs as little more than an impressive example of conditioning. Premack, who has carried out a long programme of studies teaching chimps to use a keyboard, was initially optimistic about the language potential of apes but he now concludes that apes cannot be turned into children even with the most extensive language training (Premack, 1986).

The debate about chimpanzees' abilities to learn language was re-awakened by Savage-Rumbaugh's reports of the performance of a young male pygmy chimpanzee, Kanzi, whom she was studying (Savage-Rumbaugh et al., 1986). The chimpanzees used by the Gardners, Terrace, and Premack were all common chimpanzees (*Pan troglodytes*). There is some evidence that pygmy chimpanzees (*Pan paniscus*)—also known as bonobos—are more intelligent than common chimps and that they also have a more complex social-communicative repertoire.

Savage-Rumbaugh had previously trained the chimpanzees, Austin and Sherman (Savage-Rumbaugh, 1986), who were taught to communicate through a keyboard that activated geometric symbols. She comments that they had to be given explicit training to go beyond the use of a particular visual symbol in a single context. Kanzi differed from Austin and Sherman in that he learned to use the symbol keyboard spontaneously rather than in special training sessions. This came about because he watched his mother, Matata, being trained to use the keyboard. Kanzi was not given formal training in the use of the keyboard or systematic food rewards.

Once Kanzi had learned the symbols on the keyboard, he was provided with a portable board that could be taken outside the laboratory. The board contained photographs of the symbols on the keyboard (lexigrams) and a particular symbol was selected by touching the board. Kanzi was credited with knowing a lexigram only if he spontaneously produced it on at least nine occasions and also if he provided unambiguous evidence that he was using it appropriately. For example, many of the lexigrams referred to locations and Kanzi showed that he understood them by indicating the lexigram and then taking a researcher to the correct location. Kanzi was also tested to see if he understood the items in his production vocabulary.

Kanzi comprehended lexigrams before producing them and he often comprehended both the spoken English word and the lexigram before using the latter in production. For example, when Kanzi first understood the word "strawberries", he would hurry over to the strawberry patch when the word was mentioned. Later the lexigram for "strawberry" was added to Kanzi's keyboard and he learned to use it to request a strawberry to eat, to ask to travel to the strawberry patch, and also when shown a picture of strawberries.

Overall, Kanzi's performance at learning lexigrams was impressive and over a period of 17 months he learned to understand nearly 60 symbols and produce nearly 50. He also regularly produced two and three lexigram combinations such as "Grape eat", "More drink", and "Apple me eat".

(continued)

## Teaching language to chimpanzees (continued)

Kanzi could also understand the difference in meaning between two similar combinations such as "Chase Kanzi" and "Kanzi chase". The most recent report of his progress (Savage-Rumbaugh et al., 1993) describes Kanzi's ability to make even more complex syntactic distinctions such as that between "Put the pine needles in your ball" and "Can you put the ball on the pine needles?" Overall, Kanzi's syntactic comprehension was very comparable to that of Alia, a 2-year-old child. However, there was one striking difference between them. Over the six months of testing, Alia produced increasingly long utterances, combining three or four words by the time she was 2 years old. However, Kanzi's production remained stable with the great majority of his utterances consisting of a single lexigram.

Seidenberg and Petitto (1987) have argued that Kanzi's use of lexigrams is not genuinely symbolic and that it is fundamentally different from young children's early vocabulary learning. However, both Savage-Rumbaugh (1987) and Nelson (1987) have convincingly argued that Kanzi's understanding and use of lexigrams is much closer to that of young children than Seidenberg and Petitto claim. Nevertheless, although Kanzi's performance is very impressive, it pales into insignificance when compared with the very rapid vocabulary learning that occurs in young children and their early mastery of syntactic rules.

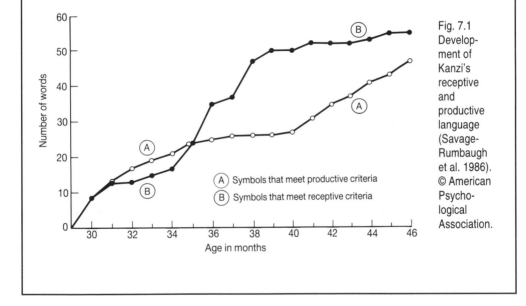

Fig. 7.1 Development of Kanzi's receptive and productive language (Savage-Rumbaugh et al. 1986). © American Psychological Association.

(A) Symbols that meet productive criteria
(B) Symbols that meet receptive criteria

been given the opportunity to acquire language (see panel above). Although the achievements of many of these chimpanzees have been impressive, they serve to illustrate that, although chimpanzees can be taught to use symbols to represent words, their ability to do so is very much less than that of a child. The same can also be said of syntactic ability. Comprehension of simple syntactic forms does appear possible at least for one bonobo (see panel on pp. 122–123) but there is, as yet, no evidence that even bonobos ever attain the mastery of complex syntax.

*Piaget*'s views about the nature of child language development are distinctive from those of both Skinner and Chomsky. For Piaget (see Piaget, 1970), language emerges in the child neither as the result of conditioning, nor as a result of the maturation of innate language-specific processes, but through the completion of the processes of development that occur in the sensori-motor stage. Language in Piagetian theory is only one manifestation of a much wider ability to represent the world through symbols, and it is intimately bound up with cognitive development. Thus Piaget's view of language is at odds with Chomsky's claim that language is acquired through language-specific mechanisms that are independent of other cognitive functions.

In some respects, both the claims of Piaget and Chomsky are correct. There is evidence that acquisition of some aspects of language, notably syntax, are independent of other aspects of cognitive development (see also p. 218). At the same time, however, there is no doubt that full understanding of a great deal of language requires other, more general, cognitive abilities. Chomsky has admitted this to be the case (see Chomsky, 1976) and has recognised that the use of language results only from the interaction of several mental faculties. For example, understanding the meaning of a word like "tiger" draws on our general knowledge of tigers, their appearance and their behaviour.

## The social context of early language development

Although the theories of Chomsky, Skinner, and Piaget are all very different, they generally take very little account of the fact that the young child does not encounter language in isolation. It is easy to get the impression from Chomsky, for example, that the child is a little linguist analysing language from randomly encountered adult utterances. However, spoken language is used in a social context for communication, and so the child comes into contact with language in a situation where, although the language is unfamiliar, many other aspects of the social context will be familiar.

Vygotsky (see pp. 21–24) placed great emphasis on the importance of social interaction in cognitive development, especially the development of language and thinking. His views had an important influence on *Jerome Bruner*, who was responsible for introducing Vygotsky's ideas to scholars outside Russia. The influence of Vygotsky can be seen very clearly in Bruner's account of early language development.

Bruner (1975a; 1975b) argued that children learn about language in the highly familiar context of social exchanges with caretakers. (Like many other researchers who have considered early parent–child interaction, Bruner talks exclusively about the role of mothers, but his arguments could apply to any adult or older child who spends a great deal of time with the child.) According to Bruner, the familiar social context helps the child to interpret the language spoken by the caretaker. This is possible because, in talking to young children, adults typically use language to interpret and comment on the social context. As Bruner expresses it, the child's knowledge of the social context and of the routines that occur within it, assist the child to "crack the code" of the language that accompanies social interaction.

Fig. 7.2  Jerome Bruner.

Bruner elaborated and revised the details of his theory over a number of years (Bruner, 1983a; 1983b), but his essential claim remained the same. What changed were his arguments about the precise relationship between the structure of the social context and the structure of language. In his original 1976 theory, Bruner argued that there was a high degree of similarity between the structure of social events and the structure of language, suggesting, for example, that children could learn about the grammatical roles of *agent* (the person who carries out an action) and *experiencer* (the person on whom an action is performed) through turn-taking games. However, by 1983, Bruner had modified his claims to argue that the social context provides support for language acquisition but it does not directly provide the knowledge that is necessary to acquire language. According to Bruner, language—particularly syntax—is an "autonomous problem space". In other words, learning the rules of grammar is a distinctive task that is separate from other kinds of learning in which the child engages.

This reformulation of Bruner's theory makes it more compatible with Chomsky's claims about the special mechanisms that are employed in the acquisition of syntax. Many researchers of child language follow Bruner's more general view that "... we shall make little progress if we adhere either to the impossible account of extreme empiricism or to the miraculous one of pure nativism" (Bruner, 1983b). Although there is much to be discovered about child language, research suggests that the processes involved are the result of a complex interaction between the child's general cognitive abilities, specific linguistic abilities, and the child's experience of language.

There is also good evidence that the social-interactional context in which children hear people talking has an important role to play in the way that young children first begin to understand and produce language. As Bruner pointed out, parents talk to their children about events and objects with which the child is currently engaged.

A study by Harris, Jones, and Grant (1983; 1984/85) showed that two-thirds of the changes in mothers' conversational topics arose from changes in their children's activity. This proportion was evident even when the children were only 7 months old and it was still present when the children had reached 16 months of age. What changed over this period was the kind of activity that prompted mothers to begin a new conversational topic. When the children were only 7 months old, mothers relied on changes in the children's direction of gaze as a cue to what to talk about. By 10 months, mothers mainly began a new conversational topic in response to a change in the child's action and, by 16 months, actions and actions accompanied by child vocalisations were the two main events that prompted mothers to change their topic of conversation.

Further evidence of the close relationship between mothers' speech to their children and ongoing activity comes from the finding that, when the children were 16 months old, 78% of maternal utterances concerned objects on which the child was currently focusing attention. This proportion was considerably lower (49%) for a group of children who had delayed language development at 2 years of age (Harris, Jones, Brookes, & Grant, 1986).

There are two possible explanations for this finding. One is that the differences in the mothers' speech in the two groups arose *because* of differences in the language ability of the two groups. In other words, the two groups of mothers might have been talking differently because the two groups of children were talking differently. The other explanation is that these differences in maternal speech were responsible, at least in part, for the differences in the children's language ability.

There is good reason for preferring the second of these explanations because, when the speech of the two groups of mothers was sampled, all of the children, who were then 16 months old, appeared very similar. All of the children were at the pre-word stage and they were not producing any recognisable words. Evidence of differences among the children did not appear until several months later. At 2 years of age, the slower developers were still producing single words but the normal developers were producing utterances that were several words long. The two groups also differed in their vocabulary size, with the normal developers knowing more words than the slower developers. Because these differences between the two groups did not emerge until several months *after* the mothers' speech was sampled, it is unlikely that the mothers' speech styles were being influenced by the speech of their children. These findings can, therefore, be seen as evidence that the close tying of maternal speech to the current social context is an important factor in early language development.

Other aspects of the developing patterns of communication between mothers and children would appear to be important for the development of language. Most notable among these are establishment of *joint attention* between mother and child, and the child's understanding of *reference*.

Collis and Schaffer (1975) and Collis (1977) have shown that joint visual attention is common in the first year of life; mothers and babies tend to look at the same objects. Their argument is that joint attention in the first year of life occurs because mothers tend to follow their children's line of regard, although, by the second year, infants pay increasing attention to where their mother is looking. Butterworth (Butterworth & Grover, 1989; Butterworth & Jarrett, 1991) has shown, however, that the looking behaviour of young infants is rather more sophisticated than the findings of Collis and Schaffer suggest. Babies as young as 6 months are able to follow their mother's line of regard successfully providing that the object of regard is in front of the infant and it is the first one that the baby encounters when turning to look. By the age of 12 months, babies are still unable to locate a target that is behind them but they can locate a target even when it is not the first one that is encountered in turning to look. By the age of 18 months, babies can successfully locate objects behind them although they are still easily distracted if there is already something in their field of view.

A significant development for the establishment of joint reference occurs towards the end of the first year when infants show signs of understanding pointing and look in the appropriate direction when someone else points (Leung & Rheingold, 1981; Schaffer, 1984). Pointing is crucial to arguments about the development of referential communication because this gesture provides an important non-verbal procedure for picking out an object in the environment both for the benefit of another person and for oneself. The ability to point is uniquely human. Even chimpanzees are incapable of using an outstretched arm and index finger

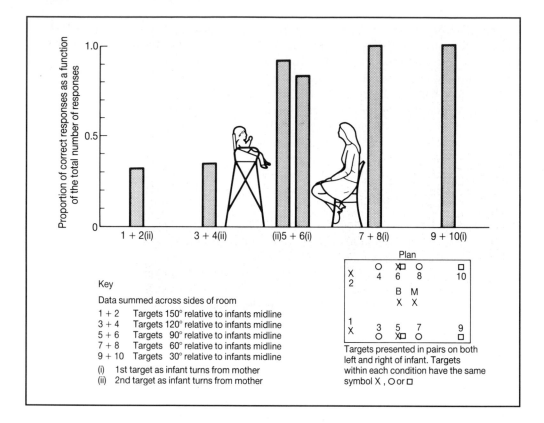

Key

Data summed across sides of room

| | |
|---|---|
| 1 + 2 | Targets 150° relative to infants midline |
| 3 + 4 | Targets 120° relative to infants midline |
| 5 + 6 | Targets 90° relative to infants midline |
| 7 + 8 | Targets 60° relative to infants midline |
| 9 + 10 | Targets 30° relative to infants midline |
| (i) | 1st target as infant turns from mother |
| (ii) | 2nd target as infant turns from mother |

Plan

Targets presented in pairs on both left and right of infant. Targets within each condition have the same symbol X, O or □

Fig. 7.3 Baby's comprehension of direction of gaze (Butterworth & Jarrett, 1991).

to indicate (Butterworth, 1994), and this difference between the chimp and the child appears to have implications for differences in their vocabulary development (see Harris, 1992; see also the panel on pp. 122–123).

Babies begin to point at around 1 year of age and, soon after doing so, they use pointing to direct attention. Infants typically check that mothers are attending to the object of interest: they point and then turn to check that the mother is looking in the direction of the point. Butterworth and Franco (1990) found that pointing and checking were invariably accompanied by vocalisation, which supports the view that pointing is communicative. They also found that, by 15 months, infants would first check to see whether the mother was looking at them and only then point in order to redirect attention.

There is a relationship between the child's production of pointing and language development. Bates et al. (1979) showed that both proffering objects and communicative pointing (pointing followed by checking) were predictive of early vocabulary development; and Folven, Bonvillian,

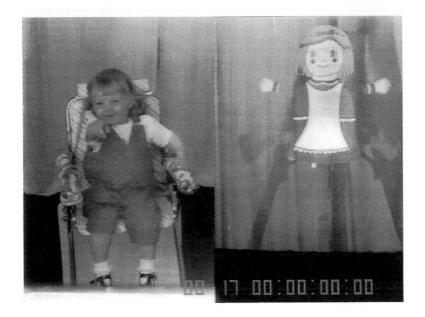

Fig. 7.4 Baby pointing at doll.

and Orlansky (1984/85) found that the frequency with which children produced communicative pointing between 9 and 12.5 months was positively correlated with the size of both spoken and signed lexicons during the second year of life.

Pointing tends to elicit very specific responses from adults. Masur (1982) investigated maternal responses to children's first pointing gestures and found that these produced a very high rate of response. Significantly, most maternal responses involved labelling the object at which the child was pointing. Baldwin and Markman (1989) have explored the significance of pointing in the child's acquisition of new vocabulary. They have shown that children as young as 10 months of age spend significantly longer looking at novel objects when they are pointed at than when they are merely presented to the child without pointing. When an object is labelled, as well as being pointed to, the amount of looking is even greater, suggesting that the young child is most predisposed to look at objects that are singled out both through pointing and through the use of an accompanying verbal label.

## Early vocabulary development

Most children show their earliest understanding of language when they respond to their own name at around 7 months. Gradually, over the next few months, comprehension increases until the point when, having

## The meaning of children's first words

The prevailing view in the mid-1980s was that the first words children produce are not the names of objects or actions. Rather, it was argued, first words are *context-bound* in that they are produced only in one specific situation or context (Bates et al., 1979; Dore, 1985; Nelson & Lucariello,1985; Barrett, 1986). Some examples of context-bound word use are reported by Harris et al. (1988). James, one of the children they were studying, initially used "mummy" only when he was handing a toy to his mother and "there" only when pointing up to a picture on a frieze. Another child, Jenny, initially used "bye-bye" only when she was waving goodbye.

There is, however, increasing evidence that not all early words are used in only a single context. Bates et al. (1979) report some early words being *contextually flexible*, that is, they are used in more than one behavioural context (see, for example, Bates et al., 1979; Dromi, 1987; Lucariello, 1987; Harris et al., 1988; Barrett, Harris, & Chasin, 1991; Goldfield & Reznick, 1990). For example, in the study by Harris et al. (1988), James used "teddy" to refer to one particular teddy in a variety of different contexts (for example, when sitting on teddy and when pointing to teddy's reflection in a mirror). This use, although restricted to a single referent (one particular teddy), is contextually flexible and it contrasts with James' use of "mummy".

Another child, a little girl called Madeleine, first used the word "shoes" in a range of situations including looking at pictures of shoes in a book, pointing at her own shoes, and also when holding her doll's shoes. Both "teddy" and "shoes" were being used as the name of the object to which they referred. In the study by Harris et al. (1988), of the first 10 words produced by four children, i.e. 40 in total, 14 were initially used as object names.

Some authors (notably Dore, 1978; and McShane, 1979) have argued that young children's first use of object names comes about because they develop an insight that words can be used to name things. The development of such an insight has been thought to underpin the "vocabulary spurt", the point at which the rate of learning new words suddenly increases (see Figure 7.5). However, the finding that children have both context-bound and contextually flexible word-uses when they first start to talk, suggests that there is no sudden development of a naming insight. Data from Goldfield and Reznick (1990) support this view. They studied 24 children from the age of just over 1 year and found that, as vocabulary size increased, there was an increasing proportion of object names. However, even before the vocabulary spurt occurred, almost half of the words used by the children were object names.

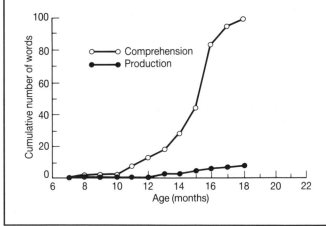

Fig. 7.5 Development of comprehension and production of words.

reached an understanding of about 20 or 30 words, children first start to talk. Children vary considerably in the age at which the first word appears. For some children it is as early as 10 months, but a significant number of children do not say their first word until they are 18 months of age or even older (Harris et al., 1986). In spite of this variation in age there is a great deal of similarity in children's first words. These are usually the names of familiar adults (e.g. "mummy", "daddy"), family pets, favourite toys, food, and body parts. Young children also soon learn to use words that are related to important actions. For example, many children use the words "no" and "more" early on in their vocabulary development (Harris, Barrett, Jones, & Brookes,1988).

There has been considerable debate about what children's early words mean. In the 1970s, the prevailing view was that the majority of early words did not have the same meaning as adult words. However, more recent research has suggested that children's first words are much more similar in meaning to adult words than had been previously supposed (see panel opposite).

Children show different patterns in their early use of words. Nelson (1973) identified two distinctive styles in early language development. These were the *expressive* style and the *referential* style. Children who adopted the referential style had a large proportion of object names in their first 50 words, whereas expressive children had few object names but more action words and people's names. Nelson showed that the kind of words that children produced was related to their subsequent development, and this finding has been confirmed by Bates et al. (1988) who found that the children who acquire more object names tend to build up a vocabulary more quickly.

Children's production of their earliest words is closely related to the speech that they hear every day. Harris et al. (1988) found a very close relationship between children's initial use of words and the way that their mothers most frequently used them. For example, James (see panel opposite) first used "mummy" only when he was holding out a toy for his mother to take. Analysis of his mother's speech to him revealed that her most frequent use of "mummy" when speaking to James was when she held out her hand to take a toy from him and asked "Is that for mummy?" Children's vocabulary development is, however, influenced by parental speech only in the very early stages. Barrett et al. (1991) compared children's initial and subsequent uses of early words and found that, whereas there was a relationship between the child's initial use of a word and the mother's use of that same word in over 90% of cases, such a relationship was present for less than 50% of subsequent uses.

# Early syntactic development

The first studies that psychologists carried out on early syntactic development were concerned with the various stages that children go through when they first start to talk. One of the most influential studies was carried out by Roger Brown, who published a book called *A first language* in 1973. Brown, and many researchers who studied with him over a long period, carried out a detailed analysis of the language of three children who were referred to as Adam, Eve, and Sarah. The study was begun in 1962, soon after Chomsky had made his first claims that children learned rules when they were acquiring language. Brown set out to describe the kind of rules that Adam, Eve, and Sarah produced. He also divided the early years of language development into several different stages (see pp. 133-134).

More recent studies of early syntactic development have placed great emphasis on individual differences among children. Children vary considerably in the age at which they first start to combine words and, more interestingly, in the number of different words that they produce before starting to combine words. There are important relationships between early vocabulary development and the child's acquisition of syntactic knowledge.

Bates et al. (1988), who studied 32 children from the time they were 10 months old until they were just over 2 years old, identified two distinguishable strands in language development. The first strand is what Bates et al. call "analysed production". This kind of production is rooted in comprehension and consists of the child learning to produce words that he or she already understands. This strand is particularly evident in children who have large comprehension vocabularies and who go on to use nouns in a flexible way in production, that is, in a variety of situations. By contrast, the second strand , called "unanalysed production", consists of words and phrases that the child has learned by rote or in fixed routines. Children do not appear to understand these latter words to the same extent that they understand words that form part of analysed production.

Bates et al. go on to suggest that these two strands of language development have their counterparts in early multi-word speech. They found that unanalysed production was closely related to variation in the average length of children's utterances at 20 months. Bates et al. explain this by arguing that variation in mean length of utterance (MLU) stems mainly from the ability to use grammatical function words such as "and", "the" and "he" and morphological inflections such as the plural "s". By contrast, analysed production was related to semantic–conceptual sophistication at 20 months, that is, the number of different semantic relationships the child expressed in both single words and multi-word utterances.

## Roger Brown's study of Adam, Eve, and Sarah

Brown, and his colleagues at Harvard, recorded the spontaneous speech of Adam, Eve, and Sarah in conversation with their parents at home. Recordings were made every two weeks and transcribed. The first recording for Eve was made when she was 18 months old and those for Adam and Sarah when they were 27 months old. The first recording for each of the children took place once they had begun to combine words.

Brown used a measure called *mean length of utterance* (MLU) in order to assess the children's increasing ability to combine words and produce more complex utterances. MLU is calculated by taking 100 utterances produced by a child (excluding all cases where an utterance is a repetition of something said by an adult) and then working out their average length in *morphemes*.

The number of morphemes in an utterance is often the same as the number of words because, in children's early multi-word speech, words usually consist of only a single morpheme. For example, the utterance "the top" consists of two morphemes. However, as children's speech becomes more complex, they begin to modify words to make nouns, for example, plural or possessive. Children also begin to use different tenses for verbs. These modifications are made by the addition of morphemes.

The most common way of making a noun plural is to add the "s" morpheme (e.g. hat–hats). Possession is also indicated by use of an additional "s" morpheme (e.g. daddy–daddy's). Thus the utterance "my mummy's hat" contains four morphemes. Verb tenses are indicated through the use of two different kinds of morpheme-auxiliaries, such as "is" and "will", that occur before the main verb, and morphemes that are added to the main verb itself (e.g. sit–sitting). Thus "the train is going" contains five morphemes. In some cases, particularly for verbs, the additional morpheme changes the whole sound of the word (e.g. run–ran). Such irregular past tenses count as two morphemes. Thus "the boy ran" contains four morphemes.

The rate at which the speech of the three children developed showed some interesting differences. Eve's development was the most precocious. By the time she was just 2 years and 2 months old, she was producing utterances that were, on average, four morphemes long. Adam and Sarah did not reach this level until they were 3.5 years old.

Brown divided language development over this period into five stages according to MLU. It is not clear whether all—or any—of the stages identified by Brown are "stages" in the sense described in Chapter 2 (pp. 27–30). His aim was merely to divide early language development into a sequence of increasingly complex levels.

In Stage I the children had an MLU of 1.75; at Stage II MLU was 2.25; at Stage III it was 2.75; at Stage IV 3.5. The final stage studied by Brown was Stage V, which occurred when the children were producing utterances with an MLU of 4. As might be expected, the longest utterances that the children produced at each of the stages were considerably longer than the MLU. For example, at Stage III the longest utterances were 9 morphemes long and at Stage V they were 13 morphemes long.

Brown noted that, in Stage I, many of the word combinations produced by the children were not grammatical by adult standards. Some of the early combinations of Adam and Eve were as follows (non-adult utterances are marked with an asterisk):

| | | |
|---|---|---|
| a coat | my stool | poor man |
| * a celery | that knee | little top |
| * a Becky | more coffee | dirty knee |
| * a hands | *more nut | that Adam |
| the top | *two sock | big boot |
| my mummy | *two tinker-toy | |

Brown argued that both the adult and non-adult utterances could be explained by assuming that Adam and Eve (and Sarah) were producing two word utterances containing nouns (noun phrases) by adopting the following rule:

$$NP \rightarrow M + N$$

(continued)

This means that they produced noun phrases (NP) by putting a modifier (M) in front of a noun (N). You can see from the examples that the nouns (e.g. "knee", "hands", "Adam") always came in second position and that the modifier class is much more general than any class of words that adults use. Among other things, it contained articles ("a", "the"), demonstratives ("that"), numbers ("two"), possessives ("my") and adjectives ("little", "poor", and "big").

Brown showed that, as the children moved into the later stages and their knowledge of English increased, words in the initially undifferentiated class of modifiers were separated into different categories such as articles (Art) and demonstratives (Dem). By Stage IV the children were selecting words from more than one category to use in front of nouns but they still followed rules even though they were now more complex:

$$NP \rightarrow Art + M + N \quad \text{e.g. the driver's wheel}$$
$$NP \rightarrow Dem + M + N \quad \text{e.g. that mommy sandwich}$$
$$NP \rightarrow Dem + Art + N \quad \text{e.g. that a page}$$

Brown argued that the order in which children acquired knowledge of different aspects of English was very similar, with the progression from simple rules to more complex ones. However, he emphasised that the rate at which children progressed through the various stages was very variable. More recent studies have shown that it is not only the rate that is variable: children also vary in the route that they follow in mastering early syntactic development.

# Language development and sensory impairment

Children who have severe visual or auditory impairments experience special problems when they acquire language. We discuss these in the next two sections.

## Early language development in blind children

Studying the early language of blind children is interesting because it reveals the influence of children's perceptual experience on their language development. Landau and Gleitman followed the language development of two children called Kelli and Carlo who were blind from birth. Both children took a long time to say their first word—Kelli was 23 months old and Carlo 26 months—and Landau and Gleitman (1985, p. 27) conclude that "relatively late onset of speech is characteristic for blind children." However, the first words of blind children were similar to those of sighted children.

There were interesting differences for some words that are concerned with seeing. Landau and Gleitman tested Kelli's understanding of the verbs "look" and "touch". When asked to "look" at an object, Kelli would explore it with her hands but when asked to "touch but not look", Kelli touched, banged, or stroked an object, but did not manually explore it. Landau and Gleitman conclude from this that there is a common basis for the meaning ascribed to "look" by blind and sighted children. For the sighted child, "looking" involves exploration with the eyes. For the blind child, "looking" also involves exploring with the dominant modality used for object perception—in this case, touch.

Mills (1987) studied a blind girl called Lisa to discover how she understood the word "see". She found that Lisa used "see" to refer to the auditory modality. On one occasion, having complained that she could not "see" the noise being made by a tape-recorder, Lisa moved into a better position to hear it. This example is similar to Kelli's interpretation of "look" in that it involves the substitution of a modality that is salient to a blind child for one that is not. The two studies suggest, however, that blind children may vary in the modality that they choose as an alternative to vision.

Dunlea (1989) also concludes that blind children make use of information about touch and sound in lieu of visual information, but she sees the lack of visual information as having much more extensive consequences. She presents a detailed account of the acquisition of the first 100 words by three blind children. Although blind children can hear what is being said to them, their opportunities for observing the social context in which words occur are severely limited. Dunlea's study shows that this limitation has some important implications for early language development.

Dunlea found that blind children acquired new words at roughly the same rate as sighted children but they did not show the same pattern of development. In comparison with sighted children (see panel on p. 130), blind children used words in a rigid way and were generally very unwilling to extend their initial use of words either beyond the scope of their own action or to unfamiliar objects. This makes them very different from sighted children who very rapidly extend their use of individual words. Indeed, one of the most striking features of the early vocabulary of sighted children is that many words are used in a contextually flexible way right from the outset. Another feature of the lexical development of the blind children studied by Dunlea was that they showed a very steady rate of vocabulary development. There was no sign of the typical burst in rate of acquisition that occurs after the first 30 or so words. Dunlea's contention is that, even by the end of the single-word period, blind children have not yet learned about the general relationships between words and objects and actions. This suggests that visual experience has an important role in guiding the development of the conceptual processes that underpin young children's early vocabulary development.

Dunlea also found that, in spite of differences in early vocabulary, the blind children progressed to multi-word utterances at much the same point as sighted children. Once they had a vocabulary of around 100 words, they began to combine words even though, at this stage, much of their vocabulary was still highly restricted. Dunlea concludes that, for the blind child, the stimulus to begin combining words appears to be independent of their state of lexical knowledge. Thus the language of blind children provides further evidence that some aspects of language development, notably syntactic development, occur as the result of language-specific processes that are not affected by social experience or more general cognitive development.

## Sign language acquisition by deaf children

The language development of deaf children varies enormously. Some deaf children acquire language just as successfully as hearing children, but a small proportion have very great difficulty and may arrive at school with almost no language (Harris & Beech, 1994). Children who have a profound or severe hearing loss generally experience greater difficulty than children with only a moderate hearing loss; and children who are born deaf, or who become deaf in the first year of life, have considerably more difficulty in developing language than children who become deaf after the first year.

Fig. 7.6 A child signing "duck" in British Sign Language.

Apart from from the extent of hearing loss and the age of onset, another factor that influences language development in deaf children is whether their parents are deaf or hearing. Most deaf children (about 95% according to Kyle & Allsop, 1982) are born to hearing parents but some have parents who are deaf. Several studies have shown that this small minority generally achieve a higher level of language competence than deaf children from hearing families (Kampfe & Turecheck, 1987).

It has been suggested that deaf children with deaf parents generally fare better than deaf children with hearing parents because deaf parents have a much greater insight into the communicative needs of a deaf child, particularly in the child's early years (Gregory & Barlow, 1988; Swisher & Christie, 1988). Also, children who are born to deaf parents are often exposed to sign language from birth just as hearing children are exposed to spoken language.

There are many different sign languages just as there are many different spoken languages. The most extensive research has been carried out on the language used by the deaf community in the United States, known as American Sign Language (ASL). There is also a growing body of research on other sign languages including British Sign Language (BSL).

Recent studies of ASL development in children growing up in a signing environment from birth have reported that ASL is acquired at much the same rate as spoken language (Caselli, 1983, 1987; Petitto, 1988; Volterra, 1981; Volterra & Caselli, 1985). First signs appear at a similar time to first words. When deaf children first use signs, they do so to refer to objects, individuals, and events with which they become familiar within the social-interactional context, just as hearing children initially use words (Folven et al., 1984/85). The learning of early sign combinations is also comparable to the learning of early word combinations as is the mastery of syntax .

# Conclusion and summary

Children's early language development is the result of a complex interaction between innate abilities and experience. The development of early vocabulary is very closely linked to young children's experience of hearing familiar adults use words in familiar contexts; but, as children gain in competence, they become more and more capable of learning new words on the basis of very little experience (Nelson & Bonvillian, 1978). By the time children reach the pre-school years, they commonly learn between 10 and 20 new words every day.

Evidence from blind children suggests that early vocabulary learning is firmly grounded in visual as well as social experience. However, learning about syntactic rules seems to be a process that is much less rooted in social and visual experience, and hearing children, blind children, and deaf children acquiring sign language show much greater similarity in syntactic development.

The findings of Bates et al., however, show that there is a continuity in development from the production of first words through to the first stages of syntactic development. Some children focus more on acquiring meaning, whereas others devote more resources to acquiring phrases and combining words.

There is no single route to the mastery of language, and children, especially in early childhood, show a large range of individual variation both in their speed of development and in the strategies that they employ. Their progress through early language might be thought of as a journey through an epigenetic landscape (see Figure 2.2) rather than a passage through a linear succession of stages.

In the next chapter, we consider two further aspects of the development of the symbolic function—play and drawing.

## Further reading

Harris, M. (1992). *Language experience and early language development: From input to uptake.* Hove: Lawrence Erlbaum Associates Ltd.

# Symbolic representation in play and drawing

# 8

**T**his chapter will extend the discussion of symbolism beyond the acquisition of language to other aspects of early childhood. Symbolic play makes its appearance early in the second year of life and undergoes well-described developmental changes. The literature on children's drawing also presents fascinating evidence on the relation between symbolism and depiction. Finally, the case of childhood autism will be discussed, which reveals a dissociation between aspects of visual–spatial experience and the social and emotional foundations of symbolic representation.

## Play

Play is a deceptively simple term that covers diverse activities. It has a biological aspect, particularly characteristic of young animals and humans, but it can be observed in various forms throughout the lifespan. Play in humans also has a cultural aspect, especially in the ritualised forms of children's games, in the artefacts available to support play, and also in other games of chance and skill.

Theorists interested in the biological aspect of play have long argued that it serves as an instinctive means of practising essential life-skills (Groos, 1901). Play, however, is not simply a matter of practice—that would be too serious a definition. Play refers to a certain quality of behaviour, rather than to any particular activity and "serious" behaviours can be performed playfully. Many species, including humans, have special signals to indicate that they wish to engage in social play. For instance, rhesus monkeys look at the play partner through their legs, whereas humans may smile, or offer objects, as an invitation to play.

Play may be carried out alone to practise individual skills or it may occur socially. Play may serve to explore inanimate objects or to explore human relationships and social roles. Play may be spontaneous or it may be rule-governed. Play stands in contrast to work; the former is intrinsically motivated, the latter has a serious extrinsic goal. Bruner (1972) has argued that technological societies make a relatively sharp distinction between the play of the young and the work of adults. However, in traditional societies, such as among African pygmies, play serves to model the adult lifestyle. The children play at hunting and climbing and their activities shade gradually into the real thing as they grow up.

All these characteristics of play may help to define it. Play is a pleasurable, voluntary activity that involves much repetition and variation as the child explores the range of possibilities of behaviour. Play often has a paradoxical goal—for example, playful aggression in kittens allows the practice of dangerous skills under safe conditions. Rough and tumble play in young children may serve the same purpose. Thus, play involves a preferred orientation to reality. In the case of simple physical play, such as play fighting, aspects of aggression are omitted and this makes the behaviour different from the "real" activity. In symbolic play, cognitive processes create an imaginary reality. Mundane objects are made to "stand for" other things as they become props for games. Symbolic processes also enter into the playful exploration of social roles, as when children play at being bus drivers, nurses, teachers, or mothers and fathers.

Unlike the simple practice of physical skills, symbolic play therefore involves imaginary reality. According to Baldwin (1905), imagination is the general power of having mental images. Baldwin distinguished *reconstructive imagination* (as when one imagines a man on a horse from previous experience) from *compounded imagination* (as when one imagines a centaur from the previously separate memories of a man and a horse).

Forming new symbolic combinations depends on giving relative freedom to the imagination in suspending reality. Much symbolic play involves suspension of belief and putting together novel combinations of elements. Children's stories about witches and dragons, for instance, involve the deliberate mingling of the factual and the fictional. The stories are often told by an authoritative adult in a tone of voice that encourages freeing the imagination from the constraints of reality. Such complex, imaginary play develops out of simpler forms which can be observed in early childhood.

## Play with objects

Even the infant will play with objects but this activity is rather too practical to qualify as symbolic. Symbolic play requires that one object stands for another, and this qualitatively new aspect of behaviour is the main evidence for the transition from infancy to a new stage.

Vygotsky (1976) gave an interesting account of how physical objects come to act as props for the early symbolic play of the child. For example, when the child uses a stick as a hobby horse, the stick temporarily loses its own identity and gains aspects of the identity of the horse. That is, the customary identity of the object is replaced by a meaning that has been designated by the child and the signifier is differentiated from what is signified. The meaning of "horse" is what gives the stick its new significance. At the same time, the child also differentiates a particular aspect of his or her mental representation of horses. Vygotsky argued that in object play, meaning is predominant over the physical characteristics of objects. The child's play will be regulated by the rules that follow from the meaning attributed to the prop object. The hobby horse must be ridden and not used for other purposes. Thus, symbolic play creates a zone of proximal development (ZPD, see pp. 22–24) in which children can explore, in imagination, the outer reaches of their understanding.

Initially, the distance between the imaginary and the real is not so great and the gap is bridged by physical props, such as the stick. The stick, in its early use as a symbolic prop, serves as an index which physically represents "horsiness" in the child's play (see the Table on p. 117). Eventually, however, almost anything can be made to stand for anything else and play becomes increasingly internalised as pure symbolism. Vygotsky afforded play an important and positive function in mental development. He particularly emphasised the internalisation of speech and the invention of stories as aspects of playful verbal behaviour in the older pre-school and school-age child.

Piaget also emphasised the fantasy element of play in pre-school children. In his terminology, assimilation predominates over accommodation. That is, the child assimilates the world to his or her own ego in play, rather than changing his or her own ideas to meet the demands of reality. In Piaget's theory, play is the opposite of imitation (where accommodation predominates over assimilation) where the child adapts to fit the demands of reality.

Piaget made extensive observations of his three children at play in early childhood. According to Piaget, the essential difference between the practice play of infancy and the symbolic play of early childhood is that symbolic play serves to exercise the imagination. He observed elementary symbolic play as early as 1 year and 1 month, when his daughter pretended to drink from a seashell. His description of the development of symbolic play in the pre-school period is summarised on pp. 142–143.

Piaget was particularly interested in rule-governed play, which stands midway between child and adult play and begins in the school years. His theory of moral development was based on observations of children playing rule-governed games, like marbles (see panel on p. 194). Piaget was most interested in how play becomes governed by logical rules. For the pre-school child, play may offer various kinds of satisfaction but it is

# Piaget's theory of play in the pre-school period

Piaget (1952) observed symbolic play in his three children during the pre-school and early school years. He divided the types of symbolic play into two main stages; up to 4 years and from 4 to 7 years, with sub-stages.

## Stage I: 1–4 years

### Sub-stage 1: Projection of symbolic schemas onto new objects

*Type 1a: Projection of familiar schemas*
A symbolic schema is a mental representation that preserves the most distinctive aspects of an object. In the earliest examples of symbolic play, the child applies familiar schemas to new objects. For example, Jacqueline at 1 year 6 months and 30 days, or 1.6 (30), said "cry, cry" to her toy dog and imitated the sound of crying. She went on to make her toy bear and toy duck cry. At 1.7 (1) she made her hat cry. Such examples are make-believe reproductions of the child's own actions applied to new objects.

*Type 1b: Projection of imitative schemas*
A second type of symbolic play, observed at the same age, involves projection of imitative schemas onto new objects. These schemas are not derived from the child's own activity but are borrowed from activities that have been observed in others. For example, Jacqueline at 1.9 (20) rubbed the floor with a seashell, then with a cardboard lid, in the manner that she had previously observed the charwoman cleaning the floor.

Piaget's play types 1a and 1b are intermediate in development, between signifiers that serve as an index, and symbolic gestures (see p. 117).

### Sub-stage 2: Separation of index and action

With further development, the gesture becomes increasingly independent of the prop. The child's action (signifier) begins to separate from what is signified. These examples, however, are still of indexical gestures (see the Table on p. 117). The developmental advance is that the identification of the pretend object precedes its use in action and hence the child achieves greater distance from the "here and now" through imagination.

*Type 2a: Simple identification of one object with another*
At 2.0 (22) Jacqueline moved her finger along the table and said, "finger walking, horse trotting". At 2.3 (10), holding a brush over her head, she said "Its an umbrella".

*Type 2b Games of imitation*
At 1.10 (3) Jacqueline pretended to play hide and seek with a cousin, Clive, who was not present and who she hadn't seen for 2 months. She pretended to be her cousin and imitated him strutting up and down. At 2.4 (8) she pretended to be her mother and said to Piaget, "Come kiss mummy", and then kissed him. Such imitative games can become very complex. By 4.3 (6) Lucienne stood stock still as she imitated the sound of bells. Piaget put his hand over her mouth in an attempt to make her stop. She pushed him away angrily and said "Don't. I'm a church".

These more complex examples certainly involve reconstructive imagination. Such re-enactments, however, still retain an element of indexical signification (see the Table on p. 117).

### Sub-stage 3: Combinations of symbols

Combinations of symbols of increasing complexity begin, in which, at the simplest level, the child transposes real scenes with imaginary ones. For example, at 2.5 (25) Jacqueline prepares an imaginary bath, using an empty box as the bath and a blade of grass as a thermometer. She plunged the grass into the big box and declared the water too hot. She waited and then tried again declaring, "That's alright, thank goodness".

By 3.6 (9) she constructed an imaginary ant's nest from pine needles, complete with imaginary furniture, a family of ants, and imaginary macaroni in the cellar.

(continued)

## Piaget's theory of play in the pre-school period (continued)

Soon, the whole character may be imaginary. At 3.11(20) Jacqueline invented a composite animal which she called "aseau" . This animal was part bird, part dog with long hair and it had moral authority ("You mustn't do that, aseau will scold you").

Piaget says this an example of "infantile totemism", also described by Freud as the invention of animals that dispense justice. Piaget also describes many other examples of imaginary play in which the child, through make-believe, comes to understand unpleasant situations, or emerges victorious against the threat of failure. In each of these cases, reality is assimilated to the needs of the ego.

Invention of the character "aseau" illustrates compounded imagination and it is certainly an example of pure symbolic play (see p. 117).

### Stage II: 4–7 years

Symbolic games of the type described here begin to lose their importance as symbols become more closely constrained by reality. Piaget argues that symbolic play becomes more orderly; there is an increasing desire for exact imitation of reality and the social roles of the participants in symbolic play become increasingly complementary.

At 4.5 (13) Jacqueline decided that she and her sister, Lucienne, would pretend to be Joseph and Therese, two of their friends. In the course of the play, Jacqueline reversed the roles so that she was Therese. The play continued with meal-time scenes and other imaginary activities. Such games slowly give way to games with rules, like marbles, by the age of 7 (see p. 194). The examples here are from Piaget (1952, pp. 118-146).

not until the period of concrete operations that these satisfactions are legitimised by an understanding of the rules of fair play.

These examples suggest that symbolic play, like language, does not emerge in an all-or-nothing fashion. Both Vygotsky and Piaget agreed that the child represents an imaginary reality initially through actions with the assistance of objects which serve as props. Such objects have the status of indices which assist the child to differentiate signifier and signified in the transition to purely symbolic play. With development, symbolic action becomes separated from gesture and bodily activity. In addition, play in the second and third years becomes social, with the beginnings of reciprocal and complementary role-taking. Furth and Kane (1992) suggest that symbolic play, while serving many particular functions in development, has one overarching purpose—to inform children of the societal framework within which they live. By the age of 4–5 years, the child in social play explores shared societal values, traditions, and customs.

The verbal imagination can create extensive imaginary worlds. Cohen and MacKeith (1991) collected adults' memories of imaginary worlds of childhood. They found that some people had invented extensive "paracosms" (imaginary worlds) as early as 3 years of age. These may be a farm, an island, whole countries, extensive railroad systems, or even Baltic states! They may be secret, or shared with siblings. The extensive detail of the work of the imagination is revealed, among the older children at least, by the maps that they draw of their imaginary societies.

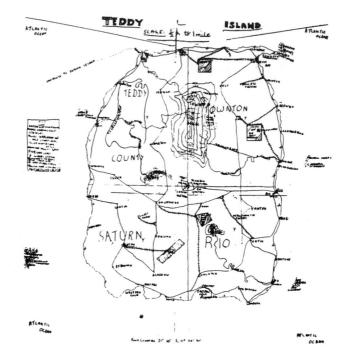

Fig. 8.1 An example of an invented island (from Cohen & MacKeith, 1991).

## Transitional objects

Not only does play have an important role in intellectual development, it is also involved in emotional development. Many children have a favour-

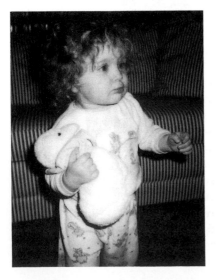

ite soft toy (e.g. Francesca 15 months, seen here with her duck), or perhaps a piece of cloth, to which they are particularly attached. The cartoon character Linus, in the Peanuts comic strip, carries his security blanket at all times. Psychoanalysts call such favourite things "transitional objects", because they are thought to help the child to bridge the transition between close physical contact with mother in infancy and the movement away from the caretaker as the toddler becomes autonomous.

Winnicot (1971) suggests that these special possessions serve as a kind of substitute for the mother. They act as imaginary companions which the child can invest with his or her own ideas, emotions, hopes, and fears. Psychoanalysts often use symbolic play as a means to reveal the causes of maladjusted children's difficulties.

## Gender identity

As we mentioned earlier, play also serves to acquire an understanding of the social and functional roles performed by adults. It is commonplace to observe the pre-school child exploring in play the actions of a cook, mechanic, bus driver, car passenger, doctor, or nurse. Such functional roles may be combined with family roles of mother or father. It is interesting that pre-school children adopt these roles along gender-appropriate lines (Garvey, 1977). Girls play roles normally occupied by females, while boys are more likely to take the male part in play. Symbolic play may therefore contribute to the acquisition of gender identity.

Gender is a biological attribute that shapes the social roles that the child can explore in symbolic play. Conventional social roles in turn provide a symbolic framework within which the developing child can explore gender identity. The biological basis of gender is becoming known through modern genetics. The sex chromosomes of female mammals, including humans, are identical XX chromosomes, whereas males have different XY chromosomes. The complex embryological processes and hormonal factors that organise masculine and feminine morphology are well described in Cairns (1979).

Social differentiation of boys and girls also occurs in the ways that they are dressed, in how they are named, and in the many ways in which parents socialise them. Toy purchases for children are sex-typed from infancy. Rheingold and Cook (1975) found that from the ages of 2–6 boys' bedrooms contained more cars and trucks, whereas girls' bedrooms contained more dolls, dolls' houses, and play household items. The girls' bedrooms contained more floral furnishings and ruffled fabrics. The boys had more sports equipment and toy animals (but there was no sex difference in the number of soft stuffed toy animals).

Symbolic representation of gender appears early on in development. Lloyd and Duveen (1990) found that children as young as 18 months understand the gender-marked nouns "mummy", "daddy", "lady", "man", "girl", "boy". These very young children could pick out a gender-appropriate photograph from a pair of male and female photographs when they heard a gender-marked noun. Four-year-old boys are better at sorting pictures of toys that adults judge to be masculine (e.g. fire-engine, garage) whereas girls are equally good at sorting pictures of typically male or typically female toys (e.g. brush and mirror set, tea set). Parents play differently with male and female offspring, fathers being more likely to engage in rough and tumble play with sons. There are therefore a multitude of ways in which biological and social influences serve to inform the young child that he is a boy or she is a girl.

How is the basic biological predisposition to be male or female channelled in the formation of gender identity? Gender identity is about how children understand and interpret their sex role symbolically. Perhaps the best known theory of the development of gender identity is that of Sigmund Freud (1938), who argued that identification with the parent of the same sex is the main process by which the child acquires gender identity. Freud conceived of gender identity as a natural outgrowth of the process of attachment of the child for the mother.

Freud took as a metaphor for gender identification Sophocles' tragedy in which Oedipus unknowingly murders his father and marries his mother. He argued that, between the fourth and sixth year, the male child must resolve the Oedipal conflict. The boy desires to take the place of his father in order to possess his mother sexually. The Electra conflict is the equivalent process for girls. In order to resolve the feelings of guilt and fear that arise from the child's fantasies about replacing the envied parent, the child represses the forbidden desire and identifies with the parent of the same sex. The concept of identification is similar in some ways to imitation, in that boys emulate the father figure, while girls emulate the mother, incorporating the admired characteristics of the sex-role model into their own identity.

There is a problem, however, with supposing that masculinity or femininity is a single bipolar dimension. The qualities associated with men and women overlap significantly and any one individual may embody some properties of each. Furthermore, some occupational roles may be arbitrarily related to gender. Some roles are filled by different sexes in different cultures, as in the case of female engineers who are much more common in Russia than in the West. The Freudian account may be limited because it tends to take as a package aspects of personal identity that can be separated. Labelling the self as male or female, the choice of behaviours considered appropriate to a particular sex, identification (wishing to be similar to the same-sex parent), and the child's sexual orientation are treated as inseparable aspects of the same process.

Piaget (1952, p. 189) addressed Freud's theory in his observations of the pre-school child's play and dreams. Although he readily admits that play may reveal unconscious symbolism in children and that their dreams and nightmares may reveal their fears, he was rather sceptical of Freud's particular interpretation of childhood symbolism. Piaget suggested that the child's conscious intellectual processes may be more important than the unconscious repression of unacceptable thoughts about the parent in arriving at an understanding of gender identity.

Kohlberg (1966), a follower of Piaget, argued that it is sufficient for children, aware of their own gender identity, to be interested in classifying other objects and persons as similarly "girlish or boyish". Kohlberg argues that development proceeds from an understanding of cognitive gender identity, to a belief in stereotypic sex roles, to the imitation of adults, and finally to a special attachment to the same-sex parent. On this view, unlike the Freudian theory, knowledge of the genital differences between the sexes comes only after the child has an understanding of gender and sex-role identity.

Fischer and Lazerson (1984) also agree that toddlers can scare themselves with their own thoughts, but that young children do not understand age or sex roles until about 4 years. Children can then think about age or sex roles considered separately but, when dealing with both at the same time, may confuse them. For instance, the little boy who says that when he grows up he wishes to become a "mummy" may simply be having difficulty in coordinating two aspects of the representation of age and gender. Such cognitive accounts of gender identification very much reduce the significance of the symbolic sexual aspects of Freud's Oedipal theory (see also pp. 247–248 on parenting).

# Symbolism in children's drawing

The third area we will explore in our overview of the acquisition of symbols is the fascinating literature on children's drawing. Drawing is particularly interesting because it combines iconic and symbolic aspects of signification (see the Table on page 117). Drawing also presents the child with a particular problem of compressing three dimensions into the two-dimensional surface of the picture. There are well-documented changes in children's drawings with age, especially in the ways that the human figure is drawn and in the representation of depth in the picture plane. However, Gardner (1978) cautions that symbolic representation in different media may develop at different rates. How children draw the human figure may differ from how they assemble a pre-drawn cut-out, or create a model in plasticine. It is necessary to be alert to the constraints on representation imposed by different media. That said, however, there is reasonable evidence for a general symbolic process in children's drawing which is not specific to that representational medium. This brief overview will concentrate on drawings and their implications for the early symbolic processes.

## From scribbles to graphic symbols

Fig. 8.3
Children's early
drawings
(Kellogg, 1969).

The earliest drawings of the child, from 18 to 30 months, are often scribbles, which may reflect little more than the energetic movements of the child making visible marks on a surface. Some theorists argue that these scribbles are not intended to be representations (e.g. Kellogg, 1969). It has proved possible to classify early drawings into 20 basic types, which are very similar worldwide (Fig. 8.3).

These simple forms include geometric shapes such as circles, squares, triangles, crosses and simple combinations such as the mandala (a cross enclosed by a circle), and sun drawings (a circle with straight lines radiating in all directions). These geometric shapes are the basic elements that, in combination, form the first graphic symbols. On this theory, graphic symbols arise from non-symbolic precursors (Kellogg, 1969).

Other theorists suggest that even the earliest geometric shapes may have symbolic significance for the child. Golomb (1992) argues that simple shapes are non-conventional signifiers in their earliest origins (see the Table on p. 117). A circle, for instance, can signify the general solidity of three-dimensional objects. On this view, the perceptual abilities and the motor skills of infancy form the foundations for graphic representation.

Golomb (1992) suggests that children move on from scribbling to the use of geometric shapes like circles in drawing, because the shapes can effectively serve as memory aids for what the representation is intended to depict.

Regardless of which view of the origins of symbolism in drawing is correct, by 3 years of age children find meaning in their scribbles and start to see them as pictures of other things. A drawing of a person may consist of a "tadpole figure" comprising a circle for the head, with two vertical

Fig. 8.4 Tadpole drawings (Cox, 1993).

lines for legs, some dots for facial features, and the arms extending horizontally from the head. A similar tadpole schema, drawn horizontally, may be used to represent animals, like a cat or dog. The combination of geometric forms has a general symbolic function in representing visual objects. It is remarkable that congenitally blind children, when asked to draw the human figure, also do so using combinations of circles and straight lines, just like sighted children, (Millar, 1975).

Fig. 8.5 Drawings by blind children. (Millar, 1975, Pion Ltd.).

## Intellectual and visual realism in child art

Luquet (1927), one of the early students of child art, argued that children's drawing passes through several stages. Following the *"fortuitous realism"* of the scribbling stage, the early symbolic period in drawing was described as the stage of *"intellectual realism"*. Although the drawing of pre-school children bears some resemblance to what is being depicted, its primary purpose is to represent an object by symbolic means. The drawing is not an attempt at a photographic type of depiction; rather it is an iconic symbol that incidentally resembles what it represents (see the Table on page 117).

Luquet argued that young children, by combining simple geometric elements, are drawing "what they know rather than what they see".

Intellectual realism gradually gives way to *"visual realism"* as the child attempts to master the intricacies of representing life-like three-dimensional objects within the spatial constraints of the two-dimensional picture plane.

Piaget and Inhelder (1956) followed Luquet's classification of stages, especially in Piaget's theory of the child's conception of space. Piaget and Inhelder argued that is not until age 7 or 8 years that children are able to coordinate conceptually different points of view. They are also not able to understand proportionality until the same age and to make use of such devices in visually realistic spatial depictions.

Freeman and Janikoun (1972) provided some evidence for a transition from intellectual to visual realism. They asked children to draw a cup which was presented in such a way that the handle could not be seen but a prominent feature, a flower decoration on the cup, was in full view. Children below 8 years of age included the non-visible handle and omitted the visible flower decoration from their drawings. They knew that cups have handles and their drawings symbolically depicted what they knew about cups. Children aged over 8 years omitted the handle and included the flower, as, it is argued, they drew realistically what they could see from a particular viewpoint. Note, however, that another interpretation of this study is simply that younger children prefer to draw the symbol for a cup rather than the cup as seen from a particular viewpoint.

Ingram and Butterworth (1989) showed that children as young as 3 years of age would attempt to draw a pair of plain wooden blocks of different size from a particular viewpoint. The blocks were presented in different positions (either vertically one on top of the other, horizontally one next to the other, or in-depth, one behind the other). The finished drawings of the vertical pile and of the in-depth file were both drawn in the vertical plane and the finished products were virtually indistinguishable. However, the process of drawing revealed that the children had different pictorial strategies for depicting height and depth. Piles were drawn with the bottom block first, then the second block drawn above and touching the first block. Files were also drawn vertically but the near block was always drawn first and the far one second and not touching the first. Thus even the 3-year-olds were preserving something of the specific spatial viewpoint in their drawings. Furthermore, the different temporal order of production of the blocks shows that different spatio-temporal 3D processes may still result in very similar 2D products. Not until about 5

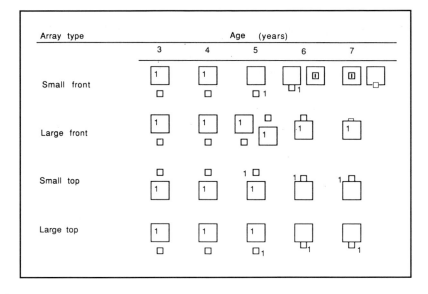

Fig. 8.6
Children's
representation of
depth in drawing
(Ingram and
Butterworth,
1989).

years of age did the children begin to represent depth by perspectival interposition of the cubes. These data, illustrated in Figure 8.6, show that even young children are attempting a visually realistic depiction which includes the point of view of the observer.

Ingram and Butterworth (1989) showed that this early visual realism can easily be suppressed in favour of intellectual realism. Facial features were added to the blocks so that the pair of blocks resembled a doll. In whatever orientation the blocks with doll features were presented, children between 3 and 7 years always drew the doll vertically. In fact, some of the youngest children drew the featured blocks as a vertical tadpole figure, just a head and legs, even though the model had a body and lacked arms and legs! Such tadpole drawings never occurred with the blocks without features.

It seems that the blocks alone lack any symbolic significance and hence, even young children can depict them realistically in a drawing. However, as soon as human features are added, the child invariably draws the person schema, in the typical frontal vertical orientation. These data suggest that drawing some types of objects does involve conceptual knowledge, consistent with Luquet's theory of intellectual realism. However, even very young children, at Luquet's stage of fortuitous realism, will draw what they see from a particular viewpoint if the overwhelming effects of the symbolic representation can be circumvented.

## Picturing numbers

Fig. 8.7
Examples of early
representations of
number (Hughes,
1986).

It is possible to think of the early period of children's drawing as one of creative invention and practice in using graphic symbols (Golomb, 1992). This can be illustrated in some studies reported by Hughes (1986), in which children as young as 3 years were invited to represent numbers by drawing. Children were given a pencil and paper and asked to put something on paper to show how many bricks had been placed in front of them. It was possible to classify the responses into three kinds: pictographic, iconic, and symbolic representations.

Mutale (4 years 3 months): 5 bricks

Emma (5 years 2 months): 6 bricks

Pamela (5 years 1 month): 3 bricks

The pictographic representations were those in which there was a close visual similarity to the actual appearance of the blocks. In the pictographic mode of depiction, the children would show both the number and the shape of the cubes. The depicted squares were drawn sequentially, in one-to-one correspondence with the cubes in the display. In iconic systems, the children would use a discrete mark of their own, often a stick used as a tally, to stand in one-to-one correspondence for each cube until the whole set was depicted. The older children would use conventional symbols to represent number (e.g. 1, 2, or 3) or they might write the words "one", "two", or "three". However, it was not until age 7 that the conventional symbolic mode of representation became dominant over the very popular, spontaneous iconic mode. As Hughes argues, iconic tallies can represent effectively whether an object is present or absent and, like fingers, they function effectively as the basis of a number system, especially for small numbers (see pp. 208–209).

A particularly interesting finding concerned the children's spontaneous representation of zero, or the absence of quantity. Hughes reports that when the table was cleared of bricks, and the children were asked to depict that there were no bricks on the table, the youngest children were puzzled. Given the task of representing the number of bricks in an empty tin, 3- to 5-year-old children would either leave the paper blank, develop idiosyncratic tallies such as a stroke with a tail on, or they used the zero (0) which can be thought of as a depiction of an enclosed, empty space. Thus, even young children develop coherent systems of notation for number. It is tempting to argue that these basic forms of depicting number become elaborated in different cultures, for example the Roman numerals I, II, and III are obviously related to simple tallies and the 0 has become the conventional form.

## Culturally defined styles of artistic representation

By the age of 5 most children can represent familiar objects in drawing, and they then go on to master the complex skills of composing pictures, realistically representing space and using pictures to tell stories.

On Luquet's theory, the young child in the transition from intellectual to visual realism faces many of the problems overcome by artists following the invention of linear perspective drawing systems. However, Luquet's developmental progression effectively restricts the definition of visually realistic pictures to the style of representation perfected in Western art from roughly the fifteenth century.

Hagen (1985) offers a radical alternative to stage theories of visually realistic drawing. She argues that there are no stages beyond the initial appearance of symbolic depiction. In her opinion, visual realism in Luquet's sense does not develop. Instead, she argues that visually realistic depiction depends on mastery of culturally defined conventions. The cultural conventions depend in the first place on gifted individuals for their invention; i.e. drawing visually realistic pictures depends on making a choice among a finite set of projection systems, some of which already exist as conventions within a culture, ready to be passed on (see pp. 154–6).

Hagen points out that these different projection systems show no consistent order of appearance in the history of art. Cave paintings of 35,000 BC, for example, were drawn in projective geometry with multiple station points (i.e. a different viewpoint for each object depicted), whereas scenes on Greek vases of 700 BC made use of orthogonal projection from multiple station points. The familiar Renaissance style, with linear projective geometry and a single station point uniting the spatial relations between objects, is a different, very effective way to depict visually realistic scenes, but it is not necessarily a higher stage in cultural development.

## Representing 3D space: Orthogonal projection

Different artistic traditions make use of different projection systems in the representation of objects in 3D space. The art of Ancient Egypt made use of the so-called *orthogonal projection* system, in which the objects depicted in the picture plane are drawn parallel and at right angles to the observer. In this system, the projected size of the objects depicted does not decrease with their distance from the observer (although relative size may serve to represent the status of the kings, queens, and slaves depicted).

Egyptian wall painting.
Copyright British Museum.

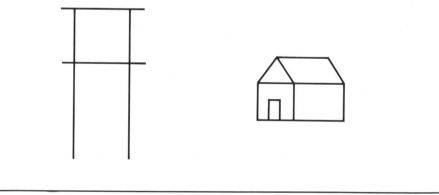

# Representing 3D space: Affine projection

In traditional Japanese art, on the other hand, the depicted object's distance from the observer is represented by its height in the picture plane (the so-called *affine projection*).

Japanese woodcut print by Harunobu (circa 1772). Courtesy of Werner Forman Archive, Prazac collection, Brno, Czech Republic.

## Representing 3D space: Projective geometry

Western post-Renaissance art makes use of *projective geometry*, in which the projected size of the depicted object in the picture plane decreases with distance from the observer. Oblique lines that converge to a vanishing point in the picture plane correspond to lines that are parallel in the world.

*A woman drinking with two men*
P. de Hooch, circa 1658.
Reproduced by courtesy of the Trustees,
The National Gallery, London.

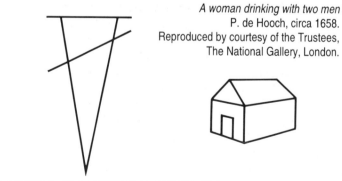

Hagen found that when American adults were asked to draw a simple picture of a house from memory, they produced a depiction in projective geometry in only 23% of their drawings (the most common projection system was affine geometry in 40% of drawings) (see the illustrations on pp. 155–156). She argues that acquiring visually realistic representation is not an inevitable stage of development but a matter of acquiring artistic skill within a culturally preferred system of projective representation. Such a radical view contrasts strongly with Piaget's emphasis on the development of intellectual abilities as the necessary condition for spatial representation.

## Anomalous development in autism

Childhood autism is a rare developmental disorder often manifest before the second year of life, which involves a profound failure in the social, linguistic, and imaginative development of the child. An important diagnostic criterion is impairment of communication and language, which is sometimes noticeable despite an adequate capacity for speech among the more intellectually able autistic children. Another important symptom is an abnormal lack of imaginative "pretend" play (Frith, 1989; Hobson, 1993). Autism is most frequent among boys and it is accompanied by mental retardation in approximately 75% of cases, although a minority of autistic children do have intelligence in the average, normal range (Frith, 1989).

It is unlikely that the particular symptoms of childhood autism involved in sufferers' social and communication difficulties are a specific consequence of mental retardation. As already mentioned, some autistic children are of normal intelligence, but they display autistic symptoms. Furthermore, autistic symptoms are not typical of other groups of mentally retarded children, such as those of children with Down's syndrome, which arises as a result of a chromosome abnormality. Rather, it seems that autistic children may have a rare disorder, an abnormal development in communication, in which their capacity for symbolism is severely affected, while some other abilities may even remain intact.

Those autistic children who do acquire speech have particular difficulties with personal pronouns ("I", "you") and with relative terms for time and space ("here", "there", "come", "go"). Such *deictic terms* are relative to who is the speaker or listener in a conversation. The use of the correct deictic terminology in conversation depends on the role (speaker, listener) and the spatial frame of reference (near or far from or towards or away from some landmark known to the speaker and listener). To communicate effectively using these deictic terms, the speaker must be sensitive to the hearer's information needs. That is, in speaking we evaluate what others need to know in order to understand our message and we also evaluate the intentions of others in interpreting the meaning of what they say to us. Even intellectually able autistic adults have difficulty with the imaginative role-taking involved in the use of deictic terminology, perhaps in part because they fail to see the need to adjust their speech for maximum communicative effect.

Some remarkable evidence for a basic deficit in symbolic functioning in an autistic child was unearthed by Selfe (1983). Selfe studied an autistic child called Nadia who was exceptionally gifted in drawing. By the age of 5 years Nadia was drawing pictures of horses, cockerels, and cavalrymen from memory, in realistic perspective (see Figure 8.11). Nadia lacked language and her gross motor development was very retarded, but she could produce these exquisite drawings. Selfe argues that Nadia's drawings differed so much from those of normal children precisely because Nadia was unable to consider the objects symbolically. She drew the objects in a visually realistic manner, altogether lacking in intellectual realism.

Fig. 8.11 Drawings by Nadia (left) and an average 6.5-year-old child (below). (Selfe, 1976).

Selfe (1983) subsequently identified a small number of graphically gifted children, for example Simon who could draw buildings as complex as the Houses of Parliament in realistic detail, both from memory and directly. Selfe argues that these gifted autistic artists attend particularly to the spatial aspects of the picture in their graphic representations. She suggests that these autistic children are concerned to represent single viewpoint, static spatial configurations and they are able to do so because there is no interference from symbolic processes that lead normal children to produce drawings that are pictographic (see pp. 149–151).

Pinpointing the early origins of autism has proved elusive. However, recent studies have begun to reveal which communication abilities may show early specific deficiencies over and above any problems that may be due to intellectual retardation. Sigman and Ungerer (1984) used the strange situation test, where a child is briefly separated from his or her mother and behaviour on reunion is studied, to measure the attachment of autistic children aged between 2 and 5 years to their mothers (see the panel on p. 108 for a description of this test). There was no major difference between the behaviours of the autistic children and mentally retarded children of the same age in attachment behaviour on reunion with their mothers. Hence the communication deficit of autism is unlikely to be a simple consequence of abnormalities in the attachment process.

Hobson (1993), however, is careful to point out that there are important ways in which autistic children do not relate normally to their parents. For instance, they may not turn to them for comfort, nor do they seem interested in sharing experiences, or in caring for their parents. The strange situation task may only reveal that gross aspects of attachment are not disturbed.

Recent studies of joint attention in autistic children, however, have shown major differences between autistic children and control groups in abilities thought to be basic to communication. Autistic children have difficulty interpreting and producing pointing as a signal for something interesting for others to see (Curcio, 1978); they have difficulty identifying emotional expressions in films (Hobson, 1993). Autistic children have specific difficulties with understanding mental states, such as beliefs, which may govern our behaviour. For instance, I may believe that the supermarket will be open for shopping on Sunday, only to discover after journeying there that it is actually closed. My behaviour was governed by a false belief. Normal children over the age of 4 can understand that people may have false beliefs but autistic children have difficulty understanding that another person can be mistaken (Baron-Cohen, Leslie, & Frith, 1985).

Leslie (1991) has argued that the core deficits of autism in emotion, play, and language dysfunction can be explained by a failure in those

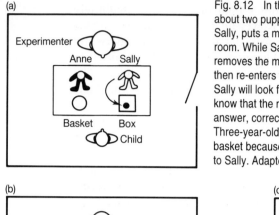

(a)

Experimenter

Anne    Sally

Basket    Box

Child

Fig. 8.12  In this false belief test the child is told a story about two puppets, Sally and Anne. The first puppet, Sally, puts a marble in the box, and then she leaves the room. While Sally is away, the second puppet, Anne, removes the marble and places it in the basket. Sally then re-enters the scene and the child is asked where Sally will look for the marble. Four-year-old children know that the marble is in Anne's basket but they will answer, correctly, that Sally will look for it in the box. Three-year-olds will claim that Sally will look in the basket because they cannot yet attribute a false belief to Sally. Adapted from Baron-Cohen et al. (1985).

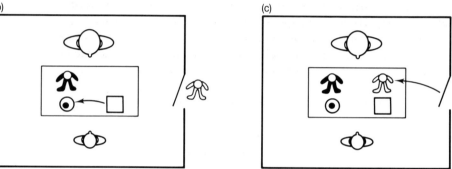

(b)

(c)

aspects of early cognitive development that allow symbolic representation of objects and aspects of experience. He suggests that autistic children lack the ability to suspend belief in order simultaneously to consider the real and symbolic properties of objects. A normal child knows that a banana remains a banana, even when pretending that the banana is a telephone.

Leslie argues that autistic children cannot "decouple" the properties of the real object from its mental representation, so that the object can take on pretend properties. This basic deficit makes autistic children excessively literal in their understanding, because they cannot consider reality "as if" it were different. Leslie therefore argues that an inability to pretend is ultimately responsible for the other difficulties of autistic children. Hobson (1993) discusses this hypothesis sympathetically, although he argues that even more fundamental difficulties may exist at the interpersonal-emotional level which could be inborn.

## Conclusion and summary

This chapter has extended the discussion of symbolism to play, children's drawing, and the case of childhood autism. According to Piaget, the emergence—almost simultaneously in development—of spoken language, symbolic play, imitation, and mental imagery are evidence for a stage transition in development between infancy and early childhood. For Piaget this is evidence that a general reorganisation of cognitive processes is responsible for symbolism.

There is certainly evidence that symbolism arises in a variety of domains in early childhood. The generality of symbolism offers support to Piaget. It is rather more difficult, however, to be sure that these symbolic abilities are not a function of the species-typical predisposition of humans for language.

Piaget would deny this interpretation. Vygotsky and Piaget actually agree that language and the intellect develop as separate streams during infancy. Comparisons across species also suggest that language and intellectual abilities are separable. For instance, some aspects of spoken language can arise without symbolic ability, as in the case of the imitative capacity of the parrot. Nor does having complex intellectual abilities, as in the case of the chimpanzee, guarantee acquisition of language. Vygotsky (1961) argues that the intellectual and linguistic streams begin to merge in early childhood, whereas Piaget maintains that language is always subordinate to intellectual operations.

The evidence from symbolic play, from children's drawing, and from childhood autism is only partially consistent with either of these broad views. In the case of drawing, there is much evidence that the drawn product is intended to be an iconic symbol. However, experimental studies have shown that the symbolic component of drawing can be dissociated from its visuo-spatial aspect, with both types of representation being simultaneously available. In normal pre-school children, the symbolic representation tends to suppress the visuo-spatial form.

Where there has been a specific deficit in the development of the symbolic process, as in the case of autistic children, the visuo-spatial representation and other intellectual abilities may nevertheless be intact. This suggests that symbolic processes must be separate and, at least to some extent, independent of other forms of visuo-spatial representation. However, the evidence from atypical development reviewed in this chapter links symbolic deficits very closely to language and social deficits.

The fact that different representational systems, symbolic and non-symbolic, can exist alongside each other in the pre-school child is also of interest for how we understand subsequent developmental processes. Multiple, simultaneous forms of representation of reality in the pre-school child may influence further development in at least two ways. First, initially independent processes may come to be hierarchically integrated, as when the child begins to be able to draw symbolic objects in realistic perspective. Second, the child may begin to select from among alternative representational possibilities already in the repertoire in elementary form, those which actually are found in the particular culture to which he or she belongs. Some speculative examples that come to mind here are the vertical representation of depth in oriental art and the use of tally systems for number. Both these styles of representation may be cultural elaborations of the spontaneous representations observed in young children. On this admittedly speculative, selectionist theory, the culture offers the child an epigenetic pathway for further development in the representation of number and art.

## Further reading

Bruner, J.S., Jolly, A., & Sylva, K. (Eds.) (1976). *Play*. Harmondsworth: Penguin.

Cox, M.V. (1993). *Children's drawing of the human figure*. Hove: Lawrence Erlbaum Associates Ltd.

Hobson, R.P. (1993). *Autism and the development of mind*. Hove: Lawrence Erlbaum Associates Ltd.

Thomas, G.V., & Silk, A.M. (1990). *An introduction to the psychology of children's drawings*. Hemel Hempstead: Harvester.

# Cognitive development in early childhood 9

O ne of the most important questions that still remains to be resolved in contemporary developmental psychology concerns the relation between language and thought. In Piaget's theory, thought is not determined by language; rather, changes in cognition are reflected in changes in the structure and complexity of the child's language. Other theorists, notably Vygotsky, suggest that specifically human, "higher mental processes" are formed by the fusion of language and thinking, a development that occurs in early childhood between the ages of about 2 and 5 years.

Questions about the relation of language and thought are important because so much knowledge depends on transmission through language. Not only do parents and schools rely on language for instruction, but also language is the repository of wisdom in both oral and written cultural traditions. Furthermore, language enters into the very methods used by psychologists to probe the mind of the child. Interviewing techniques rely heavily on language and it is not always clear what young children understand, independently of the words being used to question them. In recent years, the subtle interplay of language and thought has been extensively stressed, especially in testing the capacities of the pre-school child.

## Piaget's theory of pre-operational reasoning

In Piaget's theory, the period from 2.5 to 6 years is known as the pre-operational stage, followed between 6 and 12 years by the concrete operational stage. The pre-operational period is a time during which children gradually acquire systematic, logical thinking.

According to Piaget, the developmental task during the pre-operational period consists in organising thinking into a system of mental operations. There is continuity between the pre-operational stage and the sensori-motor stage of infancy, when the baby developed complex

## Piaget's conservation problems

Of all Piaget's contributions to psychology, the best known are probably the conservation problems. To have the concept of conservation means that the child understands that the basic properties of matter are not altered by superficial changes in their appearance. The best known example is conservation of volume, but conservation also applies to number and weight. Take, for example, two equal quantities of water in identical beakers A and B. The child will tell you that the amount of water is the same. Then B is poured into a third beaker C, of different shape, so that the water level is higher (or lower) than before. The pre-school child will say there is more water in the jar with the higher level. The child fails to compensate for a change in the height of the liquid by the change in the width that results from the water being poured into a differ-ently shaped jar. Nor can the child understand the principle of reversibility; that is, if the water is poured back into the original jar, the level will once again be the same. The pre-operational child is said not to be able to imagine the sequence of changes in the appearance of the water in the successive jars that would accompany a reversal of the height of the liquid to its original level. (See Figure 9.1, below, for examples of Piagetian conservation problems.)

The same lack of conservation arises with experiments on number (discontinuous quantity), where rows of counters are said to change in numerosity depending on their arrangement in space, and even the length of a piece of string (continuous quantity) is said to depend on whether it is stretched out straight or coiled!

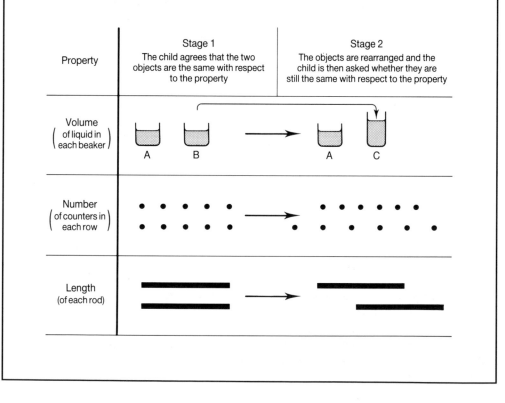

| Property | Stage 1<br>The child agrees that the two objects are the same with respect to the property | Stage 2<br>The objects are rearranged and the child is then asked whether they are still the same with respect to the property |
|---|---|---|
| Volume (of liquid in each beaker) | A    B | A    C |
| Number (of counters in each row) | | |
| Length (of each rod) | | |

coordinated actions. Mental operations, according to Piaget, are the internalised forms of actions that the infant has already mastered, for example in ordering, combining, and separating things in the physical world. However, thought is not fully logical because the child's mental "actions" on represented reality need to be made systematic and coordinated with each other. Although the young child can reason about simple problems, the system of mental operations lacks critical linkages, such that it is not totally internally consistent. For instance, the child may not be able to reverse the logic of a train of thought. So, for example, the 3-year-old knows that she has an older brother, but she may not realise that the relationship simultaneously entails her brother having a younger sister! In this example, thinking proceeds in only one direction and is irreversible.

The key feature of pre-school age thinking, according to Piaget, is that the child is able to focus only on one salient feature of a problem at a time. Piaget argues that the child is dominated by the immediate appearance of things and, as a consequence, thought is pre-logical.

The very widespread nature of the pre-school child's difficulties is illustrated in many tasks. A well-documented example is the class inclusion problem, which is a test designed to assess whether the child can simultaneously think about parts and wholes. For example, the child is shown a necklace of 10 wooden beads, seven of which are painted brown and three white. Piaget asks the child, "Are there more brown beads or beads?" The child typically answers that there are more brown beads than beads. Piaget says that when the child thinks about the whole class (beads) he or she cannot simultaneously think about the parts (i.e. the sub-sets brown beads, white beads). The child can compare parts with parts, but not parts with wholes, because thinking remains a succession of separate views of things (these are called *centrations* in Piaget's terminology), which preclude reasoning about the relations between them.

These tasks, and many more, convinced Piaget that the logical processes necessary for systematic reasoning are not yet properly coordinated in the pre-school child.

# Childhood egocentrism

There are many other Piagetian examples of the unsystematic nature of pre-school children's thinking. All have in common the idea that the pre-school child is egocentric. At its simplest, egocentrism can be defined as looking on the world only from one's own position. It implies an inability to differentiate between one's own point of view and other possible points of view.

## Piaget's "Three mountains task": A diagnostic test of egocentrism

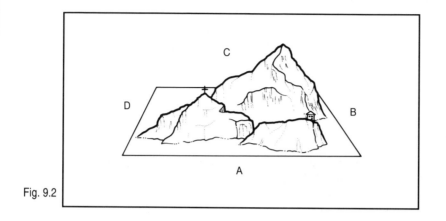

Fig. 9.2

Egocentrism is the tendency unwittingly to view the world from only one's own perspective. The task, originally used by Piaget and Inhelder (1956) to illustrate childhood egocentrism, is known as the three mountains task. It is used to find out how the pre-school child represents to itself a scene from different viewpoints.

A large mountain, called La Saleve, is visible across the lake from the city of Geneva and it is known to everyone locally, including the children tested by Piaget and Inhelder. A 3D model of the mountain and surrounding peaks serves as the test for determining whether the child can comprehend and describe other points of view. In the diagram in Figure 9.2, the child is seated at position A and asked to represent his or her own view and the view of a doll placed at positions B, C, and D. Various methods are adopted: The child is asked to either (1) arrange three pieces of cardboard shaped like the mountains; (2) select the doll's view from one of 10 pictures depicting different points of view; or (3) choose one picture and decide where the doll must sit with respect to the model to have that view.

Piaget and Inhelder described four stages in the development of perspective-taking ability:

*I*    *Below 4 years:* The child simply doesn't understand the meaning of the questions.

*IIa*    *4–6 years:* The child fails to distinguish between his or her own view and a doll's view. Consequently, children choose their own view, whatever the perspective of the observer.

*IIb*    *5–7 years:* First signs of discrimination between viewpoints, the child is aware of the distinction but cannot specify what it is.

*IIIa*    *7–9 years:* Some relationships under transformation are understood. First is the transformation "in-front–behind", but the child cannot consider simultaneously all the spatial transformations. Even if the "in front–behind" relationship is correctly represented from the doll's perspective, the left–right perspective remains untransformed from the child's perspective, so that it does not correspond to what would be seen from the doll's position.

*IV*    *8–9 years:* The first evidence of a comprehensive operational system for dealing with all perspective changes. All the transformations involved in a change of viewpoint are considered simultaneously and the child gives the right answer.

In this classic demonstration, then, children below 8 years are considered egocentric because they are "rooted to their own position", they cannot imagine any position other than their own.

As Piaget described it, this involves an inability to decentre from a particular point of view. In general, egocentrism means that the child is unable to differentiate what is *subjective* (this means what is strictly private or personal) from what is *objective* (i.e. a matter of public knowledge, something we know for certain to be true). It is just as well to be clear that egocentrism does not refer to selfishness as a personality trait. It is simply the unconscious adoption of one's own perspective through failure to realise that other perspectives exist. The panel opposite describes Piaget's famous three mountains test of egocentrism.

## Animism

Some of Piaget's most charming examples of thinking in the pre-school child are revealed by the adult asking probing questions. Piaget (1929/1973) argued that children's answers do not simply reflect lack of knowledge. He argued that children egocentrically assimilate what they don't understand to something that they do comprehend. A good example is his work on animism, which may be defined as attributing life to inanimate objects. Such a confusion is egocentric, according to Piaget, because it implies an inability to distinguish between the psychological and the physical world.

In Aristotle's original definition, animism refers to the view that the "soul (anima) is the cause or principle of life", (Baldwin, 1905). Animism is said to be characteristic of children's thinking until about the age of 10 years. According to Piaget, any event that has no obvious physical cause is believed by the pre-school child to be in some way animated. Piaget suggests that children indiscriminately take activity as a criterion for life and they consequently attribute intentions to anything that can move, even inanimate objects like the wind, or a candle flame. He gave many charming examples of animistic thinking from his interviews with young children. Here is one:

Piaget:   Can the wind feel anything?
Child:    Yes.
Piaget:   Why ?
Child:    Because it blows.
Piaget:   Can the water feel anything?
Child:    Yes.
Piaget:   Why?
Child:    Because it flows. (Piaget 1929/1973, p. 211)

Questioned closely by Piaget, the child seems to attribute life to inanimate objects because they show spontaneous movement. To be sure, this

## Piaget's observations on children's understanding of dreams

Another example of egocentrism in the thought processes of the pre-school child comes from a study of dreaming. This study was actually motivated by Piaget's psychoanalytic interests. The student may wish to follow up some of the links between Piaget and Freud on dreams by reading Piaget's, *Play, dreams and imitation in childhood* (1951).

Piaget:    Do you know what a dream is?
Child (6.6 years of age):    When you are asleep and you see something.
Piaget:    Where does it come from?
Child:    The sky!
Piaget:    Can you see it?
Child:    Yes when you're asleep.
Piaget:    Could I see it if I was there?
Child:    No.
Piaget:    Why not?
Child:    Because you wouldn't be asleep.

Piaget:    What do you dream with?
Child:    The mouth.
Piaget:    Where is the dream?
Child:    In the night.
Piaget    Where does it happen?
Child:    In the bed—on the pillow.

As we can see from this transcript, the child's understanding of the dream seems to be that something external to the self is in the room. The child seems to think that one cannot see a dream clearly because it is dark and it is night time. Yet again, childhood egocentrism is diagnosed by Piaget because there is a failure to distinguish subjective and objective aspects of experience. From the child's point of view, the dream seems to be an external visual event, like a visit to the cinema, an experience potentially visible to anyone (but, paradoxically, only so long as their eyes are closed) (Piaget, 1929/1973, p. 114).

---

is not a bad criterion for being alive, but it is incomplete. Piaget says the child assimilates the world to her own ego and in that sense thinking is intuitive rather than fully rational. Here is another example:

Piaget:    What does the sun do when there are clouds and it rains?
Child:    It goes away because it is bad weather.
Piaget:    Why?
Child:    Because it doesn't want to be rained on.
          (Piaget 1929/1973, p. 213)

This example also shows egocentrism because the child attributes both will and consciousness to an inanimate object.

The child is said to be unable to distinguish properly between how things appear and how they really are. In the case of dreaming, for example, the child cannot distinguish between a dream seeming to be external and externality itself. Having defined a dream as a picture, one can see that the child is unable to comprehend the dream as an internal aspect of self. According to Piaget (1973), the young pre-operational child is simply incapable of making the distinction between appearances and reality.

# Problems with language
# or with Piaget's tests?

At first sight, then, pre-school children are quite illogical in their failure to reason about simple conservation problems or to differentiate their own point of view from that of others. But to what extent are they being led into these answers by the manner of questioning or by the rather abstract tests of reasoning Piaget devised? We need to be careful not to assert that the child actually believes that quantity changes as the row of counters lengthens, or that dreams really are in the public domain. Piaget's results might have other explanations.

It could be that young children, with limited knowledge of the physical world and of the meaning of language, simply make an intelligent guess when confronted with a question about a phenomenon that they have never before encountered or don't fully understand. It might be that simplified versions of Piaget's classic experiments may reveal unsuspected abilities. As the child is still acquiring language, it could even be that the social interaction with the adult questioner misleads the child into giving wrong answers.

Critics of Piaget, especially Margaret Donaldson (1978) and more recently Light (1988) and Siegal (1991), take the view that much of children's difficulty in reasoning stems not from an inability to think logically but because they cannot comprehend the adult's language and because the tasks selected make little sense to them. Their arguments are quite subtle; it is not just the child's lack of knowledge of language that leads them into error. Children's errors arise in an active attempt to discover what the adult actually means by the questions being asked in the social context established for the task. This line of argument is based on Vygotsky's theory that aspects of intellectual development based in language in young children depend on the interpersonal context. Some examples will make this clear.

# Margaret Donaldson's
# critique of Piaget

The book, *Children's minds*, by Margaret Donaldson (1978) is one of the most influential critiques of Piaget's stage theory to have been written. Her basic argument is that pre-school children are very much more competent than Piaget gives them credit for. She suggests that Piaget's testing situations are too abstract and do not connect with the child's everyday social experience. Consequently, he underestimates the child's ability. Donaldson suggests, instead, that children should be tested in situations that make "human sense" to them. By human sense she means that the child should be tested on problems that are couched in the social terms familiar to the child in everyday life, rather than in the abstract rather unfamiliar ways that have been adopted.

Donaldson argues that young children do understand other people's feelings and so socially based tasks that tap this ability will give a rather different estimate of pre-schoolers' thought processes than Piaget's rather "cold-blooded" tests of intellectual development. One example, which she discusses extensively in her book, is an experiment on childhood egocentrism by Hughes, in which a child has the task of "hiding" a boy doll from either one or two policeman dolls. The task is shown in Figure 9.3. It comprises a model made of two walls, intersecting as a cross. Children aged from 3.5 to 5 years play a game which involves hiding a boy doll in one of the quadrants formed by the walls, so that the boy doll can't be seen from the position of a policeman doll, also placed in the model. In the example with one policeman, two quadrants are visible and two are hidden from the policeman's position. With two policemen, only one hiding place (location C) is concealed from the gaze of the policemen.

Fig. 9.3 Hughes' perspective-taking task. Adapted from Donaldson (1978).

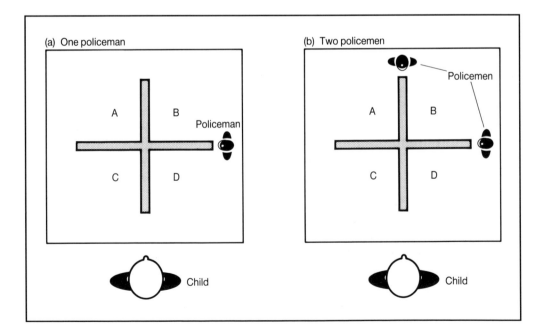

In Hughes' study, the youngest children were 90% correct in identifying whether the policeman doll(s) could see the boy. In more complex arrangements, with up to six sections of walls and three policemen stationed at various positions, 4-year-olds still showed 90% correct performance. These results seem impossible to reconcile with Piaget's theory that the egocentric child cannot understand the possibility of other points of view.

However, to evaluate Donaldson's claims about the implications of this task more carefully, it is necessary to distinguish between two aspects of the test. We need to ask (1) whether the child is aware that viewpoints exist that are independent of his or her own, and (2) whether the child can imagine what someone else would see from a different position.

Donaldson's results are consistent with (1) above. That is, even the young child appreciates the possibility of different viewpoints. This must mean that the child cannot be considered completely egocentric. However, as was discussed earlier (see pp. 127–129) babies can work out where someone else is looking or pointing. So, the ability discovered in Hughes' task may in part be explained by a relatively elementary understanding based on knowledge of lines of sight and in part by knowledge of hidden objects. The young child may be able to say whether the boy would be visible or invisible from the various positions of the policeman simply by working out whether the policeman's line of sight is blocked by a wall. Thus, the non-egocentric skills in determining whether another person's viewpoint is occluded or not, pinpointed in 4-year-olds by Hughes, may actually require only a slightly more advanced level of understanding of spatial relationships than the skills already demonstrated when babies search for a hidden object. The ability demonstrated may not require the child to imagine the particular view that would be perceived from any particular position.

In other words, Donaldson may not be correct to argue that her simplified task, in making human sense, is equivalent in difficulty to Piaget's three mountains task. In the latter case, the question is not whether something can be perceived but what can be perceived from positions other than the child's own.

In an overview of recent studies, Cox (1991) has discussed what the young child can represent. She agrees both with Piaget and with Donaldson that the three mountains task requires the simultaneous coordination and transformation of a number of spatial relations in the display. There is no question of an absolute inability of young children to understand that points of view can be different, but the spatial aspects of the task do show developmental stages (see the panel on p. 166).

However, Cox also concludes that the child does have difficulty in determining what can be experienced from a different perspective. Here the problem she identifies is that different perspective-taking tasks may be of differential difficulty. For example, with objects such as a doll that has an easily identifiable front, back, and sides the child may find it relatively easy to specify what would be seen from any position. In the three mountains task however, not only are the mountains symmetrical (i.e. they are not fronted), but the child must also imagine the relationship between them. Furthermore, the mountains occlude each other differently, from different viewpoints. The requirements of the three mountains task are thus much more complex than the policeman test.

Cox concludes that knowing how more complex scenes of this kind appear to another observer is rather a late-appearing ability. However, she does suggest that children at Piaget's stage IIa (between 4 and 6 years, see the panel on p. 166) tend to select their own view in the three mountains task because this simply happens to be the view that differentiates the three mountains most clearly. The child is not "stuck" with his or her own view, as some interpreters of Piaget imply. Rather, the child chooses the best view of the scene. All of this leaves Piaget's concept of spatial egocentrism partly intact and partly modified. The modified aspect is that even the youngest children understand that different viewpoints on the world exist. However, Piaget is on stronger ground in arguing that there are stages in the child being able to specify what can be seen from any particular viewpoint other than the child's own.

## Language and thought: Vygotsky's theory

Where Donaldson and many other critics of Piaget may be on much stronger ground concerns the relationship between social interaction, language, and the child's performance on typical Piagetian tasks. Here, the basic argument is that young children don't necessarily know what words mean in the test interview, independently of the context in which they are uttered. In fact, the context is *essential* to the child in interpreting what the adult intends. Donaldson's theoretical position is based on Vygotsky, who suggested that one of the developmental tasks of the pre-school child is to master the structure of language and internalise it as the foundation of verbal thought. A brief overview of Vygotsky's ideas in the panel overleaf will give a useful background to the more recent experiments about to be discussed.

## Vygotsky's theory of the relation between language and thought

Vygotsky and Piaget had a fundamental disagreement about the relation between language and thought. Piaget had argued in his book *The language and thought of the child* (1923) that early language is egocentric and only becomes socialised with cognitive development. He suggested that the pre-operational child fails to take into account the other person's point of view and, as a result, the early conversations of children have more of the quality of monologues than of dialogues. Only with cognitive development does speech take on a genuinely communicative function. In Piaget's theory, language and communication depend on the development of thinking.

Vygotsky argued, on the contrary, that language is communicative from the outset. He carried out an ingenious test of his theory. He compared the amount of "egocentric" speech (simply understood as how much the child apparently talks "for" itself) when hearing pre-school children are together, with the amount of speech produced when the hearing child is placed in a room with a group of deaf-mute children. Under these circumstances the hearing child has little chance of communicating and Vygotsky found that the rate of egocentric speech decreased significantly. This result would not be expected if speech had been intended by the child simply as a monologue.

Vygotsky argued that children's speech is intended to communicate, even though children are not necessarily successful in this aim. According to Vygotsky, language and thought both develop and have a mutual influence. They come together to yield a uniquely human form of thinking, "inner speech" or verbal thought. He suggested that there is a developmental progression which begins on the social plane, in the relations between the adult and child, moves to inner dialogue, and finally to verbal thought. The child first understands the adult non-verbally, in relation to the context and the perceived intentions of the adult's behaviour. This is the basic, common understanding which enables the understanding of speech and the verbal regulation, by the adult, of the child's behaviour. From the child's point of view also, words serve as a means of social contact, as a means of controlling the adult's behaviour, and they allow the child to solve problems which would be impossible unaided. The "internalisation" of this dialogue between adult and child is, according to Vygotsky, at the very foundations of verbal thought.

Problem solving with others should be thought of as a basic unit of the pre-schooler's behaviour. From the child's point of view, the roles of the adult and the child are not fully differentiated and the child depends on the adult for guidance. These aspects of children's thinking are nicely illustrated in the experiments by McGarrigle and Donaldson, discussed in the text. Vygotsky's theory is well described and explained in Cole, John-Steiner, Scribner, and Souberman (1978).

Donaldson (1978) reports an elegant experiment by James McGarrigle which has become known as the "naughty teddy " study. This is a variant on the number conservation task originally devised by Piaget. First of all, the child is asked whether two rows of counters arranged in parallel lines contain the same or a different number. The child readily agrees that the number is the same when the length of the rows is identical and each counter is opposite another. Then, under the control of the experimenter, a glove puppet known as "naughty teddy" rushes in and lengthens one of the rows of counters. This manoeuvre is carried out in such a way that one row of counters is made longer than the other row, just as in the conservation test. The child is then asked whether the longer row contains the same or a different number of counters than the shorter one. Most children between 4 and 6 years now "conserve", that is, they give the correct answer that the number of counters has not changed, even though they fail to conserve under the standard testing conditions of the conservation task.

Light (1988) has discussed these findings in relation to a series of experiments which were designed to establish whether children really demonstrate the logical requirements of conservation when giving the right answer. He suggests that children may be giving the right answer for the wrong reasons. Just as children may be misled by the adult's behaviour into supposing that length is relevant to number, they may equally be led to acquiesce that the number remains the same by the social interaction taking place around the accidental transformation. A young child doesn't really understand what the adult's question means and therefore makes a best guess at what is being asked, by monitoring closely the adult's behaviour and interpreting questions accordingly.

When the adult deliberately rearranges the display, and asks questions about number, the child reasonably takes it that perhaps a change in length may have something to do with what the adult means by "number". The implicit message given by the adult is "Take notice of this transformation, it is relevant to questions about whether the number is the same or different". When the rearrangement is made to happen accidentally, then the child interprets the adult's question, in relation to the whole context, to mean that the number has not changed. Light argues that the child is discovering the meaning of the language as applied to number through social interaction in the testing situation. This applies both to where the wrong answer is given and to the situation where the right answer is volunteered. The child learns about quantity terms by interpreting their meaning in relation to socially intelligible contexts.

These demonstrations therefore suggest that the child's difficulties with conservation tasks, at least in part, arise from difficulties in understanding what the adult means when questioning the child. However, by the time the child is 8 or 9, he or she has little difficulty with conservation tasks. There seems to have been a genuine stage transition from the pre-school period. The unresolved theoretical question is whether this stage transition is a function of acquiring coordinated logical operations in thinking, as Piaget maintains, or whether it may reflect the beginnings of verbal reasoning.

# Appearance and reality

Piaget argued that the pre-school child has difficulty in distinguishing how things appear from how they really are. Many of Piaget's examples of animistic thinking were given earlier in this chapter (see pp. 167–168) and this line of research has been extensively pursued by others. Recent studies qualify Piaget's claims.

The perceptual abilities of the baby were discussed in Chapter 6 and the idea that perception puts the child in direct contact with the real world was considered. The argument is that because perception specifies the real world, the developing child is necessarily dependent on what is perceived, in order to build up a fund of knowledge. However, appearances can be deceptive. The question Piaget asked is whether children can conceive of the possibility that perception may be misleading or whether they inevitably take whatever they perceive to be real?

Flavell (1983) and his colleagues carried out a study in which children were shown a piece of sponge that had been carefully painted to look like a rock. The children were allowed to squeeze the "rock" and discover that it was actually spongy. The children were then asked two questions:

1. *A reality question:* "What is this really, really? Is it really a rock or really, really a piece of sponge?"
2. *An appearance question:* "When you look at this with your eyes right now, does it look like a rock or does it look like a piece of sponge?"

The majority of 3-year-olds answered that the object is really a sponge (to question 1) and that it looks like a sponge (to question 2). By contrast, the majority of 4-year-olds were able to state that it really is a sponge but looks like a rock. Perner (1991) has reviewed many studies of this type and suggests that the realism of the 3-year-olds leads them to understand the question in the following fashion: "When you look at this right now, are you looking at a rock or looking at a piece of sponge?" And, naturally, they answer "A piece of sponge". By 4 years, however, children are beginning to acquire a notion of misrepresentation and can understand how the sponge can look "as if it were" a rock.

A particularly spectacular study of the appearance and reality distinction, which fully confirmed Piaget's observations, was carried out by DeVries (1969) who had a very well-behaved black cat called Maynard. Three-year-olds were encouraged to play with Maynard and get to know him. Then, Maynard's face was placed behind a screen, although his tail was still visible, and a realistic mask of a dog was strapped onto the cat's head. DeVries told each child: "Now this animal is going to look quite different. Look, it has a face like a dog". When the screen was removed she asked the child "What kind of animal is it now?" "Is it really a dog, can it bark?" Three-year-olds focused almost entirely on the cat's appearance, some said he had actually become a dog. The 4- and 5-year-olds were confused, whereas 6-year-olds did not believe that a cat could become a dog.

These apparently compelling examples of the limits of pre-operational reasoning are subject, however, to the same criticisms as the other studies we have already reviewed. The adult is deliberately misleading the child in an attempt to assess their knowledge and, consequently, an underestimate of the child's capabilities may be obtained.

Carey (1985) showed that 4-year-olds are often inconsistent in their attributions of animism. For example, children sometimes say that a table is alive because it has legs, and at other times that it is not alive because a table does not have a face and therefore cannot breathe. Such anthropomorphic justifications are as common as those couched in terms of movement or activity, and seem to reflect judgements based on the familiar properties of living people.

Carey suggests that young children may judge the meaning of the word "alive" by comparison with things being "dead" or out of existence. For example, she describes a protocol with a 4-year-old who said "A ball is living when it goes up in the air but when the ball goes down it dies dead" or "The moon is dead today but tonight it lives". Being in motion or being observable seem to be the criteria the child adopts in these cases. Functional properties are also associated with the child's concept of life: "A table is alive because you can eat on it". Such justifications, in terms of observable or functional properties, are biologically relevant in the sense that they highlight existential criteria and they also underscore the salience of other people as exemplars of living things. Thus, Carey's 4-year-olds do have an idea of animate versus inanimate objects, based on autonomous movement and functional integrity, but they do not have a well-formed concept of living things as distinct from inanimate objects. Consequently, they will sometimes deny that plants are alive because plants don't move or they will say that a button is alive because it can fasten things. The implication is that children have an intuitive biology but they simply don't know enough biology to classify plants and animals into the single superordinate category of living things.

Finally, it has been suggested by Carey that animism in childhood might be an attempt to characterise the world by an intuitive biology, rather than as the result of incomplete logical development. Both for adults and children there are unclear cases of what is alive, when it may be necessary to consult an expert biologist for a decision. Strict rules apply, based on morphology, the means of reproduction, digestion and so on. In marginal cases, to determine whether some aspects of nature are animate or inanimate is a difficult task. Young children are, in a sense, grappling with a similar problem at the outset of acquiring their biological knowledge.

## Context, cognition, and culture

When we examine young children's knowledge in real-world contexts that are familiar to them we find evidence for basic competences. One example of such an ecologically valid study, which also reveals the subtle ways in which cultural practices influence the development of reasoning, is by Inagaki (1990), on the effects of raising animals on children's biological knowledge. The panel below describes the study.

In the familiar, ecologically valid context of goldfish care, with no trick questions, pre-operational Japanese children reveal that they have acquired some general biological principles relevant to animate objects and that they can reason by analogy on the basis of these principles. The children are using their knowledge in a flexible way to generate plausible predictions. This also gives us rather a different perspective on childhood egocentrism, because it suggests that animism and the phenomena noted by Piaget may actually be the result of the extension of a perfectly valid strategy of understanding living things by analogy with oneself to non-living objects.

---

### Context-specific reasoning about biology in young children

Inagaki (1990) cleverly capitalised on the fact that Japanese parents will often buy their pre-school children goldfish. This study compared children aged 5 years 10 months, who had raised goldfish at home for at least 6 months, with an equal number who had not. They were given factual questions about goldfish and also tested about an unfamiliar aquatic animal, a frog. The kind of questions asked were "Suppose someone is given a baby frog and wants to keep it forever the same size because it is so small and cute. Can he do that? What will happen to a frog if we feed it 10 times a day?"

Not surprisingly, the children who had kept goldfish at home knew significantly more about the facts of raising them than a control group who had not had the experience. But they also had a better conceptual understanding of biological processes, such as growth, illness, digestion, and excretion, as revealed by questions on the effects on the fish of over-feeding or of failure to change the water. Almost all these children made analogies with people in offering their explanations. For example, a goldfish should not be overfed "because it will feel a pain in its stomach".

---

Carey (1985) has suggested that the young child uses an intuitive psychology to construct an intuitive biology. This is elaborated by appropriate experience with animals, through parental tuition, and eventually systematised through schooling. The school has the responsibility to connect formal wisdom about biology, which has been accumulated by the culture, with the child's intuitively based knowledge.

Another example of context-specific reasoning, a study by Siegal (1991), is discussed in the panel below. Siegal (1991) drew attention to a particularly important practical aspect of the debate about whether young children can reason about cause and effect or distinguish appearance from reality. His examples concern the young child's knowledge of causes of health and illness, and they may have important implications for training children in hygiene.

Siegal (1991) also showed that pre-schoolers understand that a scraped knee is non-contagious and that toothaches are not sent as a mysterious punishment. In these highly salient contexts, which are certainly familiar in the West, pre-school children do show appropriate reasoning. Siegal points out that such early causal knowledge might be used as a basis for preventative health education.

These examples of what quite young children can actually do in specific contexts show that intellectual development in the pre-school child is rather patchy. It depends on the particular context. These examples also illustrate how culture influences thought processes and their development. Cole and Cole (1993) suggest that the cultural context influences development in many subtle ways. For example, 4-year-old bushmen growing up in the Kalahari desert are unlikely to learn about taking baths or pouring water into differently shaped jars, whereas urban children are unlikely to know how to find water-bearing roots in the desert. Pre-school

---

### Pre-school children's understanding of contamination

Siegal (1991) showed that the majority of Australian pre-schoolers (aged 4 years and 11 months) in his sample knew about contamination. He showed children a glass of milk, with a dirty comb in it, or a dead cockroach floating on top. They were asked "Would the child get sick if he drank some of the milk with the dirty comb in it? Would you want to drink milk with a cockroach in it, even if an adult told you you could?".

The children said they would not drink the milk, even with the dead cockroach removed. Not only does this reveal a basic understanding of contamination, it also shows quite nicely the ability to distinguish appearance from reality because once the contaminant has been removed from the milk, even though it looks wholesome, the child knows it remains contaminated.

children may show adult standards of thought in highly familiar, culturally specific contexts.

Children growing up in villages with craft specialities, such as making clay pottery as happens in Mexico, are likely to show conservation of mass earlier than Western children. This is presumably because they have more experience of rolling clay in the context of making, firing, and selling pots. Moulding clay in a Western pre-school nursery is associated with completely different activities. The culture also regulates how much responsibility the child will bear and this, in turn, will have repercussions regarding the opportunity to gain and display competence.

In summary, the problem still to be resolved is whether thinking in pre-schoolers is governed by general rules or whether it is context-specific. Piaget's search was for general rules underlying behaviour at any particular stage. His tasks tend towards abstract, context-free tests of reasoning. However, recent research shows that early competence is most readily revealed in concrete, familiar contexts within which the child has had a lot of experience.

# Conclusion and summary

Pre-school children's thinking is uneven and often naive. Piaget's account, which seeks to describe universal stages of development, emphasises the child's lack of logical consistency, difficulty in adopting others' perspectives, reasoning about appearance and reality, or about cause and effect. Childhood egocentrism is said to be fundamental to all these difficulties.

Donaldson was in the vanguard of contemporary critics of Piaget in her demonstrations that pre-school children are more competent in their reasoning than Piaget gave them credit for. Although it is true that familiar everyday contexts reveal greater abilities in pre-schoolers than Piaget allowed, Donaldson's interpretation, that tasks which make human sense tap intellectual abilities that Piaget's tasks do not, may be an oversimplification.

Donaldson may be correct, however, in drawing attention to the importance of language in reasoning and to the child's difficulties in knowing precisely what an adult intends. Her findings about the interaction of the child's performance on Piaget's tasks with the behaviour and perceived intentions of the adult is what Vygotsky's theory would predict. Vygotsky argued that mental abilities are first made manifest in the social interaction between people (see pp. 21–24). Piaget's tasks tend to overlook the fact that, from the child's perspective, these tests of reasoning are also social encounters in which the child will seek guidance from the adult.

How we think of the pre-operational stage has particularly important implications for the transition from home to school, where the child must engage in the acquisition of knowledge valued in his or her culture, mainly through verbal means. Contemporary approaches to pre-school thinking stress the ecological validity of the tasks we set children. Such tasks, drawn from everyday experience, do reveal some remarkable competences in the pre-school child.

## Further reading

Cox. M. (1991). *The child's point of view (2nd edition)*. Hemel Hempstead: Harvester Press.

Donaldson, M. (1978). *Children's minds*. Glasgow: Fontana.

Siegal, M. (1991). *Knowing children: Experiments in conversation and cognition*. Hove: Lawrence Erlbaum Associates Ltd.

# PART 4

# Middle Childhood

# Cognitive development in middle childhood

# 10

**M**iddle childhood is the period from approximately 6 years to adolescence. As in the previous stages we have discussed there are both biological and social markers. Middle childhood coincides in many societies with the beginning of formal schooling and being allowed a relatively unsupervised life—on a bicycle, in a playground or in the classroom, or perhaps helping with younger brothers and sisters. There is an increasing emphasis on peer relations to complement parent–child relations in the life of the child. Cole and Cole (1993) estimate that 40% of the waking time of 6- to 12-year-olds is spent with peers.

There is continued physical growth, with a gain in height of 2–3 inches per year for both boys and girls. At 6 years of age, children are about 3.5 feet tall and weigh about 50 pounds; by 13 years of age, they are about 5 feet tall and weigh 100 pounds. Boys double in strength during this period.

A little-noticed biological marker for entry into middle childhood is the eruption of the first adult teeth as the milk teeth are replaced. It is not clear that there is any necessary psychological significance to this event, but that it is universal provides a convenient and easily observable biological benchmark for a new stage in development.

There are other biological reasons for supposing a stage transition to have occurred. There is a growth spurt of the brain between the ages of 5 and 7 years, especially in the region of the frontal lobes. This part of the brain plays an important role in planning and in the sequential organisation of actions and thoughts. The Russian psychologist Luria (1959), a student and life-long follower of Vygotsky, developed a test in which the child has to follow instructions to activate or inhibit behaviour. The simple task requires the child to squeeze a rubber ball when a light comes on, according to the following instructions: "Squeeze the ball when you see a green light. Don't squeeze the ball when you see a red light".

Pre-schoolers get confused by these instructions and tend to squeeze the ball whenever they see a light come on, regardless of its colour. Verbal instructions serve to activate their behaviour but do not serve to inhibit it. Eight-year-olds, however, have no difficulty with the task and can follow the instructions perfectly. Luria argues that children have become able to use language to regulate their own behaviour. Language now serves both to activate and inhibit activity.

In Vygotsky's theory, once language takes on this self-regulatory function, it is internalised as verbal thought. From a Vygotskian perspective, verbal regulation of behaviour is a major feature of the stage transition from early to middle childhood (see pp. 21–24).

Another factor that may contribute to the stage transition occurring in middle childhood is a change in memory capacity, or perhaps simply in the efficiency with which children use their memory. Children may become more aware of the strengths and limitations of their own memory and this may lead to conscious rehearsal of material to be remembered. Such knowledge about the operation of one's own abilities is known as *metacognition*. In the case of metamemory (knowledge about the operation of memory), children have learned that rehearsal helps in remembering information, which results in improvement on tasks requiring memory for large amounts of material (Kail, 1990).

Another consideration is the increased amount of knowledge that the child can bring to bear on problem solving in middle childhood. Chi (1978) showed that 10-year-old chess experts had better memory for the positions of chess pieces than college students who were only novice chess players. The children, having greater knowledge of chess, could remember more than the adults. This example also raises the possibility that changes in development may not always have the across-the-board quality of a stage transition but may sometimes reflect knowledge of specific domains.

The main evidence that the middle childhood period does indeed comprise a new stage of development, comes from Piaget. Middle childhood encompasses Piaget's stage of *concrete operations*, in which children begin to use logical rules to solve problems.

# Piaget's theory of concrete operational reasoning

Leaving aside for the moment the recent evidence on the intellectual competence of pre-schoolers (Chapter 9), there remains the fact that the school-age child readily solves problems that the pre-schooler finds difficult. Perhaps the best example comes from Piaget's conservation tasks, in which children are tested on their understanding that physical quantities such as mass, weight, and volume remain constant, despite changes in the appearance of the quantities (see panel on p. 164).

The school-age child comprehends conservation as self-evident and will say, in the conservation of liquid quantity task for example, that the amount of water in two differently shaped jars remains the same because nothing is added or taken away when the water in a tall, thin jar is poured into a short, fat one. Furthermore, if the water in the short, fat jar is poured back into the tall, thin one, the child knows that the level in the tall, thin one is the same as it was at the beginning of the task. The child also knows that the change in the height of the liquid is accompanied by a correlated change in its width and this accounts for the change in appearance.

According to Piaget, the stage transition from pre-operational to concrete operational reasoning is a shift from reliance on perception to reliance on logic. The conservation problems, which gave such difficulty before, are now solved because the child can reason that, if nothing is added or taken away, the amount must be the same. Similarly, mentally reversing the sequence of steps (i.e. imagining the water being poured back into the original container) enables the child to conclude that nothing can have changed simply as a result of pouring the water into a new container.

The fact that children are no longer perceptually dominated by one aspect of the display (the height of the liquid) means they can take into account the possibility that the perceived changes in height and width covary. This new-found ability to comprehend the logical necessity of conservation enables children to justify their conclusions. This qualitatively new behaviour is Piaget's main reason for arguing that a stage change has occurred in cognitive development (see panel, pp. 186-187).

Piaget defines a logical operation as an internalised, mental action that is part of a logical system. According to Piaget, thought during the concrete operational stage is more flexible than in the pre-operational child because children can mentally retrace their steps—thought is reversible—within an internally consistent set of mental operations. However, cognitive development is not yet over. The thought of the concrete operational child remains limited because of the need for a concrete object to support thinking. According to Piaget, it is not until adolescence that thinking becomes capable of tackling purely hypothetical problems.

Other important logical operations that the child acquires during the period of middle childhood are seriation, classification, and numeration. *Seriation* will be explained in the next section. *Classification* refers to the hierarchical ordering of objects into superordinate classes and sub-classes. Piaget's famous (or infamous) example is the class inclusion problem (described on p. 165), in which the child is questioned about a necklace made up of seven brown and three white beads. The 6-year-old is asked whether there are more beads (superordinate class) or more brown beads

# Logical necessity and logical justification in concrete operational reasoning

Perhaps the single best indicator that children have entered Piaget's concrete operational stage is when they can solve conservation problems. Conservation refers to the child's understanding that quantitative relationships between two objects are conserved, or remain invariant, despite irrelevant changes in the appearance of the objects. An irrelevant transformation is any change other than addition or subtraction from the original quantities.

Piaget argued that from about 7 years of age, children can logically justify their decisions when solving problems. This qualitative change shows that they have entered the concrete operational stage. An operation is defined as a mental action that is part of a logical system. Logical operations are interiorised actions which are inter-coordinated into groups. The transition for Piaget is from intuitive thinking, dominated by perception, to logical thinking based on systematic deduction. The system of logical concrete operations involves two different sets of rules which allow the child to reverse imagined sequences of actions and their observed consequences. These are Identity (I) and Negation (N) (I/N rules), or Reciprocal (R) and Correlative (C) (R/C rules).

Concrete operational children can solve concrete problems that separately involve either I/N or R/C reversible reasoning. These reversible mental operations can be illustrated by the conservation of liquid volume task (refer to the panel on p. 164 if necessary). Two identical quantities of water, initially in identical containers, are shown to the child who affirms that the amounts are the same. Then one jar is emptied into a container of different shape and the child is asked whether the amounts of water are the same or different in the two jars. Pre-operational children, who Piaget maintains are dominated by perception, mistakenly centre on the height of the liquid and conclude that the volume has changed after it is poured. However, children who have attained concrete operations are not misled by this change in the appearance of the liquid. They know the volume is the same and often justify their judgements by saying "If the water were to be poured back, the levels would be just the same as before" (justification by the Negation rule) or "The water in this jar is taller but this one is wider" (justification by the Compensation rule). A child's ability to justify his or her conclusion shows understanding of the reversibility of the actions and the associated transformations that were observed. In other words, the child knows that the volume of water must remain invariant under these perceptual-motor transformations. A limitation, however, is that the child can only justify his or her conclusions with respect to one or other of the reversibility rules. Not until formal operations are obtained are the I/N and R/C operations coordinated hierarchically (see panel on p. 229)

The I/N and R/C operations can be illustrated in the conservation of liquid quantity task as follows:

I = *Identity*. It is the same water poured into a new jar.

N = *Negation*. The water is poured back into the original jar.

R = *Reciprocal.* Two sets of operations, such as pouring the water and then pouring it back, are the reciprocal of each other.

C = *Correlative*. Changes in one aspect (e.g. the height of the liquid) are compensated by change in another aspect (e.g. the width of the liquid).

Another approach to the logical necessity of conservation, which may actually be broadly consistent with Piaget's position, has been proposed by Bruner, Olver, and Greenfield (1966) They suggest that the child reasons that the amount must be the same because it is "the same water". On this view, the qualitative judgement of identity may enable the child to arrive at a logical conclusion about quantitative identity across the observed transformation.

(continued)

**Logical necessity and logical justification in
concrete operational reasoning (continued)**

The basis of this logical justification can be expressed in the following way:

1. The child is shown two identical jars containing water to the same height and width, i.e. Jar A = Jar B. They are in 1:1 correspondence. Therefore the amount of water is the same in the two jars.
2. The water is poured from Jar B to Jar C. It is the same water (qualitative identity) and nothing is added or taken away (quantitative identity), i.e. A = C.
3. If A = B and B = C then it follows by deduction
4. that A = C.

It is logically necessary that the amount of water is the same in jars A and C. The deduction enables the child to justify the conclusion that the volume of liquid is conserved across a transformation in its appearance. On this account, the deductive inference A = C provides the sense of logical necessity that the amount *must* be the same. This in turn allows the child to offer a logical justification according to one of the I/N or R/C reversibility rules (see Brainerd,1978, for an extensive discussion). Although Piaget's and Bruner's accounts differ slightly in their emphasis, they are actually similar in that each requires the child to be in possession of an internally coherent set of logical operations for solution of the conservation task.

(subordinate class) and typically replies that there are more brown beads than beads. The 8-year-old understands that the questions refer to different aspects of the problem, the set and the subset.

*Numeration* emerges from the combination of classification and seriation. The pre-school child does understand something about number and may be able to count small sets of objects. According to Piaget, the main gain for the concrete operational child is that serial ordering and classification enable the child to comprehend numbers as a sequence and to classify them as a set of classes and sub-classes. For example, a group of eight counters can also be understood to comprise two groups of four, or four groups of two counters; and this provides the logical foundation for learning about multiplication and division (see pp. 212–213).

Again, there has been much controversy over whether children do or do not have these abilities before the concrete operational stage. As these problems have particular significance for educational practice, they have received a great deal of empirical investigation both in Western cultures and cross-culturally.

## Seriation, measurement, and transitive inference

Seriation refers to the understanding of relationships of position both in space and in time. Acquiring the logic of seriation allows the child to order objects according to spatial dimensions such as height, length, width, or according to when events occurred in time. Seriation, in turn, enables the logical operation of *transitive inference* where, for example, the child can work out the relative length of two sticks by employing a third stick of intermediate length. This type of measurement problem can be described as follows:

If stick A is longer than stick B, and stick B is longer than stick C, which is the longest? The solution is that if A is longer than B, and B is longer than C, then A is longer than C. We deduce that A must be the longest stick from the dual relationship of B with A and C. To solve transitive inference problems, the child must be able to store all the relevant information in memory and comprehend the double relationship of the comparison term, B, with its neighbours A and C. Piaget argued that children cannot solve transitive inference problems until the beginning of concrete operations and consequently they do not understand the logical necessity of the relations between the A and C terms (see the panel on pp. 186–187 for a possible link with the conservation task).

Piaget's claim generated a great deal of controversy because it had important implications for teaching about numbers and measurement. Numbers occur in a serial order. In measurement, a ruler necessarily serves as the B term in serial comparisons between objects to be measured.

Bryant and Trabasso (1971) showed that 4-year-old children could solve a version of the transitive inference task in which five rods of different lengths and colours, (A, B, C, D, E) were serially compared. The rods were kept in a block of wood with holes drilled into it, so that the longest rod (which was red, say) was at the left, with successive rods of reducing length to the right. Each rod protruded by exactly the same amount above the surface, so the children could only see how long the rods actually were when the experimenter took them from the block, in pairs, and showed them to the children.

The children were given extensive training, in which pairs of rods were serially removed from the block and the children were shown that the red rod was longer than the white one next to it, the white rod longer than the green one next to it, and so on. The children were tested on their knowledge of the relative lengths of adjacent pairs while the rods were concealed in the block.

After training, the children had learned all the relationships between adjacent pairs—that is, that the red rod A was longer than the white one B; the white one B was longer than the adjacent green one C; the green one C was longer than the blue one D; and the blue rod D was longer than the pink one E. In other words, the children knew that A was longer than B, B was longer than C, C was longer than D, and D was longer than E. Then came the critical tests in which the children were asked about non-adjacent pairs. The questions were: Which is longer A or C, and C or E? The children gave the correct answer to both these questions, showing that they had deduced that A was longer than C and C was longer than E. However, the critical question was: Which is longer B or D? The answer to this question is crucial. In the training phase, both the B and D rods had equally often been named by the children as longer or shorter than the adjacent rods A, C, and E. If children can get this B is longer than D question right, it cannot be because they are simply parroting a verbal label that they have heard before. In fact, the children did give the right answer, B is longer than D, and so Bryant and Trabasso argued that the young child's problem is not with transitive inferences but with memory limitations which conceal their underlying capacity for logical reasoning. This criticism of Piaget is similar to that of Donaldson (see pp. 169–172) in that it proposes a distinction between an underlying competence and the child's actual performance on reasoning tasks.

Russell (1978) has reviewed criticisms of the Bryant and Trabasso conclusion that children can make transitive inferences. One possibility is that the children may simply have imagined all the rods, rather like imagining all the members of a family of five people of different height; then they directly read off the relative heights of any pair from the mental image. Russell says such a solution would not require any understanding of the logical necessity of transitive inference. This solution is arguably consistent with Piaget's theory that pre-operational children rely on the appearance of things when reasoning. However, in this case, the appearance of the rods in visual imagery actually allowed the child to arrive at the correct answer, which weakens Piaget's case, as it is quite possible that inferences do require visual imagery, even in adults.

In another approach to the question of whether young children can make transitive inferences, Bryant and Koptynskya (1976) studied spontaneous measurement in pre-school children. They presented children with a wooden block with a 4-inch and a 6-inch hole bored into it. The children had to work out which hole was deeper using a 10-inch measuring stick with a red portion 4 inches long at either end and a 2-inch yellow band in the middle. When the stick was dropped into the deeper hole, the yellow band disappeared, whereas when it was dropped into the shallow hole, the yellow band protruded above the surface. The relative position of the yellow band could thus be used as a comparative measure of the depth of the two holes.

Four-year-olds had no difficulty stating that the 6-inch hole was the deeper of the two holes. Bryant and Koptynskya argued that this shows not only that children are capable of simple measurement, but that they can also use the measuring stick transitively to make the inference that the

6-inch hole is deeper. The child's reasoning would be as follows: one hole "swallowed up" the yellow band, whereas the other hole did not. As more of the stick was accommodated, that hole must be deeper.

It is difficult to decide exactly how young children are able to perform correctly in these two studies of transitive inference. However, even if children are actually solving transitive inference problems through visual imagery this may not be entirely consistent with Piaget's theory of logical development. Piaget argued that perception, in the absence of logical operations, is inadequate for understanding reality. It is only on the argument that perception is not adequate that it follows that pre-operational children are dominated by the incidental aspects of what they experience. More pertinent, perhaps, is the criticism that the tasks used to demonstrate transitive inference in pre-operational children actually structure the problem space for the child, whereas in Piaget's tests the child is expected spontaneously to come up with the right solution (Russell, 1978).

Bryant (1974) actually made a much more extensive argument for the adequacy of perception in understanding the world. His theory, based on a great deal of experimental evidence, is that perception in young children is adequate for understanding the relationships between objects but it is poor in providing absolute information. For example, a 4-year-old can easily tell which of two rows of counters contains relatively more counters when both rows are arranged so that each counter is opposite a corresponding counter in the adjacent row, but the child would have difficulty knowing the absolute value that one row contains 10 counters and the other contains 8. In fact, Bryant follows the French psychologist, Alfred Binet, in arguing that perception operates logically by a process of unconscious inference. All in all, the weight of the evidence suggests that perception in infancy and early childhood is adequate for perceiving objects and the relationships between them.

## Some possible theories of the transition to concrete operations

At least three theories of the transition from pre-operational to concrete operational thinking are possible on the evidence to date. The matter is not yet resolved, but it may be useful to list the main alternatives before going on to consider other evidence.

1. The boundary between pre-operational and concrete operational thinking may not be as strict as Piaget thought. For some problems, such as conservation, or transitive inference, younger

children may be able to reason adequately but they also have to overcome the unfamiliarity of the social situation (Donaldson) and / or limitations in memory (Bryant) to reveal this ability. This type of explanation implies that there isn't really a stage transition at age 7. In solving Piaget's tasks, children need only apply pre-existing logic to non-social situations (Donaldson) and / or develop the requisite memory capacity (Bryant).

2. A second possibility is that Piaget was wrong about perception and its relationship to the development of thinking, but he was right that concrete operational thought is nevertheless a separate stage. Given appropriate training and contextual support, younger children can solve problems that are similar to Piaget's concrete operational tasks (Donaldson, Bryant). However, they do so only under the special circumstances that apply in these studies. This competence may be restricted to the perception of the relationships among the elements of a task, and children are not able logically to justify their conclusions.

   This view combines some of the newer evidence for the adequacy of perception in young children with Piaget's arguments about the importance of logical justification. On this view, a stage transition does occur. The new-found ability for logical justification in children aged from 7 to 12 years need not mean that pre-school children lack the ability for logical reasoning but they may have difficulty with logical justification. However, this leaves unexplained the new ability for logical justification.

3. A third possibility combines (2) above with a Vygotskian alternative. There may be a stage transition from perceptually based to verbally based reasoning. This argument comes from the observation that many of the competences revealed in pre-school children's reasoning (e.g. by Donaldson, see pp. 169–172) occur only under conditions where any ambiguity between the verbal and non-verbal communication between adult and child is eliminated. A similar possibility exists in the Bryant and Trabasso training study, where the requirements of the task were made absolutely unambiguous. Hence it is possible that children move through the zone of proximal development (see pp. 22–24) from non-verbal to verbal thought when they become able to map their perceptual experience into language. This in turn might enable verbal justification of conclusions once the logical requirements of the task can be consciously formulated in verbal terms. Such an account would combine aspects of the observations of Donaldson, Bryant, and Piaget with Vygotsky's theory.

Piagetians might still argue that the onset of concrete operations enables the child more flexibly to take perspectives and to keep more than one aspect of the task in mind. They might suggest that a decline in egocentrism would contribute to more effective communication because children would be better able to select the salient attributes of the situation in justifying their conclusions. However, Piagetians would have difficulty in explaining away all the contradictory evidence we have reviewed so far.

## Cross-cultural comparisons of concrete operations

Piaget's concrete operational stage is intended to be a description of a universal feature of development. What is crucial is not the exact time at which the child enters a stage, but that the sequence of sensori-motor, pre-operational, concrete operational, and formal operational stages should always occur in the same order and universally, as they are supposedly universal modes of human intellectual development.

Dasen (1972) reviewed a large number of studies of concrete operational reasoning in non-Western children and adults. In general, children in non-industrialised societies show a 1-year lag in their entry into concrete operations, when compared with children from industrialised societies. This suggests that there may be a cultural contribution to the rate of development, but the lag does not undermine Piaget's basic argument for universality. However, detailed analysis shows there are many exceptions and variations from culture to culture. Performance on some Piagetian tasks may depend on whether children have attended school, and it could even be that Piaget's reasoning tasks reflect the cognitive style demanded by Western industrialised society (see the panel on page 193).

## Moral reasoning

Piaget was also concerned to apply his theory of cognitive development to aspects of social knowledge. He published an important book *The moral judgment of the child* (Piaget, 1932), in which he argued that a child's cognitive development is responsible for moral reasoning. He saw the beginnings of social order and morality in children's rule-governed role play, even in their simple games of marbles.

In this aspect of his theory, Piaget laid much greater emphasis on the importance of the child's experience with peers than with adults. Some definitions will help: a *role* is a particular, socially prescribed form of

# Cross-cultural comparisons of concrete operational reasoning

Looking more closely at particular concrete operational tasks reveals a surprising variation both within and between different societies in children's ability to solve concrete operational problems. Dasen (1972) reports, among other tasks, on conservation of quantity, weight, volume, and length, and the ability to carry out seriation. These tasks have been administered at one time or another to Australian rural and urban Aboriginal children, to New Guinea Highlanders, to Chinese children in Hong Kong, to Canadian Eskimos, to adults from Amazonian tribes, to schooled and unschooled members of the Wolof people in Senegal, to illiterate adults in Sardinia and to Zambian children.

Although all these groups succeeded in passing Piagetian concrete reasoning tasks, which suggests that acquiring at least some concrete operations is universal, there was a very great variation among the different groups. Rural, unschooled Aborigines, with a little training, can solve conservation tasks but they lag about 3 years behind schooled, urban children. In some tasks, even adults failed; in other tasks, children performed better than the adults, as if the adults eventually developed quite different reasoning strategies in different cultures.

In evaluating such evidence, it is important to take into account the possibility that inadequate communication from the experimenter may also contribute. Performance on Piagetian tasks by people in traditional cultures improves when native speakers are used to carry out the tests.

Dasen suggests that a combination of two major factors explain this variation in performance: (1) whether or not the children had attended school and (2) the extent of contact with Western cultures. Thus, children in New Guinea and Senegal, who attended Western-type schools, were comparable to Western children in the attainment of concrete operations, whereas unschooled children from the same cultures were much slower in attaining a similar level of performance. This suggests that schooling may have a special effect on the attainment of concrete operations. On the other hand, schooling may simply serve to bring the individual into contact with Western intellectual values. Where the society already holds such values, schooling may not significantly influence the onset of concrete operations. Thus, unschooled Chinese children in Hong Kong—a country that has had close ties with the West—performed comparably to schooled Western children on Piagetian tests of concrete operational reasoning.

Cole and Cole (1993) argue that problem-solving tasks have specific settings, or contexts, which interact with basic cognitive processes. Even if logical operations are universal, their expression depends on the particular setting. Schooling provides a particular setting for the development of memory and reasoning in Western children. Cole and Cole argue that the method of teaching in schools creates a metacognitive awareness of the basic principles for ordering information. This contributes to the child's intellectual skills in domains where much information of an impersonal kind needs to be remembered. However, where complex information of a personal kind is to be remembered, unschooled children and adults may display very good memory because they are experts in their own specialised contexts. Thus, unschooled Mayan children from Guatemala can remember better up to 20 objects placed in a diorama of a Mayan village than can schooled Western children (Rogoff & Waddell, 1982).

All this evidence raises the basic question of whether it is specific school training, or the more general demands of life in Western societies, that creates the concrete operational mode of thought with logical justification at its core. Could Piaget have mistaken a culturally specific Western form of intellectual adaptation for a biological universal?

## Piaget's theory of moral development

Piaget (1932) studied moral development in the context of children's rule-governed games. He interviewed boys about the game of marbles and found that they showed several stages in understanding the game. Pre-schoolers enjoyed rolling the marbles but they had no idea that the game is governed by rules. During middle childhood, they began to play to win but they did not understand that the rules of marbles are conventional. Instead, they behaved as if the rules must be inflexibly obeyed and that rules cannot be changed.

Piaget questioned a child at this stage about the possibility of making up a new rule. The child replied: "It would be cheating to make up a new rule because I invented it—it isn't a rule. It is a wrong rule because it is outside the rules. A fair rule is one that is in the game".

The child entering concrete operations believes that the rules of marbles are immutable and provided by external authority. Between the ages of 9 and 11 years, children are less in awe of the rules and they begin to realise that the rules are social conventions governed by mutual consent. They understand that it is permissible to alter the rules if everyone agrees.

behaviour, e.g. shopkeeper, doctor, nurse; a *peer* is someone of the same age and status as the child. Piaget's argument is that, in children's games, the interaction of role play in rule-governed contexts, reveals a contribution of cognitive processes to social development (and vice versa).

In playing games, children regulate their own social interactions, rather than being under the control of adults. Piaget argued that the pre-operational child plays games based on social roles (e.g. mummies and daddies), but by the time of the concrete operational stage, the child's games are based more on rules (see panel above). These rules not only reveal the child's concrete logical operations in the social sphere, but they also provided Piaget with a model for the development of morality, as children must subordinate their own wishes and behaviour to the social group.

Another method adopted by Piaget, which has also been used by Lawrence Kohlberg (1927–1987) who built extensively on Piaget's theory of moral development, is to pose dilemmas for the child to solve. Piaget told the following story:

> John accidentally broke 15 cups.
> Henry purposely broke one cup.
> Who is naughtier, John or Henry?

At age 7 years, children choose John. They take the view that responsibility is a function of the amount of damage done. By age 9 years, however, they choose Henry because he was deliberately naughty.

Kohlberg (1982) used a similar technique. One dilemma he posed was as follows:

A woman was near death from cancer. One drug might save her, a form of radium discovered by a chemist living in the same town, who was selling the drug at 10 times what it cost him to manufacture it. The sick woman's husband tried to borrow the money but could raise only half the price. He told the chemist that his wife was dying and asked him to sell the drug more cheaply or, at least, let him pay later, but the chemist refused. The desperate husband broke into the chemist's shop to steal the drug for his wife. Should he have done that?

It is important to note that moral dilemmas are not presented on the assumption that there is a correct answer; rather, they are designed to tease out the qualitatively different arguments offered to justify or to oppose, for example, the theft of the expensive drug. From the various responses to this dilemma, Kohlberg described six stages of moral development, extending from childhood to adulthood. The three developmental levels each have two sub-stages: the levels are pre-conventional, conventional, and post-conventional. Both Piaget and Kohlberg assume that there is a close link between moral reasoning and intellectual development. Hence the development of moral thought should be closely correlated with the stages of cognitive development.

The first level, *pre-conventional*, corresponds to Piaget's pre-operational stage. In Stage 1, children judge actions to be good or bad by their outcome. An action is good if it is rewarded and bad if it is punished. In Stage 2, whatever satisfies one's own needs is considered good.

The *conventional* level coincides with Piaget's concrete operational stage. Children judge actions to be good or bad according to the intentions of the actor, within a framework of social rules. In Stage 3, children consider that whatever pleases or helps others is good, and are able to take into account the points of view and intentions of other people. By Stage 4, children take the view that maintaining the social order and doing one's duty is good.

The third level is the *post-conventional*. This corresponds to Piaget's formal operational stage. The adult judges actions to be good or bad according to transcendent moral principles. In Stage 5, what is morally correct is determined by values agreed on by society, including individual rights. Laws are no longer viewed as fixed but as relative. In the final stage, Stage 6, what is morally correct is a matter of personal conscience guided by morally transcendent principles.

A contemporary development of the method of posing a moral dilemma comes from work on the child's theory of mind. Work in this area is directed to discovering what children understand about other people's thoughts and emotions. Nunner-Winkler and Sodian (1988) told children aged 4–8 years a story about a child who was tempted to steal some sweets. The children were asked whether the thief felt good or bad. Children of 6 years and below reasoned that the thief felt good, as she had obtained the desired sweets. Eight-year-olds judged that the child who had succumbed to temptation felt bad, because one should not steal. This difference in reasoning corresponds rather well with Kohlberg's shift from the pre-conventional to the conventional level.

## Moral understanding

Piaget's account of moral development was derived from his typical method of the semi-structured interview. It depends entirely on the child's capacity for verbal expression and relies heavily on the assumption that cognitive development determines moral judgement. This is a rather abstract approach to the question of morality, almost as if Piaget wished to distance himself from moral behaviour in real life. An alternative approach is to make naturalistic observations of children in their own families, to see how they behave.

Dunn (1987) studied children from 2 years of age and found that, even as young as this, they may be distressed if they fail to meet adult standards. For example, a child aged 24 months was observed crying after a conflict with her sibling. Her mother asked, "What happened?" The child replied, "Amy bumped me". In her own way, the child is referring to her sister's responsibility for violating the prohibition on violent physical contact.

With increasing frequency during the second year, Dunn noted examples of children teasing the mother, laughing while jokingly carrying out a forbidden act or deliberately avoiding mother while carrying it out. For example, one child went behind a sofa to pick her nose after being forbidden to do it; another child took a piece of brandy butter from the fridge and hid herself away to eat it.

Dunn offers many such examples of awareness of transgression of rules. She argues that adults refer to acceptable standards of behaviour and children learn a great deal from this about moral rules. Of course, Piagetians might argue that all this shows is that moral reasoning in pre-operational children, who are at the pre-conventional level, is based on parental authority. However, Dunn's naturalistic observations also show the role that the child's emotions play in acquiring a principled morality. Pre-school children are increasingly distressed when they fail to meet adult standards: they are ashamed or anxious after a transgression. They also make jokes about rule violations as if positive emotions, not just negative ones, heighten their understanding of other people's feelings in the family context. Dunn suggests that the communication of moral rules to young children may reside very much in the non-verbal emotional aspects of their interactions with adults.

Another of Dunn's observations links the affectionate emotions with rule-governed play. In families where a warm, affectionate relationship exists between siblings, even 2-year-olds will participate in simple rule-governed games, and recognise and negotiate the roles and rules involved. This type of play was only ever observed with siblings and never with mothers. Different interpersonal relationships within the family may have different potential for growth of understanding of the standards, roles, and rules that govern the adult world.

Perhaps, using Vygotsky's line of argument, in sibling play where the intellectual differences between the children are smaller than between children and adults, early moral reasoning may be revealed more readily than in the more abstract context of interviews about moral dilemmas. Children do learn about cultural rules in conversations with other family members. Dunn found that such conversations are common within families and they usually occur in emotionally loaded situations, such as when a child is distressed. The emotional context provides much information on which even the young child can base an understanding of moral rules, for example in curbing aggression or jealousy.

## Conclusions on moral development

Dunn (1984) argues convincingly that naturalistic observation of children in families reveals powers of understanding much greater than is attributed on the basis of experimental studies. The emotional intensity of the relationship between siblings may reflect the fact that both children depend for love on the same parents, and hence they may come to read each other's moods and intentions very accurately. Comprehension of moral rules may develop within peer relationships, with their accompanying emotional processes. There is an emotional urgency and significance to family relationships which may lead children to moral understanding well in advance of their capacity to reason about moral dilemmas. Everyday social interactions provide the child with direct experience of a justified moral and social order. The development of "moral emotions" such as pride, shame, and guilt is well described by Paul Harris (1989).

Piaget, Kohlberg, and Dunn emphasise everyday games as a source of understanding roles and rules. However, the distinction between moral reasoning and moral understanding needs to be borne in mind. Family contexts may foster moral understanding where emotional appraisal and self-esteem in the eyes of others are particularly important in heightening the child's early awareness of right and wrong. Perhaps moral reasoning, as Piaget and Kohlberg describe it, may reflect children's ability to think about their direct culturally organised and morally salient experience, already extending over many years. The developmental evidence suggests that moral reasoning may need to be distinguished from moral understanding and moral behaviour.

## Conclusion and summary

Middle childhood is the period from 6 years to the onset of adolescence. The main evidence that this period does indeed mark a separate stage of intellectual development, discontinuous with reasoning in the pre-school period, comes from Piaget, who described the concrete thinking typical of the school-age child. The major logical operations the child acquires are conservation, seriation, classification, and numeration. Although there is much controversy about the relationship between these and earlier abilities, the main reason for supposing that some new capacities have been acquired is that the child is now able logically to justify the necessity of the conclusions drawn. The nature of the transition and the extent to which it involves specifically verbal reasoning processes remains a matter of debate.

Cross-cultural studies of concrete operational reasoning suggest that there may be an impact of schooling and of contact with the West on the expression of reasoning in Piagetian tasks, even if their basis is biologically universal, as Piaget supposed.

Concrete operational reasoning also has social implications, especially in the domain of moral development. Piaget and Kohlberg outlined three main stages in moral reasoning—the pre-conventional, conventional, and post-conventional stages. The Piagetian method of studying moral reasoning involves asking the child to offer solutions to various moral dilemmas and to justify the conclusions drawn. This approach tends to equate morality with the ability to reason. Another, more naturalistic approach, especially evident in the work of Judy Dunn, distinguishes moral understanding from moral reasoning. Even pre-school children show evidence of understanding moral rules, especially in intimate family contexts, although they would have difficulty with reasoning on Piaget's tests.

### Further reading

Brainerd, C.J. (1978). *Piaget's theory of intelligence*. Englewood Cliffs, NJ: Prentice Hall.

Dunn, J. (1984). *Sisters and brothers*. London: Fontana.

Harris, P.L. (1989). *Children and emotion*. Oxford: Blackwell.

# The impact of school

# 11

**C**hildren's progress through middle childhood is greatly affected by their experience of school. Formal schooling provides children with the opportunity to master new skills that are relevant to the solution of concrete operational reasoning problems. In particular, school introduces children to the skills of literacy and numeracy. Literacy—the ability to read and write—has important implications both for language and the acquisition of knowledge. Children who can read are able to learn new words and to build up sophisticated vocabularies. They can also use reading as an important new way of gaining knowledge of the world. Numeracy provides the opportunity for acquiring the ability to work within a formal system that uses rules and symbols.

Success in these two areas of literacy and numeracy largely determines how successful a child is in school. Mastery of reading, writing, and arithmetic also affects performance in many conventional IQ tests which, for children of school years, contain an increasingly large number of items that test understanding of language and mathematics.

## Literacy

### The relationship between sounds and letters

One of the most important tasks that confronts the child on entering school is to learn to read and spell. How easy it is to do this varies very much from one language to another depending on the relationship between the the sound of words (phonology) and the way they are spelled (orthography). In some languages, such as Italian or Spanish, there is a very consistent relationship between phonology and orthography. This means that a particular sound always has the same spelling, so that once you have learned all the relationships between spelling and sound it is possible to spell any word that you hear and to pronounce any word that you see written down.

Unlike Italian and Spanish, English has irregular orthography; that is, there is an inconsistent relationship between spelling and sound. For example, the letter sequence OUGH is pronounced very differently in *cough, bough,* and *enough;* and there are two different ways of pronouncing AVE as in *have* and *wave.* There are, however, some regularities in English orthography in that, for many letter sequences, one pronunciation is more common than any other. Words that contain only letter sequences (graphemes) with the common pronunciation are called *regular* words whereas words that contain at least one less common pronunciation are known as *irregular.* Almost all words are regular in languages like Italian and Spanish with consistent orthography.

The three examples so far considered—Italian, Spanish, and English—all make use of an *alphabetic writing system* in which a small number of letters are used to represent the sounds of a word. There are, however, some writing systems that do not make use of letters but, instead, represent a word by means of a symbol. The most well-known examples of writing systems of this kind—known as *logographic*—are Chinese and Japanese. Learning to read a logographic writing system is a very time-consuming process, because these systems contain a very large number of symbols and each symbol (or group of related symbols) has to be learned individually. Indeed, the majority of Chinese and Japanese adults never learn to read all of the symbols and it takes children considerably longer to become fluent readers of Chinese or Japanese than Italian or Spanish. As a result, various simplifications have been introduced into the writing systems of both China and Japan, including the development of a syllabic system of writing in which each syllable in the language is represented by one symbol (DeFrancis, 1989). In China, the syllabic system was introduced in 1958 and known as Pinyin. In Japan, the syllabic script is known as kana and the original logographic script is known as kanji (see the panels on pp. 204–205).

## Stages in learning to read English

There are several different theories about how children learn to read, but they all have one thing in common: they were developed to explain how children learn to read English. As you might expect, there are some important differences between learning to read an orthographically irregular language and more regular systems such as German and Italian.

One of the most influential theories about how children learn to read was developed by Frith (1985), who revised an earlier theory devised by Marsh (Marsh, Friedman, Welch, & Desberg, 1980). Frith proposed a three-phase theory of development in which the child uses a different reading strategy in each phase. In the initial phase, children use a *logographic* strategy in which they learn to recognise words on the basis of their overall appearance rather than paying attention to individual letters. During this phase, children are unable to make any attempt at reading words that they have not already learned. When children learn to read words on "flash cards"—cards with single words printed on them in large letters—they are using a logographic strategy. As they learn each new word, they can always recognise it on the flash card but they do not have any idea about how to pronounce words that are unfamiliar.

In the second phase of learning to read, children begin to pay attention to individual letters and they learn how to convert graphemes (letters and letter strings) into phonemes using an *alphabetic* strategy. This new strategy of using letter-to-sound rules means that children can guess how to pronounce unfamiliar words by looking at the sequence of letters they contain. However, children will only be successful at pronouncing regular words. They will continue to mispronounce irregular words that they have not already learned.

Frith's final reading phase is called the *orthographic* phase. Children develop an orthographic strategy where words are broken down into orthographic units, strings of letters that commonly go together such as IGHT. These orthographic units are larger than those used in the alphabetic phase and they are not converted to individual phonemes. By using an orthographic strategy, children are able to pronounce irregular words that are similar in structure to words that they already know. For example, if a child can already read LIGHT, then it is possible to make a good guess about the pronunciation of words such as MIGHT and SIGHT. The orthographic strategy does not, however, replace the alphabetic strategy which children will continue to use for pronouncing new regular words.

Many experiments have shown that children learning to read English do normally develop these three strategies, although the teaching methods used in school have an important influence on the early strategies used. For example, in a study in Scotland, Seymour and Elder (1986) found that children taught to read by a whole word method used a logographic strategy when they first began to read. (The whole word method is where children are taught to recognise whole words—as with flash cards.) However, Connelly (1993) has shown that, if children are taught to sound out letters when they first begin to read, then they will pay much more attention to individual letters in words and will not use a purely logographic strategy.

Children's use of an alphabetic strategy was demonstrated in an experiment by Doctor and Coltheart (1980). Children were given sentences to read and they had to decide whether or not they made sense. Some of the sentences sounded correct but were not—for example, "The sky is

BLEW" and "She BLUE up the balloon". Doctor and Coltheart argued that if the children were using an alphabetic strategy and converting letters to sounds, then both of these sentences would seem to make sense. However, if the children had moved on to using an orthographic strategy, in which words were no longer sounded out, these sentences should have been correctly identified as not making sense.

Children between the ages of 6 and 10 were tested and the results showed that the 6- and 7-year-olds were fooled by the sentences that sounded correct but the older children were not. They correctly rejected sentences that merely sounded correct. This suggests that children make use of an alphabetic strategy before going on to use an orthographic one.

This experiment by Doctor and Coltheart (1980) has attracted a great deal of criticism. For example, Goswami and Bryant (1990) have argued that the study does not really test how children learn to read because it is not possible to be sure that the younger children in Doctor and Coltheart's study were actually sounding out words when they were reading them. One of the conditions in the experiment used nonsense words that sounded correct. For example, a sentence in this condition was, "She BLOO up the balloon". If the children were merely sounding out words in order to read them, then a nonsense word should have seemed just as correct as an incorrect real word (BLUE) that sounds correct. Goswami and Bryant point out that even the 6-year-olds did not treat these two types of incorrect sentence in the same way. They were much more likely to say that sentences with correct sounding nonsense words did not make sense than they were to reject sentences with incorrect real words.

One possible explanation of Doctor and Coltheart's result is that children use both visual and phonological strategies as they learn to read. Indeed, it is unlikely that, even at 7 years of age, children only rely on one kind of strategy, because they will have learned a significant number of words visually. A study by Kimura and Bryant (1983) investigated the use of visual strategies by 7-year-olds through presentation of picture–word pairs. Each picture–word pair was on a card and children were asked to sort the cards into two piles according to whether the word corresponded to the picture or not. In half of the cases where the word did not match the picture, the word looked very similar to the correct word. Children took longer to sort pairs where the word did not match the picture but looked very similar to the correct word, than they did to sort incorrect pairs where the word did not look like the correct one. This shows that 7-year-olds are making use of a visual strategy.

The finding that children seem to use more than one strategy in learning to read English, and that strategies are affected by teaching methods, has led to a recent change in theories of learning to read. Rather than arguing that all children pass through a fixed series of stages or phases (as in Frith, 1985), the most recent theories tend to emphasise that the process of learning to read is the result of an interaction between the child's predispositions for certain strategies, the method of teaching, and the child's experience. Another important development has been to see that the process of learning to read varies according to the particular script that a child is attempting to master.

## Learning to read and spell in other languages

If a child is learning to read a language that is more orthographically regular than English, then we might expect to find that reading progress is faster. This is not only because learning the relationship between sounds and letters will be easier if that relationship is consistent; it is also because, once children have learned all the links between letters and sounds, they will be able to pronounce most or all of the new words they come across.

Thorstad (1991) found that Italian children learn to read much faster than English children of comparable ability. He also found that all the Italian children he studied, even those who were 10 years old, used an alphabetic strategy and converted letters to sounds in order to read an unfamiliar word. In Italian, such a strategy is successful, so there is no need for children to acquire strategies for reading irregular words.

There was another interesting difference between Italian and English children. Italian children could spell all of the words that they could read and even some that they could not read. For the English children, however, spelling always lagged behind reading: there were many words that they could read but could not spell. The most likely explanation for this difference is that the letter-to-sound rules that Italian children learn can be applied equally easily to both reading and spelling. This means that they can be taught to spell words at the same time that they learn to read them. Thorstad found that Italian children spent most of their first year at school writing and then reading what they had written.

The irregularity of English orthography, by contrast, means that children not only have to learn how to read many irregular words but also how to spell them. For this reason, the first year at school tends to concentrate on reading with spelling being introduced only later.

Other evidence of the influence that the orthographic regularity of a script exerts on reading comes from a study of children learning to read in Japan. As we noted earlier, Japanese writing makes use of both a logographic script (kanji) and a syllabic script (kana). The advantage of kana, which is used in teaching children to read, is that it is very easy to learn. All that is necessary is that children learn how to pronounce each

## Two Japanese scripts

The Japanese writing system was borrowed, over several centuries, from different areas of China. The borrowed Chinese characters were used in two ways. Sometimes both the symbol and an approximation of its Chinese pronunciation were used in Japanese. These characters were known as *kanji*—a name derived from the Chinese term for Chinese characters which was pronounced "kanzi" (DeFrancis, 1989). In other cases, Chinese characters were used to represent the sounds of Japanese. These characters were known as *kana* and they stood for the syllables within a word. A multi-syllabic word would thus be represented by two or more kana characters.

From the outset, the Japanese writing system contained both kanji and kana characters. Over time, the use of kana to represent Japanese syllables became standardised and, in modern Japanese, there are 46 syllabic kana symbols.

Modern Japanese writing still combines the use of kanji and kana but this makes the system very difficult to learn. Popular publications, aimed at a mass audience, and some children's books, make use of a technique in which every kanji character has small kana characters (called *furigana*) placed vertically to the right of it to assist in pronunciation.

In the 1950s, the number of kanji characters used in published material was greatly reduced and the abandoned characters replaced by kana. Since then, there has been a gradual increase in the use of kana. Bank statements and bills for gas and electricity are all in kana and word processors are designed for the typing of kana even though they can output the equivalent kanji characters. As a result, some Japanese people are forgetting how to write many of the kanji signs and it is possible that, sometime in the future, the traditional Japanese writing system may fall into disuse.

symbol and from then on they can read any word that is written using kana symbols.

It is common for Japanese children to be able to read and write all the characters in the kana script by the time they go to school. Initially, reading instruction is restricted to the mastery of kana but, once children are fluent in this, they are slowly introduced to kanji. Sakamoto and Makita (1973) report that Japanese children are expected to learn 46 kanji characters in their first year at school, 105 in their second year, 187 in their third year, 205 in their fourth, 194 in their fifth and 144 in their sixth year. In junior high school they learn another 969 characters. Children's books sometimes use kana characters next to unfamiliar kanji characters to assist reading (see the panel above and Figure 11.1 opposite).

Kimura and Bryant (1983) compared Japanese children reading kanji and kana, and showed that they use different strategies for reading the syllabic kana script and the logographic kanji script. Kimura and Bryant were able to demonstrate this by giving 7-year-old Japanese children cards with words and pictures on them. The children had to sort the cards as correct or incorrect, where a correct pair was one in which the word and picture corresponded and an incorrect pair was one in which they did not. For half the incorrect pairs, the word looked very similar to a word that

|  | OBI graph | modern character | modern reading | meaning |
|---|---|---|---|---|
| 1. |  | 象 | xiàng | 'elephant' |
| 2. |  | 求 | qiú | 'pelt'  (mod. 裘 ) |
| 3. |  | 口 | kǒu | 'opening, orifice, mouth' |
| 4. |  | 目 | mù | 'eye' |
| 5. |  | 月 | yuè | 'moon, month' |
| 6. |  | 田 | tián | '(cultivated) field' |
| 7. |  | 女 | nǚ | '(kneeling) woman' |
| 8. |  | 其 | qí | '(winnowing) basket'  (mod. 箕 ) |
| 9. |  | 天 | tiān | 'overhead'  >  'sky, heaven' |
| 10. |  | 羊 | yáng | 'sheep, ram' |
| 11. |  | 馬 | mǎ | 'horse' |
| 12. |  | 龜 | quī | 'turtle' |
| 13. |  | 魚 | yú | 'fish' |
| 14. |  | 鼎 | dǐng | 'tripod, cauldron' |

Fig. 11.1 Changes in the form of Chinese symbols. The first column shows the original form of the characters dating from 1200-1045 BC. These early forms were pictographic and resembled the objects to which they referred. The second column shows the modern forms of the Chinese characters. These are much less pictographic, and do not look like the objects to which they refer (De Francis, 1989).

matched the object. Children who were using a logographic (visual) strategy should be affected by visual similarity and tend to count a similar-looking word as correct. Kimura and Bryant also tested to see whether the children were using an alphabetic strategy by getting them to repeat a syllable out loud while they were doing the sorting task. Repeating a syllable over and over again—concurrent vocalisation—makes it much more difficult to convert letters to sounds and so should interfere with alphabetic reading.

Kimura and Bryant found that the vocalisation task did not affect the children while they were reading the kanji words, but visual similarity did. This suggests that the children were using a logographic strategy for reading kanji. However, the reverse pattern occurred with kana. Here the children were not affected by visual similarity but were affected by the concurrent vocalisation task, and performed more slowly and less

Fig. 11.2 The combination of kanji and kana characters in Japanese. Modern Japanese makes use of both kanji and kana symbols. In these examples the kanji meaning "to eat" (borrowed from Chinese) is combined with a range of kana inflections to express different tenses and forms of the main verb (De Francis, 1989).

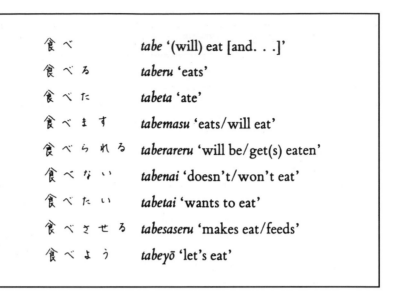

| | |
|---|---|
| 食 べ | *tabe* '(will) eat [and. . .]' |
| 食 べ る | *taberu* 'eats' |
| 食 べ た | *tabeta* 'ate' |
| 食 べ ま す | *tabemasu* 'eats/will eat' |
| 食 べ ら れ る | *taberareru* 'will be/get(s) eaten' |
| 食 べ な い | *tabenai* 'doesn't/won't eat' |
| 食 べ た い | *tabetai* 'wants to eat' |
| 食 べ さ せ る | *tabesaseru* 'makes eat/feeds' |
| 食 べ よ う | *tabeyō* 'let's eat' |

accurately. Thus they appeared to be using an alphabetic strategy for reading kana.

## Reading and phonological awareness

Children normally learn to read some time after learning to speak. This means that, when children first encounter written words, they already know a great deal about how words sound when they are spoken. As we have just seen, one aspect of learning to read involves learning how to convert letters to sounds. It has been suggested that what children know about the sounds that make up their language—phonological knowledge— affects the rate at which they learn to read.

One study was carried out in Sweden by Lundberg, Olofsson, and Wall (1980). Pre-school children were tested on a variety of tasks involving phonological knowledge. One year later, the children who were more successful at these tasks had made more reading progress than children who were less successful.

Another longitudinal study was carried out in Oxford by Bradley and Bryant (1983). They investigated pre-reading children's sensitivity to rhyme and alliteration by presenting them with sets of monosyllabic words (such as "hill", "pig", and "pin") and asking them to say which was the odd one out. (The correct answer is "hill" because the other two words both begin with the sound "pi".) Bradley and Bryant found that, when the children's subsequent reading performance was measured after 3 years of schooling, those children who had initially been good at judging the odd word out were better readers than those children who had been less good at this task.

Bradley and Bryant also carried out a training study. This showed that children who were trained to analyse words in terms of their sounds learned to read more successfully than a group who had been trained to classify words by meaning. A third group, who had received the sound training and who had also been taught about letter–sound relationships, made even greater progress.

Further evidence for the importance of sound awareness in learning to read comes from studies of children with severe or profound hearing loss. Such children, who have little or no hearing, generally have great difficulty in learning to read (Kampfe & Turecheck, 1987). Gaines, Mandler, and Bryant (1981) report that only just over 1% of deaf children read at a level appropriate for their age by the time they leave school.

One major reason for the difficulty that deaf children experience in learning to read is that they often have a very poor understanding of the relationships among speech sounds and, in particular, they find it almost impossible to understand the nature of rhyming. Harris and Beech (1994) gave a group of pre-school deaf children a version of the Bradley and Bryant (1983) test that measures sensitivity to rhyme and alliteration. Overall, the deaf children performed much worse than a comparison group of hearing children, but there was considerable variation, with some of the deaf children performing as well as the hearing children. When the deaf children were followed up over their first year at school, it turned out that the children who had performed best on the rhyme and alliteration test generally made faster reading progress than the children who had performed poorly.

This finding reinforces the view that, when children first begin reading, their ability to make judgements about the similarity of sounds at the start and end of words has an important influence on their rate of progress. Goswami and Bryant (1990) argue that children are sensitive to the sounds in words long before they begin to read, and children who are sensitive to rhyme eventually do better at reading. Furthermore, as Bradley and Bryant (1983) showed, children who are trained in rhyming skills go on to read better than children who are not trained in such skills. Unfortunately, in the case of deaf child, the scope for such training is severely limited. Most severely and profoundly deaf children find the concept of rhyme impossible to grasp so, for them, the teaching of reading needs to exploit other—more visual—strategies.

# Numeracy

As well as providing the opportunity for learning to read, entry into school also introduces the child to mathematics. An essential component of mathematical ability is an understanding of the number system that is used by the community in which the child is growing up. It is not until children have mastered the number system that they can begin to learn about mathematical operations such as addition, subtraction, and multiplication.

## Representing numbers

Systems for representing number can be divided into formal systems, which use written numerals, and more informal systems which make use of objects or body parts to represent numbers. The most widely used formal system employs Arabic numerals in which the underlying unit of the counting system—10—is explicitly represented. This contrasts with another formal system for representing numbers that you may have come across, the Roman numeral system, in which the counting base is not explicitly represented.

In the Roman system, the number 10 is represented by the letter X and the number 100 by C. The use of these letters does not reveal anything about the numerical relationship between the two numbers, notably that the second (C) is 10 times as big as the first (X). By contrast, the equivalent Arabic numerals tell you a great deal about the relationship between the two numbers once you understand the convention that the first column represents units (the numbers from 0 to 9), the second, tens, and the third, hundreds. The transparency of number representation in the Arabic numeral system facilitates simple mathematical operations and also allows complex operations with large numbers to be carried out.

In some societies, more informal systems for representing number are used. These do not have a corresponding written form but they may, nevertheless, allow simple arithmetic calculations to be carried out. For example, the Oksapmin of New Guinea use body locations to represent numbers (see panel opposite) and can carry out simple addition and subtraction. Somewhat similarly, children often use their fingers as an aid to counting both when they first learn to count and, later, when they use counting to carry out simple mathematical operations (see pp. 210–212).

Other informal systems that make use of objects as the basis of counting can be used to carry out arithmetic operations (at least addition and subtraction) on larger numbers. Cole and Cole (1993) report that West Africans, who used cowrie shells as counters, could calculate sums running into tens of thousands when trading with Portuguese merchants. It

## Learning to count among the Oksapmin of New Guinea

The Oksapmin, who live in a remote part of New Guinea, use body locations to represent numbers (Saxe, 1981). They start counting on the thumb and fingers of the right hand, work up the right arm and round the head, and finish by working down the left arm, finally using the fingers of the left hand. In this way, the Oksapmin are able to represent numbers up to 27 in sequential order ending with the little finger of the left hand. Numbers greater than 27 can be represented by continuing down the left wrist and then ascending back up the body (see Figure 11.3).

The names of the numbers are the names of the body parts. For example, the number 14—the middle of the sequence—is called "aruma" as it is located on the nose. In order to distinguish a number from its symmetrical counterpart on the other side of the body a prefix—"tan"—is attached to the higher numbers. Thus the twelfth number is called "nata" and is located on the right ear, whereas the sixteenth number, located on the other ear, is called "tan-nata".

Saxe (1981) found that Oksapmin children's understanding of numerosity was influenced by their number system. He tested children aged between 7 and 16 and found that the younger children tended to treat different numbers that were located on the same body part as being equivalent. It was not until the children were more than 9 years old that they were able to treat numbers as independent of their physical location on the body. Another confusion that some of the younger Oksapmin children exhibited was to start counting from the left side of the body rather than the right side. Even when it was explained that counting always started on the right, some children remained confused.

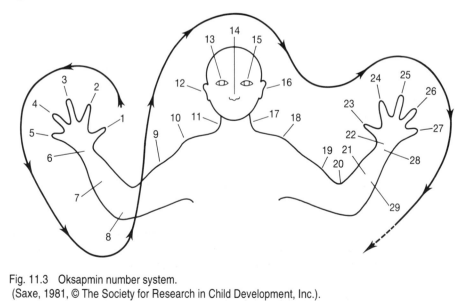

Fig. 11.3   Oksapmin number system.
(Saxe, 1981, © The Society for Research in Child Development, Inc.).

is interesting to compare a system of number representation using counters with one—like that of the Oksapmin—that uses body parts. The use of counters provides the basis by which large numbers can be represented and manipulated, and allows the development of a number system that is closer to a formal system.

## Learning to count

The key to mastering a number system and to carrying out simple arithmetic operations is to learn to count. This involves learning the name of individual numbers and the sequence in which they occur.

Recent research has shown that even young babies know something about number, although they do not, of course, know anything about counting. Antell and Keating (1983) demonstrated that newborns are able to discriminate "two" from "three", and sometimes "three" from "four", when they are shown sets of objects. The technique that Antell and Keating used was *habituation* (see p. 64) in which the baby was repeatedly presented with a picture of a number of objects and then, once habituation had occurred, with another picture that had either the same number of objects or a different number. The babies tended to look significantly longer at the new picture if it depicted a different number of objects than if the number of objects was the same.

The knowledge that allows infants to distinguish among numbers of up to four is not restricted to visual perception. Infants can also detect correspondences between the number of items that they see and the number of sounds that they hear. Starkey, Spelke, and Gelman (1983) played infants aged between 6–9 months a tape of either two or three drumbeats and then showed them two pictures, one with two items and the other with three. The babies preferred to look at the picture with the number of objects that corresponded to the number of drum beats.

A recent study by Wynn (1992) has shown that young babies also understand that when one object is added to another object there are two objects, and when one object is removed from two objects only one remains. Wynn tested babies aged 5 months and presented them with one of two conditions. In the first, the babies were shown one toy figure which was then occluded by a screen; a mechanical arm then placed another figure behind the screen. In the second condition, the babies initially saw two figures which were then occluded by a screen; then the mechanical arm moved behind the screen and came out holding one of the figures. The screen was then lowered and each group of babies was shown one of two test conditions, either two figures or only one figure. The babies looked longest when the test condition was not in accordance with the rules of addition and subtraction. Thus, babies in the first condition

(1 + 1 = 2) looked longer when they saw only one figure after the screen was removed, whereas babies in the second condition (2 − 1 = 1) looked longer when there were two figures.

The ability to determine the relative numerosity of small numbers—up to four—comes from an ability known as *subitising*. Antell and Keating (1983) showed that young babies can discriminate the number of dots in two rows providing that the number in a row is not greater than four. This ability to make comparative judgements about small numbers does *not* entail verbal counting and it continues to be the basis of young children's numerosity judgements until they learn to count verbally.

Estes and Combs (1966) showed that children of 3 and 4 years old still tend to make comparative numerosity judgements on the basis of overall size and density. If these are not reliable indicators of relative numerosity, children will make mistakes. Thus, if children of this age are asked to compare two sets containing equal numbers of dots, they will think that the sets are different if one set is more widely spaced than the other. This is the same kind of confusion that children display when they fail number conservation tasks (see panel on p. 164).

Learning to count greatly improves children's ability to compare numbers of objects. There are two important aspects to counting—knowing the number sequence (one, two, three, etc.) and knowing the relationship between numbers and objects. This second skill involves not only one-to-one counting (being able to relate each number in the sequence to a separate object), but also knowing that the final number in the counting sequence—once all items have been counted—is the total number of items.

Children usually learn these various aspects of the number system separately. Pre-school counting games help children to learn the sequence of low numbers, but this knowledge is often not related to knowledge of numerosity, except for very small numbers where this has been specifically taught. Thus a child may be able to count up to 10 without understanding that the number 10 can be related to 10 objects in a set.

By about 4 years of age, children have generally mastered the principle of counting and use their finger to point at each object as they count (Fuson, 1988). However, children are initially only successful at counting objects if these are lined up in a row and they can point at each in turn. This strategy allows children to make a vital distinction between counted objects and those that have not yet been counted. Pointing at objects in turn does not provide an accurate way of making this distinction unless the objects are systematically ordered so that children can keep track of which objects have been counted. Another more flexible strategy, which does not rely on the position of objects, is to move objects as they are counted. (This is the strategy that bank tellers use when they are counting money.) Fuson found that children did not adopt this strategy of moving objects until they were over 5 years old.

## Addition and subtraction

Initially, verbal counting plays an important role in children's ability to deal with arithmetic operations even though they are often not taught these methods as formal strategies. Three developmental stages in the solution of simple addition problems have been identified. These are counting all, counting on, and retrieval of number facts.

The simplest strategy, used when children first start to add up, is *counting all*, in which each addend (the numbers to be added up) is represented on the fingers and the overall total counted. Thus to add 3 + 4 the child holds up three fingers and then, while still holding up the first set of fingers, holds up another four fingers. The total number of fingers is then counted to give the answer.

The counting all strategy cannot easily be applied to addition where the sum is greater than 10. Children thus move on to a *counting on*, strategy in which they still use their fingers but now they count upwards from one of the addends. Now, to add 3 + 4, the child would start from three, hold up four fingers and count 4, 5, 6, 7. It is more efficient in the counting on strategy to count on from the larger number rather than the smaller, as it involves less counting. Groen and Parkman (1972) found that primary school children naturally count on from the larger number, for example, counting on from 7 rather than 2 in 7 + 2. However, it is possible that when children first employ the counting on procedure they always start with the first number in an addition and count on according to the size of the second number. Selecting the larger number as the starting point requires the child to realise the numerical equivalence of, say, 15 + 7 and 7 + 15. Although this equivalence is obvious to someone who is familiar with arithmetic, it is not immediately apparent to a child.

Counting aloud is usually replaced by subvocal (silent) counting as children reach the end of primary school. It is more difficult to study the use of subvocal counting in the solution of arithmetic problems but reaction time studies, comparing the time taken to solve addition problems involving numbers of different magnitudes, show that subvocal counting continues to be used to solve arithmetic problems throughout the early school years (Gallistel & Gelman, 1991). This method is later supplemented by the *retrieval* of number facts from memory, in which the addition of numbers is carried out by recalling the answer from previous additions.

For *subtraction*, the most common method used by primary school children is the *choice algorithm* (Woods, Resnick, & Groen, 1975), which can be seen as analogous to the counting on method used for addition. There are two ways of employing the choice algorithm. The first involves counting the number of steps required to get from the minuend (the number from which the subtraction is to take place) to the subtrahend (the number to be subtracted). For example, the solution to the sum 8 – 6 is obtained by counting up from 6 to 8 (7, 8) and seeing how many steps are involved (i.e. two). In the second method, the child counts down from the minuend the number of steps specified by the subtrahend. The answer to 8 – 2 is obtained by counting down from 8 two steps—that is, 7, 6 (6 being the correct answer). The use of the choice method is demonstrated both by reaction-time data (which shows that reaction time increases with the difference in size between the minuend and the subtrahend) and by interviews with children in which use of these methods is spontaneously reported (Gallistel & Gelman, 1991). As in the case of addition, these counting methods are finally replaced by the use of retrieval of number information.

## More complex arithmetic

Two particular aspects of arithmetic pose problems for the primary school child—dealing with fractions and multi-digit numbers. Fractions present problems because, as we have just seen, children initially rely on counting when they are performing addition and subtraction. Counting involves whole numbers and the learning of the relationship between numbers and objects: children have learned that the number 1 corresponds to one object and the number 2 to two objects.

Gelman (1991) has shown that primary school children have great difficulty both in ordering fractions and in realising that there is an infinite number of fractions. The concept of fractions that are less than 1 is particularly difficult to grasp. Gelman reports one puzzled 7-year-old explaining "You can count one, one and a half, two, two and a half, but you can't count zero, zero and a half".

Problems with the addition and subtraction of multi-digit numbers mainly arise from faulty carrying procedures. Dockrell and McShane (1992) summarise the findings of Brown and Burton (1978), who analysed nearly 20,000 multi-digit additions and subtractions carried out by school children. Brown and Burton found that 40% of children made procedural errors with subtraction. The most common errors occurred when the children had to deal with zeros—for example, borrowing from 0 in order to subtract a larger number from a smaller number but failing to carry the borrowing over to the next column, or writing the bottom digit in a column as the answer whenever the top digit was 0. Another common error was to subtract the smaller from the larger digit regardless of which was on the top line and which on the bottom.

Several studies have shown that many children find the abstract nature of formal arithmetic to be difficult to deal with. Such children often demonstrate an understanding of basic mathematical principles when asked to solve a concrete problem even though they cannot solve an identical problem when it is presented as formal arithmetic. The most striking example of this difference between knowledge of mathematical principles in a practical context and the ability to carry out formal arithmetic in a school setting comes from studies of Brazilian street children (see the panel opposite).

# Intelligence testing

As we have seen, schooling is an important context for acquiring skills in problem solving, reading, writing, and arithmetic. The means of acquiring such skills are closely linked to universal education, as has been the development of intelligence tests. In fact, it has been said that what intelligence tests measure is what makes for success in school. Put more subtly, intelligence tests measure individual differences in skills that are highly valued by society and hence, to a greater or lesser degree, such tests predict the performance of individuals, relative to the population as a whole, on a number of culturally valued verbal and spatial skills.

The origin of intelligence testing in the Binet scales has already been described (see panel on p. 9) and it was noted that, from the outset, intelligence and educational provision were intertwined when decisions about the provision of special education for the mentally retarded had to be made.

Binet and Simon constructed a test that revealed age-graded regularities in children's answers to test items. Their tasks were simple, such as naming colours, copying geometric figures, counting backwards from 20. Contemporary intelligence tests are similarly constructed, although they contain many more types of items. The method involves creating a set of test items that produce a normally distributed range of performance at any particular age level. Then items are selected to form an age-graded sequence of difficulty, and the tests are validated against other measures of ability, including performance in school.

Intelligence test items that predict individual abilities well are considered *valid* measures of intelligence and they are retained in constructing the final version of the test. The test items should also yield the same rank order of responses on successive occasions of testing the same person. Such items are considered *reliable* measures and they are retained in

## Mathematical skills in the street children of Brazil

Carraher, Schliemann, and Carraher (1988) carried out a study of children in Brazil who made a living from working in street markets, selling fruit, drinks, and popcorn. In the course of these activities, the children had to carry out quite complex additions, subtractions, and multiplications in their heads in order to work out the cost of the goods that they were selling and the change that they had to give their customers. The children also attended school where they carried out addition, subtraction, and multiplication of equal complexity using formal mathematical notation and working with pencil and paper.

The children were fast and accurate at working out the answer to mathematical problems when selling goods. For example, when asked to work out the total cost of two coconuts each costing 40 cruzeiros and the change that a customer would be due from a 500 cruzeiros note, a child replied unhesitatingly: "Eighty, ninety, one hundred, four hundred and twenty." This correct answer was obtained by adding on from 80 up to 500 in a way that is rather similar to the choice algorithm (see pp. 212–213). The same child was unable to solve a similar formal addition problem. When asked: "What is 420 + 80?" the child wrote down the sum and obtained the answer 130. (This answer was arrived at by adding 0 + 0 to get 0, then adding 2 + 8, carrying 1 and adding this to the 4, and finally adding 8 + 5 to get 13!)

Carraher et al. give many other examples which show that the children used different methods for arithmetic calculations in the street and classroom contexts. One of the most common methods used for mental calculations in the street markets was decomposition, in which numbers were broken down into parts and each part dealt with in turn. For example, when asked to find the answer to 200 – 35, one girl solved this in her head as follows: "If it were 30, then the result would be 70. But it is 35. So it is 65, 165". The steps involved in this calculation were, first, to split 200 into 100 + 100, then to split 35 into 30 + 5 and to subtract these sequentially from 100 ($100 - 30 = 70$; $70 - 5 = 65$). The 100 that had been "set aside" was then added back on to give the correct answer of 165.

The formal subtraction method used in school involved "borrowing" from each column as appropriate and "paying back" in the next column, a procedure that often led to the kind of mistakes noted by Brown and Burton (1978). Another difference between the methods used in mental calculation and those adopted with pencil and paper was that, in the former case, the children worked from hundreds to tens and then units, whereas the formal procedure worked in the opposite direction from units to tens then hundreds. Carraher et al. suggest that this is one reason why, in using the formal procedure, the children tended to lose track of the sort of answer that they should have obtained. Their other difficulty was that they looked on the school procedures merely as rules to be followed, and they often had little or no understanding of why the procedures would, if correctly applied, produce the right answer.

---

constructing the final version of the test. The tradition of intelligence test construction has been rather a pragmatic one, and hence the assertion that intelligence is what intelligence tests measure. The most widely used intelligence test is that of Wechsler (see panel overleaf).

Intelligence testing has come under some criticism in recent years. For example, although tests are constructed in such a way as to eliminate test bias due to differences in social class or ethnic origin, they may nevertheless unwittingly incorporate items that are culturally specific to the dominant social group within the larger community. To the extent that

## The Wechsler intelligence scales

The Wechsler Intelligence Scale for Children (WISC) is among the most widely used tests of intelligence. It was developed in the United States in 1949 from the Wechsler Adult Intelligence Scale (WAIS), a widely used test for adolescents and adults. The tests were extended to younger persons by identifying items suitable in difficulty for children aged from 5 to 15 years. More recently, a similar test for pre-school children has also been developed by the Wechsler Corporation (the Wechsler pre-school and primary test of intelligence or WPPSI). The set of Wechsler scales therefore offer a measurement system for intelligence throughout the lifespan (Wechsler, 1967).

The WISC test consists of 12 scales divided into two groups identified as Verbal and Performance tests. The Verbal scales measure aspects of general knowledge and the child's understanding and use of language. The scales and some example questions are:

Information: How many legs does a dog have?
Comprehension: Why are criminals locked up?
Arithmetic: A boy had 4 pennies and his mother gave him 2 more. How many did he have altogether?
Similarities: Lemons are sour but sugar is ...?
Vocabulary: What is a bicycle?
Digit span: This test scores how well the child remembers a series of numbers presented in a sequence, e.g. 6-2-3. The child has to repeat the sequence in forward order and, in another version, in backward order to establish the maximum run length held in memory.

The Performance scales reduce the reliance on language in favour of tasks that can be carried out non-verbally. The tests that make up the performance scale are:

Picture completion: The child is shown pictures of familiar objects with parts missing, e.g. a table with a missing leg. The child must point at or name the missing part.

Picture arrangement: A series of pictures that tell a story must be arranged in the correct order.
Block design: Four wooden blocks with different colours on each side must be arranged, as quickly as possible, to correspond to a second model made by the tester.
Object assembly: Wooden cut-outs must be arranged as quickly as possible to build simple standard figures.
Coding: A series of abstract lines corresponding to the numbers 1–9 must be inserted in a matrix of numbers, as quickly as possible.
Mazes: The child must draw the route through pencil and paper mazes of increasing difficulty, as quickly as possible.

Ordinarily, five verbal and five performance tests are administered (usually the Digit span and Mazes tests are omitted to save time). The IQ is calculated from standardisation tables based on the performance of a large sample of children in each year age group, selected to be representative of the whole population. That is, the IQ score is a measure of the child's ability, relative to children of the same chronological age, taking into account social class differences.

The method of scoring the intelligence quotient differs from the earlier definition of intelligence developed by Binet and Simon who compared mental age (MA) with chronological age (CA) (see panel on p. 9). The average IQ score on the Wechsler scale is also set at 100, and the child's score on the set of tests is converted to an IQ score according to how many items are passed, relative to the average number passed by children in the same year age group. This method of scoring intelligence is known as a deviation score, because it measures by how much the child's answers deviate, above or below, the average score for his or her age group.

This method of sampling the whole population avoids a problem that arises when IQ is defined as MA/CA x 100. This results in identical scores for

(continued)

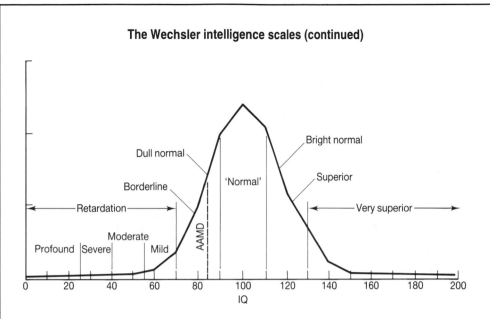

**The Wechsler intelligence scales (continued)**

Fig. 11.4   IQ test categories. (Matarazzo, 1972, © Williams & Wilkins).

example, when a 5-year-old has a MA of 6 years or when a 10-year-old has an MA of 12 (120 in both cases). The first child is one year ahead of chronological age, while the second child is two years ahead. Furthermore, it is not correct to suppose that children of different chronological ages (CA) and the same mental age (MA) have qualitatively the same mental abilities. Defining IQ relative to the same age group controls for the possibility that development leads to changes in intellectual abilities.

There are problems with IQ tests of this type. For example, the Wechsler scales were stand-ardised in the United States, under the particular cultural conditions of that country. However carefully standardised in the USA, the test is not directly applicable in other countries unless re-standardised on the new population and translated into the local language. Some test items need to be changed to allow for the different context of testing. The Wechsler scales have been re-standardised for the British population. However, a completely new set of scales has been developed, called the British Ability Scales (BAS), to meet the particular requirements of intelligence testing in Britain (Elliot et al., 1983).

test scores may be used to allocate pupils to different kinds of educational provision, for example in "streaming" children, IQ scores may underestimate (or overestimate) a child's educational potential, depending on the precise details of the test and the personal characteristics of the person who is being tested (Nash, 1990, discusses these rather technical issues extensively).

Another problem concerns the relationship between intelligence as measured by IQ tests and other talents, such as artistic, musical, or athletic ability. Intelligence as classically conceived is defined as a general ability, whereas the talents listed above are rather specific. Of course, general intelligence enters to some extent into specific talents, but these more rare aspects of human talents are separable from IQ. Gardner (1983) has argued that there are multiple intelligences, which develop along different paths. For example, musical ability often appears early, as in the cases of Mozart, Chopin, Mahler, and Berlioz who played musical instruments by the age of 4 years. Mozart gave his first public concert at the age of 5! Exceptional graphic artistic ability may not be apparent until the child is rather older, as in the case of Picasso who, by the age of 13, was much better at painting than his artist father (Radford, 1990). In both the cases of musical and artistic ability, IQ may be high but it need not be much above the population average.

Another source of evidence for the separation of IQ and specific talents comes from *idiots savants*. These are individuals who are mentally retarded (IQ below 70) but who may nevertheless exhibit remarkable, isolated abilities such as knowledge of calendar dates. There are mentally retarded calendar calculators who can say on which day of the week any particular date may fall, but the same people may have difficulties with the most elementary of life's tasks, such as tying shoelaces. Another example comes from the exceptional drawing ability of a mentally retarded child, Nadia, who drew horses in realistic perspective at the very early age of 8 years (see p. 158).

Smith and Tsimpli (1991) have recently reported the case of a savant, Christopher, who has an unusual ability to learn foreign languages. Although he has a low IQ (scoring between 42 and 75 on a range of intelligence tests), Christopher is able to speak 16 languages in addition to English, many of them fluently. He is also able to learn new languages very quickly and was able to take part in a Dutch television programme after only a few days learning Dutch from a book.

In idiots savants, despite very low general intelligence, there remain islands of normal or even exceptional ability which suggest that such abilities involve processes over and above those that occur in general mental development.

The same problem of explanation arises in cases of exceptional achievement or genius. How is genius to be explained? Is it simply the extreme of a normal process of the development of intelligence or does some special explanation apply? Is genius inherited or is it a result of a particular kind of upbringing? Talented people often come from talented families and it is difficult to establish cause and effect. Francis Galton (1869) considered genius to be inherited. He went to some trouble to show that exceptional achievement tends to run in families. Galton was Charles Darwin's cousin and himself came from a talented family, so he had a personal reason for supposing that intellectual abilities may be inherited. He studied the family trees of eminent contemporaries, such as judges, painters, and other less obvious cases, such as north-country wrestling champions. He showed that these people were disproportionately likely also to have had eminent ancestors in similar professions.

Of course, it might be argued that such correlations are simply effects of growing up in a particular environment. Galton addressed this question by comparing the probability that the son of a gifted man and the man's nephew, both reared under similar, favourable social circumstances, achieved eminence. He showed that the son had a higher probability of achieving eminence than the nephew. He therefore argued that genius was inherited, because the eminent men from successive generations of the same families were more closely related.

Modern studies compare the abilities of genetically identical twins, with fraternal twins (who are no more alike genetically than ordinary brothers and sisters) in an attempt to separate effects of genetic inheritance from the effects of a favourable environment on the development of intelligence. In such studies, twins reared together may be compared with twins who have been reared apart, to distinguish shared effects of the environment. Most studies show some effect of inheritance of intelligence but the estimates for the extent of heritability vary widely and are a matter of great controversy.

Another controversial question concerns the comparison of intelligence across different cultures. There have been attempts to develop "culture free" tests of intelligence that do not require verbal formulation. The best known such test is the Raven Coloured Progressive Matrices (Raven, 1962), which requires matching the missing portion of a coloured pattern from one of a set of six alternatives. The task is rather like fitting a piece of patterned wallpaper into a larger sheet of wallpaper with a hole cut in it. This task would seem to depend very little on verbal skills, and a lot on spatial skills, requiring merely the ability to match patterns to exemplars of increasing difficulty. Performance on this task correlates highly with scores on more conventional tests of intelligence, and hence it would appear to offer a means of bypassing language-specific processes.

However, as Cole and Cole (1993) point out, some cultures have no tradition of writing or drawing, and non-literate people may not automatically interpret two-dimensional pictures appropriately. Hence, tests that rely on pictures might be just as inappropriate in non-literate societies as tests that depend on the ability to read and speak English. A possible

Fig. 11.5
Raven's
Progressive
Matrices. From
J.C. Raven
(1975), *Coloured
progressive
matrices.*

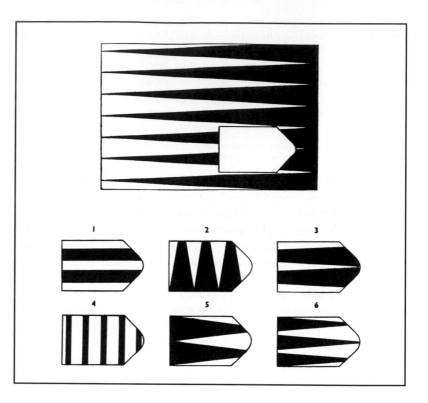

alternative to the idea of "culture-free" measures of intelligence is that intelligence is always measured relative to performance in the culture that gave rise to the test. Such a context-specific definition of intelligence is bound to set limits on the extent to which comparisons in IQ across widely different cultures are possible or logically defensible.

Ceci (1990) reviews several studies that have shown the important effect that schooling has on IQ scores. For example, Sarason and Doris (1979) show that first-generation Italian-American children, early in this century, had IQ scores generally ranging between 76 and 100. As Ceci points out, the origins of this deficit in comparison with native-born white Americans were generally considered to be non-environmental. However, what many commentators failed to notice was that these children also had a relatively low level of schooling compared with native-born white Americans and, as levels of school completion among Italian-American children increased over the first 50 years of this century, so did their IQ scores.

Others studies reviewed by Ceci show that children's IQ scores are significantly depressed if they start school later than 6 years of age or if they miss out on a significant period of schooling. Most strikingly, IQ scores actually decline slightly, but reliably, over the summer vacation. On the basis of such evidence, we might conclude that school not only has an important influence on the acquisition of literacy and numeracy, but that it even affects the success with which children perform on intelligence tests.

## Conclusion and summary

Two major achievements of middle childhood that occur within the school setting are numeracy and literacy. Both are taught through formal instruction, although the skills that children require in each case usually begin to develop in the pre-school years. Success in learning to read has been shown to be related to pre-schoolers' ability to compare the sounds that are contained in different words; and the foundation for the development of mathematical skills is laid through children's increasing familiarity with the number system and their developing ability to count.

The processes involved in learning to read vary according to the orthographic regularity of the writing system that the child is learning. Theories of learning to read have taken English as their starting point and have shown that children adopt different strategies as their reading progresses. Although there is some disagreement about the precise nature and interrelationship of children's reading strategies, there is general agreement that, having built up a sight vocabulary often before starting school, children then develop an alphabetic strategy in which they convert letters to sounds. The extent to which children rely on such a strategy depends, in part, on the way in which they are taught to read. For example, some children are explicitly taught about the relationship between sounds and letters, and this makes them more likely to use such a strategy when reading.

An alphabetic strategy can be used to pronounce all new words that are orthographically regular, and in a script such as Italian or Japanese kana, where all words are orthographically regular, children can learn to read fluently after as little as one year of formal reading instruction. For children learning to read an orthographically irregular language, such as English, ultimate success in learning to read depends on the development of an orthographic strategy in which new words can be read without sounding out individual phonemes.

Children's progress in the mastery of their number system is also affected by the characteristics of the system in question. For example, Oksapmin children learning to count make confusions between numbers located on the same part of the body. This problem does not arise for children who are learning a number system that does not locate numbers on body parts.

The use of fingers in counting is, however, a useful device that young children generally make use of, both when they learn to count and, later, when they use their knowledge of counting to perform simple addition and subtraction. Being able to make mathematical problems more concrete generally improves performance, and a study of the difficulties that children encounter with more complex arithmetic reveals that concepts that cannot be related to the familiar world are the most difficult to grasp. Children have particular difficulty in understanding the infinite nature of fractions, how to treat zeros in arithmetic, and how to subtract a larger number from a smaller one. The study of Brazilian street children (Carraher et al., 1988) also shows that children's ability to perform mental arithmetic in a familiar context may be greatly superior to their ability to deal with the same problems couched in formal mathematical terms.

Issues about the way that children's abilities are assessed occur repeatedly in a consideration of intelligence testing. Intelligence tests were originally devised in order to select an appropriate level of education for children. Even today, intelligence tests such as the WISC or the BAS are mainly used to assess children for educational placement. However, there is a complex relationship between success and length of schooling and performance on intelligence tests, as Ceci (1990) has shown.

## Further reading

Goswami, U., & Bryant, P. (1990). *Phonological skills and learning to read.* Hove: Lawrence Erlbaum Associates Ltd.

Nash, R. (1990). *Intelligence and realism.* Basingstoke: Macmillan.

Radford, J. (1990). *Child prodigies and exceptional early achievers.* Hemel Hempstead: Harvester.

PART 5

# Adolescence and Adulthood

# Adolescence 12

A s in the developmental stages already discussed, there are both biological and cultural markers for the onset of adolescence. Reproductive maturity at puberty marks the biological transition from childhood, although cultural markers of adolescence vary widely from society to society. In Western societies, there is typically an interval of 7–9 years between the biological and cultural markers of maturity. An important cultural marker is being free to marry without parental consent. Western societies require the young adult to master many skills in order to shoulder the social responsibilities that come with adulthood.

The most obvious biological markers of adolescence are the rapid changes in physical development that comprise the "growth spurt" typically correlated with the onset of puberty. The growth spurt refers to the accelerated rate of increase in height and weight that occurs in adolescence. This physical change has many of the features of stage transition predicted by the epigenetic landscape model (see pp. 19–21). There is a wide variation, both between and within the sexes, in the onset and rate of change during the transition to adolescence. In boys, the growth spurt may begin as early as 10 years of age, or as late as 16 years. In girls, the same process may begin as early as 8 years or not until 12 or 13 years. Other physical changes include increases in strength, a doubling in the size of the heart, greatly increased lung capacity, and the release of sex hormones by the pituitary gland of the brain, including testosterone in males and oestrogen in females.

On average, sexual maturity is reached 18–24 months earlier in girls than in boys. In girls, rapid change in height usually precedes the development of secondary sexual characteristics, whereas in boys, the height spurt generally occurs after the genitals have begun to grow (Coleman, 1980). These biological differences between males and females may have important consequences for psychological development, especially for aspects of identity formation, such as the body image, which are differentiated between the sexes (Brooks-Gunn & Warren 1988).

Another interesting aspect of adolescence is the secular trend in wealthy societies towards earlier onset of the growth spurt, with earlier attainment of full stature and an increase in the average adult height. Coleman (1980) points out that mediaeval European armour would fit the average 10- to 12-year-old American boy today. The average male today wears a 9–10 size shoe, whereas the shoe worn by his grandfather was a size 7! Thus the rate and course of development can be significantly altered, within biological limits, by circumstances such as improvements in health care and living conditions.

In traditional societies, there may be virtually no gap between sexual maturity and adulthood. Cole and Cole (1993) point out that, among the !Kung San people of the Kalahari Desert, the children learn hunting and gathering skills in middle childhood, so that they are self-sufficient by the time of puberty. Consequently, there is no direct equivalent to the stage of adolescence, as by the time of puberty these people are economically independent.

Although adolescence is often thought to be a particularly stormy and personally preoccupied period, this is not necessarily the case. Margaret Mead, the cultural anthropologist, made an important contribution to the study of adolescence with her books, *Coming of age in Samoa* (1928/1963) and *Growing up in New Guinea* (1930/1963). She studied adolescent females in Samoan society in the 1920s and found there was little distinctively different in the behaviour of the young women across the transitional years from childhood. Love affairs were tolerated among young men and women. The tranquil Samoan society may have provided a context for the biological changes of early adulthood, allowing developing sexuality to be readily accommodated. Subsequent studies in Samoa, carried out since the 1940s by an Australian anthropologist, Freeman (1983), did not support Mead's conclusions. It is possible that Samoan society may not have been as permissive as Mead portrayed it. It has been argued that Mead was not sufficiently rigorous in her methods of interviewing the adolescents. Because different cohorts were involved, it is difficult to be sure that changes in society may not have been responsible for the differences in results obtained by Mead and by Freeman.

In New Guinea, adolescent girls also lived rather quiet lives. Mead said that the adolescent years there were not stormy or stressful either, although in New Guinea, unlike in Samoa, adolescent girls were strictly supervised and there was little possibility for sexual experiment. In New Guinea society, the transitional years of adolescence were described as a rather unexacting time bridging the free play of childhood and the obligations of marriage.

Adolescence, therefore, varies from culture to culture (and indeed from one period to another within the same culture; life in the South Pacific islands has changed significantly since Mead studied the people there in the 1920s). At least in part, the transition to adolescence may therefore be a reflection of the requirement, in industrialised societies, for prolonged education for non-traditional occupational roles.

Adolescence propels the child into a new semi-adult social status whose onset carries new rights and responsibilities. Adolescence is also marked by new forms of thinking, with special sensitivity to received wisdom, and moral and ethical ideals. Some of the commonplace phenomena of adolescence, at least in Western society, seem both to require and to tap new intellectual abilities. Hero worship, a deep understanding of literature, religion, or art, and an understanding of aspects of cultural history all require systematicity in thinking.

Keating (1980) has distinguished five aspects of adolescent thought which distinguish it from concrete operational thinking of middle childhood:

1. Thinking about possibilities that are not immediately available.
2. Thinking ahead, planning.
3. Thinking-through hypotheses. Thought requires the generation and systematic thinking-through of hypotheses. This is particularly characteristic of scientific enquiry.
4. Thinking about thought. This is known as metacognition, or second-order thinking.
5. Thinking beyond conventional limits, perhaps linked to adolescent idealism.

# Piaget's account of adolescent thinking

In many ways, Keating's description of the characteristics of adolescent thought matches Piaget's description of formal operational reasoning. Piaget defined this new stage in development as the systematic way in which the child becomes able to consider all possible combinations in relation to the whole problem, and to reason about an entirely hypothetical situation. By contrast, the concrete operational child has acquired some organised systems of thought but proceeds only from one concrete link to the next.

Another example of the difference between formal and concrete operations can be seen in the logical process called transitive inference. The concrete operational child can infer that if A = B and B = C then A = C. This type of logic enables measurement, for example, where one concrete object, a ruler, is used to measure the relative lengths of two rods (see pp. 188–190). Concrete operational children cannot solve the transitive inference problem if it is placed on a purely verbal and hypothetical plane: John is taller than Mary, Mary is taller than Jane. Who is the tallest?

Other examples of stage-like transitions come from systematic experiments in scientific reasoning, carried out by Inhelder and Piaget (1958). Children were asked to explain physics problems such as working out how a pendulum operates, or how a balance beam works (see the panel on p. 229). Concrete operational children, operating on only one variable at a time, have great difficulty solving such problems, whereas the formal operational child, who treats the problem as a whole and systematically varies the elements, often succeeds.

## Criticisms of Piaget's theory

In the system of formal logical operations, thinking about binary problems (i.e. where two variables must be considered simultaneously) should be totally internally consistent if adult thought is indeed characterised by a fully coordinated internal logic. Formal operations are typical of the kind of thinking used by scientists—hypothetico-deductive reasoning. Formal operational reasoning, however, is far from universal. In fact, adults often have great difficulties with problems such as the balance beam (see Girotto & Light, 1992). Piaget had difficulty in explaining the non-universal nature of formal operations.

Alternative accounts of the stage transition include the possibility that adolescent thinking changes quantitatively but not qualitatively. That is, children may simply become able to process more information, perhaps as a result of biological growth of the brain. With more information-processing capacity they develop better memory and hence become able to relate more elements of a problem to each other. This type of theory denies that there has been any qualitative change in development and explains the difference in performance of children simply as a quantitative consequence of brain growth. This general type of explanation is similar to the maturationist theories of the turn of the century (see p. 13) and it is subject to the same criticisms, in that the notion of maturation may describe but fails to explain why changes that are merely the result of growth should occur.

Another explanation for change in adolescent thought focuses on the role of language. The idea that higher mental processes are based on verbal

## Piaget's formal operational stage and the INRC group

The transition from concrete to formal operations involves the hierarchical coordination of the two logical forms of reversible thought. These are Identity/Negation (I/N) and Reciprocal/Correlative (R/C), which separately become available in the concrete operational period (see panel on pp. 186–187 for the concrete operational aspects of reversible operations). These operations are hierarchically integrated into a totally internally coherent logical structure known as the INRC group. This advance enables the child to take into account two frames of reference at the same time.

Following Piaget's theory is difficult in the abstract, so let us take a concrete example. The height of water in jars in the conservation of liquid volume task will serve, starting with two identical levels of water in two identical jars; their volumes are identical. When the contents of one tall thin jar are poured into a second, short fat jar the level of water drops. The child is asked, "Does the water in each glass take up the same amount of room?" Concrete operational children will say "yes".

Then the child is given a new test. A ball of clay is dropped into the water, the child is asked to note how the water rises, and the glass is marked at the new water level. The clay ball is withdrawn and flattened into a pancake. The child is then asked to predict how high the water will rise if the pancake is dropped into the water. Children do not solve this problem until 11 or 12 years of age. Piaget argued that it is only then that children can deal with two sub-problems (conservation of volume of water and conservation of volume of clay) that will allow the conclusion that the change in the height of liquid must be proportionate to the volume of clay dropped into the water.

Figure 12.1 (below) shows the balance beam task used by Inhelder and Piaget (1958). Children are tested on a series of problems in which different weights are hung at different distances on each side of the fulcrum. Two equal weights placed at equal distances from the pivot are obviously in balance. The child has to work out whether the balance beam will be in balance or not when equal (or unequal) weights are placed at the same or different distances from the fulcrum, and state which side of the balance will drop.

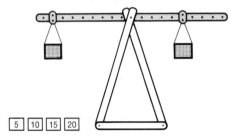

Eight-year-olds will say that the beam will balance if the weights are the same, regardless of the fact that the weights are not equidistant from the fulcrum. The adolescent, through systematic variation of the weights and distances, discovers that the weight needed to balance the beam is inversely proportional to the distance from the pivot. What is required is that one weight must be increased in the exact proportion that its distance from the fulcrum is decreased, in order to balance the other weight. Proportional reasoning is said to be characteristic of formal operational thought (see Brainerd, 1978).

reasoning was most extensively proposed by Vygotsky. One example of the verbal form of transitive reasoning was given earlier (see p. 228). Another kind of reasoning is the ability to build verbal analogies such as "Day is to night as light is to … ?". The ability to reason by verbal analogy develops rapidly during adolescence and it is possible that it depends on being able to coordinate word meanings into a logically coherent system.

Goswami (1993) has argued rather convincingly that where younger children have a well-organised body of knowledge, they have no difficulty in reasoning by analogy. However, in many of her examples, the analogical problems had concrete support in the form of pictures of all the elements in the task. For example, "A whole lemon is to a slice of lemon as a whole loaf is to … ?". (The child was shown a picture of a whole lemon, a lemon slice, and a whole loaf, and had to choose among several pictures including one of a slice of bread.)

Children from 4 to 6 years of age solved this problem correctly. Goswami (1993) argues that the common denominator that allowed the children to solve the problem was their understanding of the causal property of cutting (slicing) whole objects. She points out that children of this age do not spontaneously adopt analogical reasoning but that they can engage in it where these simplified circumstances allow.

Piagetians might argue that such abilities are simply the precursors of formal operations. Another possibility is that the younger child recognises the relations among the elements and solves the problem by identifying the associated element, rather than by analogical reasoning. For example, if a child is asked "Bird is to air as fish is to … ?", he or she might answer "water" simply because he or she knows that fish live in water. Goswami (1993) carried out studies that nicely controlled for this possibility. She showed that children aged 4–7 years could solve problems that involve identifying the similarity between different geometric shapes which had been divided into equal proportions (Figure 12.2). In this type of problem,

Fig. 12.2 A proportional analogy (Goswami, 1993).

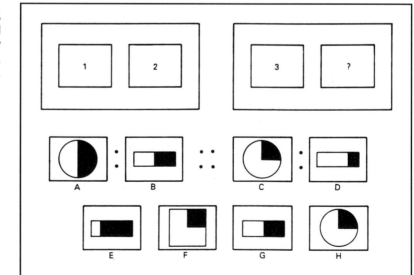

the children had to identify the analogous picture from four alternative pictures.

Children as young as 4 years correctly identified the quarter rectangle as the right answer. Thus, very young children can engage in analogical reasoning, but this perceptually based competence may not be the same as Piaget's argument that a logical understanding of analogies and proportions requires formal operations, if such problems are to be solved at a purely hypothetical level. As in previous chapters, investigators are beginning to unearth examples of reasoning in very young children which have some adult-like qualities, but which require unambiguous perceptual support to reveal the underlying competence.

## Culture and context specificity

The most interesting information about the forms of adult thinking that begin with adolescence, however, comes from comparisons of people in different cultures. Whereas Piaget emphasised the new logical form of adult thought, the cross-cultural approach emphasises the contribution of the context to thought processes. That is, the life-setting may require different degrees of systematic thought. Cultural differences in important variables like how available schooling is, or levels of literacy, may have a profound impact on whether or not one observes formal operational reasoning in particular societies or whether concrete operational problem solving is sufficient for everyday needs. Furthermore, life-settings may create specific opportunities for problem solving. Several examples are informative. The panel overleaf illustrates the complex reasoning involved in navigation by South Pacific island natives.

The example of reasoning among the Pulawat navigators illustrates very nicely a principle that is beginning to emerge in recent studies. That is, that reasoning in everyday situations may be quite different from what it is in formal testing situations. In the former case, it is not always necessary to consider all possible combinations of hypotheses and often people develop heuristic devices to solve particular problems.

Some very striking examples have recently come from Brazil where many unschooled people carry out complex reasoning tasks (see also the panel on p. 215). For example, Schliemann and Nunes (1990) studied proportional reasoning in fishermen, who catch and store shrimps, which may either be sold fresh or dried. They need to know what weight of fresh shrimps will produce what weight of dried shrimps. When working out the price of their product as a function of its weight, they also have to allow for inflation, so they can't simply apply the same solution to repeated

## Pulawat navigators

In the Polynesian islands, natives would sail from one island to another in small outrigger canoes using a compass based on 14 distinctive star paths. These are sets of stars that always rise at the same place on the eastern horizon and set at the same place in the west. The navigator, who is trained from adolescence, also has a "reference island", which may actually be purely hypothetical but whose bearing on the compass is known for any starting position (see diagram, adapted from Goodenough, 1953). Navigation involves mentally combining star paths with location of the reference island and with information about speed. The investigator, Gladwin (1970), found that the Polyne-

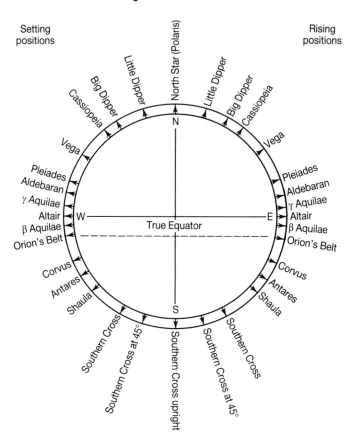

sian islanders seemed not to talk logically about how they solved the navigation problem. It was obvious to Gladwin that the canoe moved across the water while the islands remained still. However, the natives' system depended on imagining that the reference island moved while the boat stayed still. That is, they demonstrated formal operational

reasoning within the frame of reference that was culturally specific for the purpose. Gladwin found that, unless they had attended high school, the same expert navigators were unable to solve a simple Piagetian problem in which all combinations of sets of colours in a pile of poker chips had to be worked out (Gladwin, 1970).

transactions but must work out each time what the cost should be. Schlie-mann and Nunes tested the fishermen on simple proportion problems. For example:

> How much shrimp needs to be caught for a customer who wants 2 kilos of processed shrimps when 18 kilos yield 3 kilos of processed food?

Without pencil and paper, the problem is solved as follows: One and a half kilos processed would be 9 kilos fresh (i.e. halves the initial values) … and a half kilo processed is 3 kilos unprocessed (i.e. finds the proportion needed for the remaining half kilo) … then it would be 9 plus 3 is 12 (unprocessed) to give 2 kilos processed. The situated reasoning about proportionality proceeds by decomposing the problem into smaller units and using addition to arrive at the final answer.

The problem can be represented formally as follows:

$$a/b=c/x$$
$$a \times ?=b \times c$$
$$?=(b \times c)/a$$
$$?=18 \times 2/3$$
$$?=12$$

Most of the fishermen have had little or no schooling. They cannot solve the problem using the written arithmetic method. The implication is that intuitive schemas of proportionality may actually conflict with algorithms used for teaching proportionality in schools. When the authors went on to study students from the same town, who were familiar with much of the commercial transactions in fishing, the students themselves scored better when using the intuitive methods they had learned in the market place than when using the formal notation.

When we compare individuals from different cultures we gain the impression that perhaps Piaget's theory of formal operational reasoning is in a way too formal, it is overly abstracted from what people actually do. As Margaret Donaldson complained with respect to early develop-ment, disembedded thinking, as exemplified by Piaget's account, may underestimate what adolescents are actually capable of.

# Is there a transition to adolescent thought?

So once again we are faced with the question, is there a transition or not? There is evidence that adolescents do actually reason differently from younger children in familiar contexts. For example, Cole and Cole (1993) discuss a study by Adelson (1972) of social and political reasoning in adolescents.

When Adelson asked, "What is the purpose of laws?", 12- and 13-year-olds said, "If we had no laws, people could go around killing people". At this age, Cole and Cole argue, the children respond in terms of concrete people and events. They use concrete operational reasoning to come to a conclusion. However, 15- and 16-year-olds reply, "To ensure safety and enforce the government. To limit what people can do". Older adolescents can reason hypothetically and take many facets into account, and Cole and Cole suggest that they respond in terms of abstract principles based on hypothetical reasoning.

The search for inconsistency among belief systems, an awareness of contradictions in the behaviour of adults or in the rules governing behaviour, is also revealed by the ability to think hypothetically. The idealism of (some) adolescents can also be explained by the ability to reason hypothetically. What is to replace the imperfect institutions the adolescent observes? Such questions may lead to an ideal or utopian project. Some authors (e.g. Cole & Cole, 1993) emphasise the formal operational nature of such reasoning in explaining, at least in part, certain adolescent forms of thought.

So, is adolescence a stage? It is by no means certain that adolescence is a stage. In many societies, the onset of puberty marks the beginning of adulthood, marriage, and the adoption of adult roles. In Western societies, the biological shift does not coincide very closely with the acquisition of adult role status, which is conferred mainly by entering the world of work. Perhaps adolescence is not a stage but a culturally defined period of transition to adulthood.

Is adult reasoning different from that of children? Carey (1985) argues that taking all the evidence into account, there is evidence that stage transitions do occur between children's and adults' reasoning. The panel opposite summarises the evidence.

## Is children's thinking fundamentally different from that of adults?

Theories of development presuppose both continuity and discontinuity between stages. Piagetian theory, which has dominated the field, supposed that adults are qualitatively different kinds of thinkers from children and that there are major transitions between the forms of organisation of thought in the various stages of childhood. Carey (1985) made a critical assessment of the proposition along five lines of argument:

1. *Is there evidence that children represent information differently from adults?*
Piaget argued that there are stage differences in the way knowledge is organised, which arise from changes in the logical structure of thought. Others such as Vygotsky argued that knowledge comes to be represented through language and gives rise to "higher mental processes" based on verbal reasoning. It is clear that infants cannot represent what they know through language, because they don't yet speak. So it seems reasonable to conclude that the representation of knowledge through language is one major difference in development between early and later childhood, but this alone need not entail logical differences between child and adult thought.

2. *Children may differ from adults in their foundational concepts for acquiring knowledge.*
Children's basic understanding of space, time, causes, and objects may be different. This is Piaget's view, but it is not shared by contemporary developmentalists, especially those working with babies. Here there are more grounds for continuity from childhood to adulthood in processes of perception that are organised around these fundamental categories. This might explain why children reveal unexpected competences when reasoning problems are couched in perceptual terms.

3. *Children may lack metacognitive knowledge.*
Metacognitive knowledge means understanding how one's thought processes operate so that these insights can be put to use in problem solving. For example, adults may know enough about their memory limitations to rehearse material by reciting it to themselves, or they may tie a knot in a handkerchief as a reminder, or write the problem down. Children may not be as aware of their memory limitations. Differences in their performance may arise because they don't have strategies to deal with them. This type of account leaves unexplained how metacognitive knowledge arises.

Furthermore, children lack some metacognitive knowledge that is predicted by Piaget's theory. For example, the average 5-year-old does not know what is meant by a word. When asked which word is longer "Snake or caterpillar?" the child answers "snake". When asked "Is the word needle sharp?", the child answers "yes". This error is known as nominal realism in Piagetian theory. The child has difficulty focusing on the word itself rather than on its meaning, or its syllabic structure.

4 *Domain-independent versus domain-specific knowledge.*
Piaget was mainly concerned with general, domain-independent reasoning. The stages of development are supposed to apply "across the board". However, recent concern with culturally embedded forms of thinking suggests that knowledge and reasoning may be domain-specific and that some intellectual competences will be revealed, both among children and adults, only when the context is taken into account. Domain-specific knowledge might also explain why the inabilities of children may also be seen among adults under some circumstances. A domain-specific view of cognitive development may also explain why

(Continued)

**Is children's thinking fundamentally different from that of adults? (continued)**

intellectual abilities may dissociate, as in the case of idiots savants.

5. *Intellectual skills are tools of wide application.* Children are novices whereas adults are experts. This may simply mean that adults know more than children. However, Carey also suggests that becoming an expert may involve reorganising knowledge in a way that may be very stage-like. Stages are inferred because knowledge becomes reorganised so that otherwise diverse phenomena can be explained as economically as possible.

The idea that acquiring knowledge depends on specific domains acquired in specific contexts can be combined with the shift from novice to expert. This results in a modified theory of discontinuity in development. Different stages can be observed from infancy to adulthood but some forms of adult-like competence may be acquired in specific contexts. Such an account denies that the cognitive system is a single, uniform structure. Instead, the cognitive systems of children and adults would be seen as an amalgam of different levels of development which have taken place along parallel pathways. Cognitive development is better understood as content- and context-specific. However, the growth of the different subsystems might still be understood in terms of stage-like growth, just as in the metaphor of the epigenetic landscape (see Figure 2.2). Contemporary theories of cognitive development are being constructed in terms of the dynamic interactions of subsystems which develop at different rates (see van Geert ,1993).

# The Freudian view of adolescence

Against the view that adolescence is merely a function of a particular form of social organisation; the Freudian view is that the pre-adolescent, during the latency phase, identifies with members of the same sex, whereas one of the tasks of adolescence is to identify with the opposite sex. This might be thought of as a universal feature of development.

The acquisition of a strong psychosexual sense of personal identity is often thought to be one of the universal tasks of adolescents. The shift towards peer relationships requires emotional disengagement from the family. Erikson (1968) describes a series of stages in the formation of personal identity from infancy to adulthood (see panel opposite). During adolescence, the tasks are establishing trust in an ideological view of the world; establishing autonomy; taking initiative and setting goals for what one might become; and taking responsibility for one's own industry. The process of identity formation depends on the simultaneous integration of these problems in the individual and social spheres. Individuals judge themselves in the light of what they perceive to be the way in which others judge them, in comparison to themselves and to a typology significant to

# Erikson's theory

Erik Erikson (1902–94) was a student of Sigmund Freud. He offered a modified Freudian view of development of personal identity through the lifespan. His theory presents a progression through eight psychosocial stages. Erikson differed from Freud, however, in giving more emphasis to social and cultural forces in development.

Freud believed that personality is formed mainly in the first 6 years, through unconscious processes under the influence of one's parents, and that personality formation is irreversible. Erikson considered personality formation to be more malleable and to continue throughout life, to be influenced by friends, the family, and society. It follows from his theory that aspects of personal identity will be formed and influenced by childhood experience in the family and in other cultural settings, such as school. Identity formation and maintenance continues throughout life, again influenced by experience of parenting, or with grandchildren. Another important factor in adult identity development is experience at work.

## Erikson's psychosocial stages

| Age (years) | Stage | Description of Stage |
|---|---|---|
| 0–1 | Infancy | Parents must maintain a nurturant environment so that the child develops basic trust in others (corresponds to Freud's oral stage) |
| 1–3 | Early childhood | Child develops autonomy through bowel and bladder control (corresponds to Freud's anal stage) |
| 3–6 | Early childhood | Child must initiate own actions in a socially acceptable way (corresponds to Freud's phallic stage) |
| 6–14 | Later childhood | Child must learn to feel competent, especially in relation to peers (corresponds to Freud's latency stage) |
| 14–20 | Adolescence | Child must develop a sense of role identity, especially in selecting a future career (corresponds to entry into Freud's final adult, genital stage) |
| 20–35 | Young adulthood | Formation of adult sexual relationships |
| 35–65 | Maturity | Adults develop themselves through guiding their children |
| 65 | Old age | Adults achieve wisdom and a sense of well-being from a life well spent |

them. Adolescents must simultaneously consider their own and other people's judgements, plus the perspective of society. The intellectual demands of this achievement may well require formal operations

## Gender identity in adolescence

Puberty marks the onset of sexual maturity. In some societies, puberty is accompanied by initiation rites for members of one or both sexes, whereas other societies make little fuss. Among girls in traditional societies, initiation ceremonies are likely to be related to the onset of menstruation, often involving the seclusion of the girl from men for a time. At the conclusion of the period of segregation, there may be a ritual ceremony where the girl publicly dons the clothes of a mature woman. Ceremonials whose purpose is to confer adult status on boys, such as the Jewish Bar Mitzvah, are also widespread in different cultures (Conger & Petersen, 1984). In some traditional societies, puberty is accompanied by marriage; Mahatma Ghandi, for example, was married at the age of 12. But in modern, Western societies sexual maturity is dissociated, to varying degrees, from the opportunity to enter into sexual relationships.

Adolescence marks an intensification in the processes of gender identification already begun in early and middle childhood. Biological, cultural, and social processes all contribute in various ways to this increase in awareness of gender. The chromosomal and hormonal bases for gender were briefly discussed on p. 145. The contribution of biological processes is usually consistent between chromosomal, hormonal, morphological, and social factors and this combination of influences gives rise to a normative sense of gender identity. Taken to an extreme, social definitions of gender-appropriate behaviour may lead to a restriction of academic and life choices along sex-typed lines.

In some cases, however, the normal combination of components of the complex system contributing to the development of gender identity may be dissociated from others, including those involved in sexual identity. Biological males with undescended testicles may be brought up as females, and chromosomal females with deceptive morphology have occasionally been brought up as males. Under these circumstances, the gender role orientation of the individual was consistent with the assigned sex and inconsistent with the chromosomal sex (Money, Hampson, & Hampson, 1955).

In Freudian theory, adolescence marks the end of the latency period of childhood. Establishing a strong sense of gender identity is thought to depend to a large extent on the child's relationship with his or her parents. Adolescent boys and girls identify with the parent of the same sex, and positive identification is especially strong where the relationship between the parents confirms the gender-specific role models being displayed (see pp. 248–250). Negative aspects of sex role stereotyping, such as domination of one parent by the other, or mutual hostility between the parents, may lead to difficulties in identity formation for the child. Parental warmth, nurturance, and involvement with the child, all have positive consequences for gender role identification (Conger & Petersen, 1984).

Peer groups also influence gender identity. Obvious examples of the strong influence of the peer group include fashions in clothing and in hairstyles. Same-sex friendships are particularly important in early adolescence and it is thought that such close, confiding relationships may have an important part to play in coming to understand complex, personal feelings. Opposite-sex friendships generally begin in later adolescence, with dating, "going steady", and intense emotional involvement between boys and girls being more typical of the 15- to 18-year age group.

Gender identity, what sex one feels and knows oneself to be, needs to be distinguished from sexual orientation. Neither gender identity nor sexual identity develop merely through social influences acting on basic sex differences. Indeed, in the case of homosexuals, individuals may be content with their gender identity, as males or females, despite the difference in their sexual orientation. Transsexuals, however, complain of being trapped in a body of the wrong sex. Thus, gender identity and sexual identity are dissociable, although they usually develop congruently (Conger & Petersen, 1984).

## Conclusion and summary

The introduction of formal schooling in Western societies, in the nineteenth century, resulted in an extension of the period of economic dependence and a delay in the acquisition of adult roles. This gave an opportunity to study development in the period of adolescence between the biological and economic attainment of adult status. The concept of adolescence more flexibly combines biological, social, and historical factors than do preceding developmental stages. The transition to adulthood generates a need to come to terms with sexual maturity and the need to adopt adult roles. This transition will be experienced differently according to one's cultural circumstances and according to one's gender.

Formal operational reasoning marks Piaget's final stage of cognitive development. As in his previous stages, a great deal of conflicting evidence exists as to the intellectual capabilities of young adults. Contemporary theory suggests that across-the-board stage transitions do not adequately capture the forms of thought available to children and adults. However, a modular, content- and context-sensitive approach to cognitive development suggests that stages may still be a useful way of describing systematic changes in the development of thinking.

Gender identity undergoes a period of intense development in adolescence, with biological, social, and cultural factors having an influence on establishing a masculine or feminine sense of personal identity.

## Further reading

Goswami, U. (1993). *Analogical reasoning in children*. Hove: Lawrence Erlbaum Associates Ltd.

# Development in adulthood 13

**M**ost textbooks on developmental psychology end with adolescence and the transition to adulthood. It seems intuitively obvious that adulthood marks the terminus for development and so, one might suppose, there would be little to say after adolescence is over. It is true that age-related changes in physical, social, and cognitive development in adults are much less marked than in childhood, but there are nevertheless general trends that can be studied.

As in the childhood stages we have discussed, the scientific study of adulthood has received its greatest impetus from the social and economic factors that have necessitated greater understanding. Perhaps the most important and obvious reason for the study of adulthood is the very much prolonged expectation of life for the majority of the population in Western industrialised societies. In fact, the term *gerontology*, meaning the study of ageing, was only coined in 1914, which suggests that it is only in the twentieth century that populations reaching old age have existed on a large scale.

In the United States, the population over 65 years of age was 4% in 1900, 13% in 1984, and by 2030 it is expected that the figure will exceed 20%. The average lifespan in the USA at the turn of the century was 49 years, whereas now it is 77 years. The figures for other Western industrialised societies are similar, with an average life expectancy of 70 for men and 76 for women, and a further expectancy of 10 years for those who have reached 70 (Bromley, 1988). According to the *Guinness book of records*, the oldest person for whom acceptable proof of age was available was Jean Calment of France who died in 1997 at 122 years of age.

That ageing has a fundamental biological basis seems probable from experiments which show that cultured human cells divide and replicate only a limited number of times. The older the donor of the cells, the fewer times they divide. The upper limit of the lifespan, based on such biological considerations, is thought to be about 130 years (Hayflick, 1980).

Until relatively recently, the number of people surviving even to the biblical limit of three score years and ten was limited. With changes in medical social and economic circumstances, unprecedentedly large numbers of people are surviving into healthy retirement. The number of people surviving into great old age (80+ years) has perhaps provided the initial motive for studying the elderly. This in turn created a gap to be bridged between early adulthood at 17 years and development into old age, which has led developmental psychology finally to study the whole lifespan.

## Defining adulthood

Defining adulthood is not as straightforward as it may seem, as it is not simply a matter of reaching a particular age. Adulthood is defined biologically by the capacity for reproduction, socially by economic independence, and psychologically as a quality of maturity in one's personal identity.

Both Piaget and Freud saw adulthood as relatively long plateaus with little further development. However, there are many significant life-events in adulthood—marriage, becoming a parent or grandparent, success at work, perhaps the loss of work through unemployment, retirement, the loss of parents and other forms of bereavement—all of which constitute major biological and cultural transitions in the life-cycle.

It is not clear that such life changes themselves constitute stages of development in the same sense that stages were defined for the various periods of childhood (see pp. 27–30). Certainly, we can expect much greater variability in the way such changes occur, and much less universality in their effects. Of course, there is also great scope for cultural variation in the ways in which societies manage these adult life changes, both in terms of the social organisation for reproduction (e.g. through marriage), or in the ways in which work is allocated through the education system, or in the role given to the elderly in society. Contemporary developmental psychology addresses such life changes in adulthood, as well as the more traditional area of child development.

## Biological and physical development in adulthood

Biological growth continues into young adulthood. For example, between 17 and 30 years of age, the long bones of the skeleton and the vertebral column continue to grow and this may add up to 1/4 inch to men's height (less for women). Some bones of the skull continue to grow throughout life (Tanner, 1978). Visual and auditory acuity are usually at their peak in young adults (20 years for vision and 13 years for hearing), with changes in vision and hearing being well documented from 25 to 70 years.

Physical strength increases to peak efficiency at between 25 and 30 years. Rutter and Rutter (1992) give two examples from athletics: the 10,000 metre runner Paavo Nurmi ran his fastest race at the age of 27, and the hammer thrower Karl Hein reached his peak at age 30. However, both athletes showed less than a 5% decline in performance over the next 20 years, possibly because they continued to take vigorous physical exercise

There are important gender differences in the ways people age, which may have different consequences for men and women. For example, women reach the menopause between 45 and 55 years of age, whereas men continue to be fertile into old age. Examples such as these illustrate a number of points: that the peak of physical prowess occurs in early adulthood; that a significant physical decline need not occur; and that protective factors, such as physical exercise, may be important in success-ful ageing. Finally, sex differences in life-expectancy and during the life course may have important consequences for development in adulthood.

# Theories of adult development

Adulthood has been less systematically studied than child development. Erikson suggested that there are three stages of adult development—young adulthood, maturity, and old age—each defined psychosexually in relation to adult relationships and becoming a parent (see Table on p. 237). His theory has been criticised because it seems to suggest that adults who remain childless are not fully developed. It has also been criticised as sexist, especially as it relates to the development of women.

In an extension of Erikson's theory, Vaillant (1977) and Levinson (1986) have suggested that once men aged between 20 and 35 marry, they focus on their careers, sometimes to the detriment of their personal lives. This stage of "career consolidation" often involves the support of an older friend or mentor who helps with career development. From their mid-30s, men begin to strive for more career independence and to "become their own man" as they acquire seniority. These aspects of the theory have been criticised for being too much modelled on male development.

Gilligan (1982) suggests that women are more influenced by the need to be nurturant, especially in unequal relationships. This means that women's psychosocial development may be different from that of men both at home and in the workplace. This type of gender-differentiated theory is important in suggesting that male and female children, adoles-cents, and adults may work out aspects of their identity differently through their personal relationships. This type of argument can be ex-tended to offer an explanation, at least in part, for sex differences in mathematical and scientific interests and achievements. These are contro-versial but important topics in an egalitarian society (Walkerdine, 1988).

The contemporary emphasis in Western societies has been against stereotyped, traditional gender roles with more opportunity for men and women to explore their natural talents. Women in particular have entered traditionally male preserves, such as the law, banking and accountancy, science, and engineering in increasing numbers. In the United States, the number of women employed in these professsions increased from approximately 20% to 30% of those employed in each category between 1972 and 1981. The number of female bus drivers rose from 34% to 44% in the same period. However, nearly all secretaries continue to be females and electricians are almost all males (Conger& Petersen, 1984).

There are currently two major approaches to adult development: (1) *Lifespan development*, which traces the ways in which psychological phenomena, such as intelligence, vary across the lifespan; (2) *the life course approach*, which is more concerned with the impact of life-events, such as becoming a parent or retirement, on the individual.

## Lifespan development

One of the main methodological contributions of the lifespan approach has come from the study of ageing. It was discovered that people may age differently because they grow up under different circumstances. For example, people born during the Great Depression of the 1930s may have received poorer nutrition than those born during more affluent times, and may therefore differ in health and physical stature from other groups because of this early experience.

Other cohort effects can also be identified. For example, the median time between starting work and age of first marriage for men fell from 18 years in 1900 to 8 years by 1939. There are complex reasons for this, including changes in the education system, economic trends, and the onset of war. Rutter and Rutter (1992) point out that by 1960 young people in the United States were starting to work a year before they left school and on average girls were married 2 years later.

A particularly interesting example of how cohort differences may influence our assessment of the effects of ageing comes from measures of mathematical abilities of the very elderly, made by Schaie (1990). Determining whether elderly people are functioning optimally will depend on how they compare with younger groups. Schaie studied 3442 adults born between 1889 and 1959 on the Thurstone test of Primary Mental Abilities, an intelligence test that measures verbal, spatial, number, and reasoning skills. The adults were divided into successive cohorts with a difference of 7 years between their birth dates.

Schaie then drew a graph plotting the differrence between the average scores of successive cohorts. He found that reasoning skills showed a linear increase with birth cohort throughout the twentieth century. In number skills there was an increase between successive cohorts from 1889 to 1910, a period of stability from 1910 to 1924 and a decline thereafter, so that by the 1959 cohort number skills had actually fallen below the level of those born in 1889! This example shows very clearly that intellectual performance on number problems is not simply a function of how old a person is, it is also a function of when they were born.

Schaie (1990) retested 1357 of his sample four times over 28 years from 1956 to 1984. Between the ages of 25 and 53 there was virtually no decrement in a composite score of primary mental abilities (0.07 points on average), whereas from 53 to 81 the average score fell by 8.75 points. Between the ages of 60 and 74 years, approximately 33% of his sample showed some decline in primary mental abilities. Above 81 years up to 40% did so. It is interesting to note, however, that even among the oldest age group, less than half showed any decline in their scores relative to seven years earlier.

Although general indices of health did not predict any decline in mental abilities, Schaie found that people who had been diagnosed as at risk for cardiovascular disease (those with hypertension) showed an earlier decline in primary mental abilities than those not at risk. Among the very elderly, the greatest impact on intellectual functioning came from Alzheimer's disease, a degenerative disorder of the brain which has a prevalence rate of about 5% at 70 years, rising to 30% at 90 years. Normal ageing, however, is without biological or mental pathology.

## Selective optimisation

Another contribution of the lifespan approach has been the suggestion that old people maintain their intellectual abilities by selective optimisa-tion (Baltes & Baltes, 1990). That is, old people tend to concentrate their resources on what they can do well. Baltes and Baltes quote the Roman philosopher, Cicero, who asked "Have you heard of an old man who forgets where he hid his treasure?" to make the point that even memory loss may be selective and designed to maintain the quality and quantity of life.

Old people have reserves of ability which can be used for learning new skills or maintaining old ones. These reserves may be less than are avail-able to a younger person, but still sufficient to maintain an adequate quality of life. The effects of age may only become apparent when indi-viduals are functioning close to the limit of their abilities. Baltes and Baltes suggest that the key to successful ageing is selective optimisation and compensation; selectivity means restricting progressively one's activity to what one does best and compensating for specific losses, such as in physical strength, by other strategies.

### The life course approach

The life course approach is less explicitly developmental than the lifespan approach. This method identifies important events, or benchmarks, in the life-cycle which serve to give new direction to an individual's life. A highly probable example is becoming a parent, whereas some examples of low probability are dropping out of school, losing a limb in a car accident, or winning the football pools. Any of these events would make a big difference to the course of one's life and the changes engendered in the individual can be considered as developmental processes. The most frequently encountered life-events occur in four contexts: the family, work, health, and marriage (Reese & Smyer, 1983). We will illustrate the life-events approach with some examples from parenting and work.

## Marriage and parenting

Of all social institutions, marriage shows the widest range of historical and cultural forms. The Western ideal of romantic love followed by monogamous marriage and a traditional family is by no means the only way in which society regulates procreation. In the West, the traditional two-parent family with children now forms a minority of households, and customs such as long engagements and the dowry, which served to provide an economic foundation for the marriage, are also in decline. In the West, the choice of life partner is a matter for the individual, whereas in traditional Indian societies, the parents choose the partner when the child is ready for marriage.

Notwithstanding the different ways in which marriage may be arrived at, there remains the contribution of the personal characteristics of the partners to the marriage. The age at marriage is an important predictor of the success of the marriage, with teenage marriages much more likely to result in divorce. Economic factors could be important here but personal characteristics can also contribute. Very young couples may simply grow apart, as their personalities diverge. In fact, almost half of all marriages in the USA and Great Britain end in divorce within the first seven years. Marital incompatibility is a widespread phenomenon revealed by the advent of "no-fault" laws which allow relatively easy divorce.

For successful marriages there is some evidence that the partners have shared or complementary attitudes, similar physical health, physical attractiveness, education, and family backgrounds. These complementary aspects of the relationship are likely to prove particularly important as initial passion wanes and the relationship between man and wife becomes mutually supportive, compassionate, and companionable.

# Becoming a parent

The transition to parenthood also involves further changes and personal adaptation both in the husband and wife. The panel below lists the key elements of the transition to parenthood.

Pregnancy introduces major hormonal and physical changes in the female. Most pregnant women report feeling very well once the initial "morning sickness" of early pregnancy is over. There are, of course, risks in reproduction, although these are much diminished by modern medicine. For example, the age of the mother may introduce some anxiety, because the risk of a Down's syndrome birth increases from about 1 in 500 for women under 20 years to 1 in 20 for women aged 45 years. But, with modern methods of prenatal screening, more women are delaying the birth of their first child as they pursue personal career goals.

About one-quarter of couples in a British study said that their marriage had improved consequent upon having their first child; rather more spoke

---

## Key elements in the transition to parenting

Rutter and Rutter (1992) list six key elements in parenting:

1. Parenting requires skills for providing an environment conducive to the adaptive development of the child, in relation to the child's needs and demands. These include knowing how to play and talk with children and the appropriate use of disciplinary techniques.
2. Parenting requires not only skills but also positive social relationships, both between parent and child and more generally within the family.
3. Parenting reflects the quality of psychosocial functioning of the mother and father and is likely to be affected by the state of mental health of the parents.
4. Parenting is the outcome of learning. Previous experience of bringing up other children may be important as well as the experience of one's own upbringing.
5. Parenting a particular child is influenced by earlier experiences of the same child.
6. Parenting occurs in a broader nexus, influenced by whether the parent is alone, with the other parent, or with other children.

Parenting therefore involves many factors which culminate in the successful or unsuccessful upbringing of children. Parenting is a series of life-events that offer the mother and father many new challenges and responsibilities. These responsibilities may be held solely by one parent, or be shared with others in the family, or with the larger community. How these responsibilities should be apportioned between the family and society are matters of continuing controversy. Controversies as diverse as the sharing of responsibility for punishment between the family and the schools, the adequacy of single-parent families, and whether children should be paid for work carried out at home do not have simple solutions. However, they are beginning to be studied from the perspective of the parent (Goodnow & Collins, 1990).

of negative effects (loss of sleep, loss of personal freedom) and about 10% claimed that their marriages had been weakened, especially where the infant was proving difficult to manage (Moss, Bolland, Foxman, & Owen, 1986).

Perhaps the most important aspect of parenting is the love of a parent for their child. This is in many ways the reciprocal of the psychology of attachment in infancy, which we have already discussed (see pp. 24–27 and 107–110). Babies are physically very attractive both to adults and children; they look and they smell good, and it is easy to like them. Attachment to one's own children follows both from biological predispositions and as an aspect of personal, adult fulfilment. Indeed, attachment theory, or as Bowlby put it "the making and breaking of affectional bonds", may have important applications to falling in love and for establishing warm and welcoming marital relationships which meet the emotional needs of the parent and the child

Bowlby's theory has also been applied to the emotional problems that arise in coming to terms with separation, divorce, and bereavement (Bowlby, 1971; 1973). Grief at the death of a loved person is a universal emotion, which may even be experienced in other species, such as dogs and chimpanzees. A regular pattern of behaviour is often observed in which the surviving partner is at first shocked, sad, and anxious. For about a year there is a feeling of loneliness, self-blame for the death, and an impulse to search for the deceased. About two years after the death the recovery phase begins and the person makes a conscious, positive decision to go on with their life.

Grieving is common but it does vary with the circumstances of the death and the particular relationship between the partners. The pattern described by Bowlby occurs where the death is expected. In unexpected, sudden death the situation is more complex and individuals may not be able to resolve their loss, even after several years.

## Mothering and fathering

The maternal role has received wide study, especially in relation to such issues as day care. Bowlby considered the mother to be the all important caretaker and this has had repercussions for the provision of day care, because it was widely assumed that the mother would provide more adequately for the child than a paid carer.

Intensive research has not put an end to the continuing debate over "mother care or other care", but it is now widely accepted that high-quality day care is not detrimental to the quality of attachment of the baby to the mother. However, some babies spend many more than 20 hours a week in rather poor quality day care, where they receive little individual attention; and this may affect the infants' emotional and social development, as reflected in later adjustment to school (Scarr & Dunn, 1987). Good child care may depend most importantly on the caregiver's knowledge of child development and the provision of care appropriately tailored to the unique personality and needs of the child.

Fathering has been less widely studied, although changing social patterns are bringing the father's role under scrutiny too. For example, paternity leave from work is offered to expectant fathers in Sweden. Up to 60% take advantage of this opportunity to be with their newborn baby in the first weeks.

In their traditional gender role, fathers are more likely to engage their children in rough and tumble play, and to provide different sex-role models for their male and female children (see pp. 145–147). The mechanisms whereby gender roles are transmitted from adult to child are complex and depend not only on the relation between the father and child, but also on the father's relationship with the mother. For example, paternal and maternal warmth increases femininity in girls, whereas paternal but not maternal warmth increases traditional masculinity in boys.

Boys who fit the masculine stereotype have fathers who play a dominant role in family decision making, whereas when the mother plays a more dominant role boys are less likely to use the father as a role model. Fathers affect the sex-typing of their daughters in a different way, by the encouragement of their daughters in feminine activities and through their relationships with the mother. Fathers may also emphasise the importance of occupational and educational success more than mothers and more for boys than for girls. Such findings may well reflect social expectations that were common before women entered the workforce (Parke, 1981).

In one of the more recent studies of fathering, Lewis (1986) gathered a great deal of evidence for a fundamental change in paternal involvement in British families between 1960 and 1980. For example, fathers attended 60% of the births of their children in Lewis's study, by contrast with only 10% in the 1960s. By 1980 more men put their children to bed regularly (48%) than in 1960 (35%). However, not much has changed in the nappy department. Of the 2000 nappies worn by the baby over the first year, 40% of the men changed fewer than 13 nappies, both in 1960 and 1980! This can be taken as evidence for inter-generational constancy, at least in this aspect of the division of labour between mothers and fathers.

Grandparenting is also beginning to receive serious study. In the West, people become grandparents, on average, in their early 50s. Grandmothers may often serve an important role in assisting young mothers with their children and grandparents may serve an important role in family cohesion and in providing a sense of continuity over time for children and grandchildren. Reciprocally, grandparents may gain some sense of immortality through their grandchildren. Mutual love between grandparents and grandchildren has been identified by Erik Erikson as an important factor in personality formation in late adulthood.

# Entering employment and the effects of unemployment

The second major criterion for the transition to adulthood is achieving economic independence. Although entering work is obviously a life-event, it is not necessarily a developmental stage. Nevertheless, stage theories of occupational development have occasionally been proposed (see panel below), but these accounts rather presuppose a stable career pattern and early entry to work. Contemporary experience is often rather different, with people frequently changing jobs up to the age of 35, and women entering work in their 30s, when their children are less dependent. Furthermore, cycles of economic recession put many millions of people out of work, sometimes repeatedly.

---

### Stages of occupational development

Super (1957) suggested that people pass through five stages in their occupational development:

- *Crystallisation:* In adolescence, people begin to make broad choices which will affect their future careers. For example, an individual may choose to go to university and study either arts or sciences, or may enter work directly on leaving school. Ideas about the type of job that suits one will begin to crystallise (e.g. working with people, computing, nursing, commerce).
- *Specification:* From 18 to 21, the individual enters a period of training, either on the job or in further education.
- *Implementation:* From 21 to 24, the individual enters work, may receive further training and will often change jobs.
- *Stabilisation:* From 24 to 35, the individual establishes a career.
- *Consolidation:* From 35 to retirement, the person achieves as much as possible in his or her chosen career.

This general sequence may bring some order to understanding career development in some cases but it can be criticised in many ways. The sequence does not meet the strict criteria for "true" stages of development of an underlying structure which changes in an invariant, hierarchical order (see pp. 27–30). Super's stages are merely descriptive and do not offer an explanation for the different phases of working life in the same way that a developmental stage theory attempts to account for the underlying order between widely differing phenomena in development. Furthermore, Super's model presupposes stability in employment and cannot account for different career progressions of men and women. Indeed, many people may have much less choice in deciding what work to do, or in receiving training in the 1990s than in the 1950s when Super proposed his model.

---

Why do we work? Given the need to work in order to attain and maintain economic independence, are there any other psychological benefits? Many people would rather work even when their economic needs are satisfied. Jahoda (1981) has argued that paid work is a social institution with both manifest and latent, perhaps unintended, functions in people's lives. The manifest function of work is to earn a living but the latent consequences are many, including social contact, acquiring status, purposefulness, the use of skills, and living one's life in a time-frame. In other words, satisfying work can contribute significantly to an adult's sense of personal identity.

The latent consequences of work may also contribute to mental health. Research on unemployment, both in the Great Depression of the 1930s and in the 1980s, has begun to tease apart the effects of poverty brought about by loss of work, and loss of work itself. People who lose their jobs not only become poorer, they lose the opportunities provided by the latent functions of work. It is important therefore to establish whether poor people in employment are psychologically more healthy than equally poor unemployed people.

Fryer (1990), in a carefully controlled British study, showed that the long-term unemployed do suffer more mental health problems than low-paid but employed workers. It is possible, of course, that people with mental health problems are more likely to be unemployed. Contemporary longitudinal research, which follows people from employment through prolonged unemployment, suggests that unemployment can itself lead to problems such as alcoholism and other mental health difficulties (Fryer, 1992).

It has been suggested that the loss of a job is followed by four stages: shock, as the realisation of loss of the job strikes home; optimism, as the individual makes strenuous efforts to find another job; pessimism as the reality of mass unemployment sinks in; and finally fatalism and depression, as the person gives up hope of finding work. Such a cycle of emotional and intellectual responses may often occur following a major life transition but strictly speaking these are not stages. Even though unemployment may result in loss of self-esteem, it does not invariably do so, nor is the sequence typical in all communities, or the same for men and women. Women may cope better with such stresses than men, and those living in communities of high unemployment, or holding jobs they dislike, may not be so personally involved in their jobs, that becoming unemployed has the same distressing consequences (Fryer, 1985). Nevertheless, unemployment, unlike retirement, is not an experience that most people enjoy.

# Conclusion and summary

Adulthood is the longest phase of the lifespan but development in adults has only recently begun to be studied scientifically. In terms of the epigenetic landscape metaphor (see pp. 19–21), change continues but at a slower rate than in childhood. The use of stage terminology to describe adult changes is not usually appropriate, because much adult development concerns the continuous building on structures formed in childhood and adolescence. Changes are not typically the rapid, wide-ranging reorganisations that define the stage transitions of childhood. Nevertheless, life-events such as becoming a parent, or entering employment or unemployment may induce novel changes in the sense of personal identity. Adults will typically have a number of developmental "tasks" which they will wish to accomplish, both with respect to personal relationships, having a family and parenting, and with respect to the world of work. Experience gained in these important domains of adulthood provides a broader basis of knowledge and perhaps, ultimately, confers wisdom with maturity.

# Epilogue

This brief introduction to some of the major themes in developmental psychology would not be complete without a glimpse of the future. In just a few years, developmental psychology will enter the twenty-first century. We are close enough to the millenium to hazard a guess at the developmental psychology of the future. What themes are likely to preoccupy developmentalists? We will not attempt to see too far ahead, but it is possible to predict where some current theories and empirical questions are leading. The panel on pages 253–254 offers a few speculations on important theoretical and empirical issues in the developmental psychology of the near future.

## Developmental psychology in the twenty-first century

We have argued that developmental psychology is simultaneously concerned with biological and cultural processes that shape human development. This overall perspective will not change.

One prediction is of an ever closer link between developmental psychology and developmental biology. Developmental psychology as a scientific discipline has come a long way since the mid-nineteenth century, but, as this book has shown, it remains inspired and informed by evolutionary biology. We have not had space here, except occasionally, to illustrate the extensive links that can be made between developmental biology and developmental psychology. Advances in evolutionary theory, in genetics, and in the biology of the developing nervous system are beginning to give evidence that converges with the behavioural and cognitive measures typical of developmental psychology. For example, particularly important work on the development of the nervous system is beginning to reveal how brain development is influenced by experience, and it is now beginning to be possible to link behavioural measures with aspects of brain maturation. Many important articles on brain development and cognition are reproduced in Johnson (1993).

A second prediction concerns the link between developmental psychology and new theoretical models in biology. Models are being proposed which attempt to explain how self-organising systems are built up as a result of the close interaction between the growing nervous system and the particular qualities of feedback provided by perception and action systems. One particularly influential model is called "selectionism" or "neural Darwinism" (Edelmann, 1992).This approach supposes that development in self-organising systems occurs by selection from inherently diverse systems. On this view, feedback through experience serves to reduce the variability inherent in highly evolved systems. Our discussion of phonological development, where the particular phonological structure of the language of upbringing comes to be selected from a wider repertoire (see pp. 74–75), or the example of motor development (see pp. 83–86),

where successful reaching and grasping actions are selected from initially less successful swiping movements, are examples where selectionist theory applies. Selectionism offers a means of integrating evolutionary, embryological, and developmental processes. More generally, selectionist models have been proposed for early perception and cognitive development (Butterworth, 1993; Van Geert, 1993).

Another theoretical movement, "connectionism", takes its inspiration from modern computers which can operate on many streams of information in parallel (PDP or parallel distributed processing). The link with developmental psychology comes from the fact that connectionist systems change their configuration over time. The PDP computer system changes its configuration according to the structure it detects in the incoming information. The configuration of the network of computer connections undergoes sudden changes called "non-linearities" which are, in some ways, analogous to the stage transitions with which developmental psychologists have long been concerned. PDP systems therefore offer, for the first time, the possibility for computational modelling of development as a process taking place over time. Connectionist models are already available for speech acquisition, and no doubt other developmental phenomena will be modelled in this way in years to come (Plunkett & Sinha, 1992).

Computers also have important implications from a cultural perspective. In modern societies children come into contact with computers very early in development and this continues throughout the school years, into adulthood. A number of important issues arise in connection with computers as cultural artifacts that support developmental processes both in play (computer games) and in the serious business of schooling where computers are used as aids to teaching. Gender differences in affinity for and in the use of computers may also prove increasingly important. Research on children's use of computers and other

(continued)

electronic media has begun and there seems little doubt that this area will be increasingly important in the twenty-first century (Greenfield ,1993).

With modern transportation and communication systems, and the social and economic reorganisation that follows, the world is becoming a smaller place. These changes also pose new problems for developmentalists. For example, the European Community presents children with a new geographical concept but what do children from the different countries concerned understand about being European? Early evidence suggests that English 5- to 10-year-olds already have positive (and negative) concepts of French, Italian, German, and Spanish people. Children's knowledge of foreigners is formed partly through personal contact on holiday, partly through the media, and partly through schooling (Barrett & Short, 1992).

The study of development in adulthood in the twenty-first century may begin to offer a perspective on the different experiences of men and women, both as parents and in the world of work. Developmental psychology has not always taken sufficient trouble to distinguish between the development of males and females. This omission promises to be redressed as our theories become more differentiated with respect to alternative pathways for development.

## Further reading: Adulthood

Dworetzky, J.P., & Davis, N.J. (1989). *Human development: A lifespan approach*. St Paul, MN: West Publishing.

Goodnow, J., & Collins, W.A. (1990). *Development according to parents*. Hove: Lawrence Erlbaum Associates Ltd.

Rutter, M., & Rutter, M. (1992). *Developing minds: Challenge and continuity across the lifespan*. Harmondsworth: Penguin.

Scarr, S. & Dunn, J. (1987). *Mother care—other care*. Harmondsworth: Penguin.

Schaffer, R. (1977). *Mothering*. Glasgow: Fontana.

## Further reading for the twenty-first century

Edelmann, G. M. (1992). *Bright air, brilliant fire: On the matter of the mind*. New York: Basic Books.

Johnson, M. (1993). *Brain development and cognition: A reader*. Oxford: Blackwell.

# References

Adelson, J. (1972). The political imagination of the young adolescent. In J. Kagan & R. Coles (Eds.), *Twelve to sixteen: Early adolescence*. New York: Norton.

Ahrens, R. (1954 ). Beitrage zur entwicklung des physiognomie- und mimerkennes. *Zeitschrift für Experimentelle und Angewandte Psychologie*, 412–454.

Ainsworth, M., & Bell, S. (1970). Attachment, exploration and separation: Illustrated by the behaviour of one-year-olds in a strange situation. *Child Development, 41,* 49–67.

Antell, S.E., & Keating, D.P. (1983). Perception of numerical invariance in neonates. *Child Development, 54,* 695–701.

Archer, J. (1993). *Ethology and human development*. Hemel Hempstead: Harvester.

Aslin, R. (1985). Effects of experience on sensory and perceptual development. In J. Mehler & R.Fox (Eds.), *Neonatal cognition: Beyond the buzzing, blooming confusion*. Hillsdale, NJ: Lawrence Erlbaum Associates Inc.

Atkinson, J., & Braddick, O.L. (1989). Development of basic visual functions. In A. Slater & G.Bremner (Eds.), *Infant development*. Hove: Lawrence Erlbaum Associates Ltd.

Baillargeon, R. (1991). The object concept revisited: New directions in the investigation of the infant's physical knowledge. In C.E. Granrud (Ed.), *Visual perception and cognition in infancy.* Carnegie-Mellon Symposia on Cognition, Vol. 23. Hillsdale, NJ : Lawrence Erlbaum Associates Inc.

Baillargeon, R., Spelke, E.S., & Wasserman, S. (1985). Object permanence in five-month-old infants. *Cognition, 20,* 191–208.

Baldwin, D.A., & Markman, E.M. (1989). Establishing word–object relations: A first step. *Child Development, 60,* 381–398.

Baldwin, J.M. (1905). *Dictionary of philosophy and psychology*. London: Macmillan.

Ball, W., & Tronick, E. (1971). Infant responses to impending collision: Optical and real. *Science, 171,* 818–820.

Baltes, P.B., & Baltes, M.M. (1990). *Successful aging: Perspectives from the behavioral sciences*. Cambridge: Cambridge University Press.

Baron-Cohen, S., Leslie, A.M., & Frith, U. (1985). Does the autistic child have a theory of mind? *Cognition, 21,* 37–46.

Barrett, M. (1986). Early semantic representations and early semantic development. In S.A. Kuczaj & M. Barrett (Eds.), *The development of word meaning*. New York: Springer-Verlag.

Barrett, M., Harris, M., & Chasin, J, (1991). Early lexical development and maternal speech: A comparison of children's initial and subsequent uses. *Journal of Child Language, 18,* 21–40.

Barrett, M., & Short, J. (1992). Images of European people in a group of 5 to 10 year old English schoolchildren. *British Journal of Developmental Psychology, 10,* 339–364.

Bates, E., Benigni, L., Bretherton, I., Camaioni, L., & Volterra, V. (1979). *The emergence of symbols: Cognition and communication in infancy.* New York: Academic Press.

Bates, E., Bretherton, I., & Snyder, L. (1988). *From first words to grammar: Individual differences and dissociable mechanisms.* Cambridge: CUP.

Bell, S.M.V. (1970). The development of the concept of object as related to infant–mother attachment. *Child Development, 41*, 291–311.

Berkeley, G. (1709). *A new theory of vision.* (Reprinted 1963, London: Dent.)

Bertenthal, B.I., & Bai, D.L. (1989). Infants' sensitivity to optical flow for controlling posture. *Developmental Psychology, Vol. 25, 6*, 936–945.

Boden, M. (1979). *Piaget.* Glasgow: Collins Fontana.

Bornstein, M.H., Kessen, W., & Weiskopf, S. (1976). The categories of hue in infancy. *Science, 191*, 201–202.

Bower, T.G.R. (1966). The visual world of infants. *Scientific American, 215*, 80–92.

Bower, T.G.R. (1971 ). The object in the world of the infant. *Scientific American, 225*, 31–38.

Bower, T.G.R. (1982). *Development in infancy (2nd edition).* San Francisco, CA: Freeman.

Bower, T.G.R., Broughton, J.M., & Moore, M.K. (1970). The coordination of visual and tactual input in infants. *Perception and Psychophysics, 8*, 51–53.

Bowlby, J. (1969). *Attachment and Loss, Vol. 1.* Harmondsworth: Pelican Books.

Bowlby, J. (1971). *Attachment and Loss, Vol. 2.* Harmondsworth: Pelican Books.

Bowlby, J. (1973). *Attachment and Loss, Vol. 3.* Harmondsworth: Pelican Books.

Bradley, L., & Bryant, P.E. (1983). Categorising sounds and learning to read—a causal connection. *Nature, 301*, 419–521.

Brainerd, C.J. (1978). *Piaget's theory of intelligence.* Englewood Cliffs, NJ: Prentice-Hall.

Bremner, J.G. (1994). *Infancy (2nd edition).* Oxford: Blackwell.

Bretherton, I., & Waters,E. (1990). Growing points of attachment theory and research. *Monographs of the Society for Research in Child Development, 209*, 1–2.

Bromley, D.B. (1988). *Human ageing: An introduction to gerontology.* Harmondsworth: Penguin.

Brooks-Gunn, J., & Warren, M. (1988). The psychological significance of secondary sexual characteristics in 9 to 11-year-old girls. *Child Development, 59*, 1061–1069.

Broughton, J.M., & Freeman-Moir, D.J. (1982). *The cognitive developmental psychology of James Mark Baldwin.* Norwood, NJ: Ablex.

Brown, G., & Harris, T. (1980). *The social origins of depression.* London: Tavistock.

Brown, J.S., & Burton, R.R. (1978). Diagnostic models for procedural bugs in basic mathematical skills. *Cognitive Science, 2*, 155–192.

Brown, R.W. (1973). *A first language: The early stages.* London: George Allen & Unwin Ltd.

Bruner, J.S. (1972). Nature and uses of immaturity. *American Psychologist, 27* (8). Reprinted in J.S. Bruner, A. Jolly, & K. Sylva (Eds), *Play.* Harmondsworth: Penguin.

Bruner, J.S. (1974). The organisation of early skilled action. In M.P.M. Richards (Ed.), *The integration of a child into a social world.* Cambridge: Cambridge University Press.

Bruner, J.S. (1975a). The ontogenesis of speech acts. *Journal of Child Language, 2*, 1–19.

Bruner, J.S. (1975b). From communication to language—a psychological perspective. *Cognition, 3*, 255–287.

Bruner, J.S. (1983a). *Child's talk.* Cambridge: Cambridge University Press.

Bruner, J.S. (1983b). The acquisition of pragmatic commitments. In R.M. Golinkoff (Ed.), *The transition from prelinguistic to linguistic communication.* Hillsdale, NJ: Erlbaum.

Bruner, J.S., Jolly, A., & Sylva, K. (Eds.) (1976). *Play.* Harmondsworth: Penguin.

Bruner, J.S., & Koslowski, B. (1972). Visually preadapted constituents of manipulatory action. *Perception, 1,* 3–14.

Bruner, J.S., Olver, R.R., & Greenfield, P.M. (1966). *Studies in cognitive growth.* New York: John Wiley.

Bryant, P.E. (1974). *Perception and understanding in young children.* London: Methuen.

Bryant, P.E. (1991). Empirical evidence for causes in development. In G.E. Butterworth & P.E. Bryant (Eds.), *Causes of development.* Hemel Hempstead: Harvester.

Bryant, P.E., & Koptynskya, H. (1976). Spontaneous measurement by young children. *Nature, 260,* 773–774.

Bryant, P.E., & Trabasso, T. (1971). Transitive inferences and memory in young children. *Nature, 232,* 456–458.

Bushnell, I.W.R., Sai, F., & Mullin, J.T. (1989). Neonatal recognition of the mother's face. *British Journal of Developmental Psychology, 7,* 3–15.

Butterworth, G.E. (Ed.) (1982). *Infancy and epistemology.* Brighton: Harvester.

Butterworth, G.E. (1993) Dynamic approaches to infant perception and action: Old and new theories about the origins of knowledge. In L.B. Smith & E. Thelen (Eds.), *A dynamic systems approach to development: Applications.* Cambridge MA: MIT Press.

Butterworth, G.E. (1994). Infant perception and the explanation of intelligence. In F. Khalfa (Ed.), *Intelligence.* Cambridge: CUP

Butterworth, G.E., & Castillo, M. (1976). Coordination of auditory and visual space in newborn human infants. *Perception, 7,* 513–525.

Butterworth, G.E., & Cicchetti, D. (1978). Visual calibration of posture in normal and Down's syndrome infants. *Perception, 5,* 155–160.

Butterworth, G.E., & Franco, F. (1990). Motor development: Communication and cognition. In L.Kalverboer, B. Hopkins, & R.H. Gueze (Eds.), *A longitudinal approach to the study of motor development in early and later childhood.* Cambridge: Cambridge University Press.

Butterworth, G.E., & Grover, L. (1989). Joint visual attention, manual pointing, and preverbal communication in human infancy. In M. Jeannerod (Ed.), *Attention and performance XIII.* London: Erlbaum.

Butterworth, G.E., & Hopkins, B.N. (1993). Origins of handedness in human infancy. *Developmental Medicine and Child Neurology, 35,* 177–184.

Butterworth, G.E., & Jarrett, N. (1991). What minds have in common is space: Spatial mechanisms serving joint attention in infancy. *British Journal of Developmental Psychology, 9,* 55–72.

Butterworth, G. E., Jarrett, N.L.M., & Hicks, L. (1982). Spatio–temporal identity in infancy: Perceptual competence or conceptual deficit? *Developmental Psychology, 18,* 435–449.

Butterworth, G.E., Rutkowska, J., & Scaife, M. (1985). *Evolution and developmental psychology.* Brighton: Harvester.

Cairns, R.B. (1979). *Social development: The origins and plasticity of interchanges.* San Francisco, CA: W.H. Freeman.

Cairns, R.B. (1983). The emergence of developmental psychology. In W. Kessen (Ed.), *Handbook of child psychology, Vol. I.* (Series Ed: P.H. Mussen). New York: John Wiley.

Carey, S. (1985). *Conceptual change in childhood.* Cambridge, MA: MIT Press.

Carraher, T.N., Schliemann, A.D., & Carraher, D.W. (1988). Mathematical concepts in everyday life. In G.B. Saxe & M. Gearhart (Eds.), *Children's mathematics.* San Francisco, CA: Jossey-Bass.

Caselli, M.C. (1983). Communication to language: Deaf children's and hearing children's development compared. *Sign Language Studies, 39,* 113–114.

Caselli, M.C. (1987). Language acquisition in Italian deaf children. In J.G. Kyle (Ed.), *Sign and school: Using sign in deaf children's development.* Clevedon, PA: Multi-Lingual Matters.

Castillo, M., & Butterworth, G.E. (1981). Neonatal localisation of a sound in visual space. *Perception, 10,* 331–338.

Ceci, S.J. (1990). *On intelligence ... more of less: A bio-ecological treatise on intellectual development.* Englewood Cliffs, NJ: Prentice-Hall.

Chi, M.T.H. (1978). Knowledge structures and memory development. In R.S. Siegler (Ed.), *Children's thinking: What develops?* Hillsdale, NJ: Lawrence Erlbaum Associates Inc.

Chomsky, N. (1959). Review of *Verbal Behavior* by B.F. Skinner. *Language, 35,* 26–58.

Chomsky, N. (1965). *Aspects of the theory of syntax.* Cambridge, MA: MIT Press.

Chomsky, N. (1976). *Reflections on language.* London: Temple Smith.

Chomsky, N. (1986). *Knowledge of language: Its nature, origins and use.* New York: Praeger.

Cohen, D., & MacKeith, S.A. (1991). *The development of imagination: The private worlds of childhood.* London: Routledge.

Cole, M., & Cole, S.R. (1993). *The development of children (2nd edition).* New York: Freeman.

Cole, M., John-Steiner, V., Scribner, S., & Souberman, E. (Eds.) (1978). *Mind in society: The development of higher psychological processes.* Cambridge MA: Harvard University Press.

Coleman, J. (1980) *The nature of adolescence.* London: Methuen.

Collis, G.M. (1977). Visual coorientation and maternal speech. In H.R. Schaffer (Ed.), *Studies of mother–infant interaction.* London: Academic Press.

Collis, G.M., & Schaffer, H.R. (1975). Synchronization of visual attention in mother–infant pairs. *Journal of Child Psychology and Child Psychiatry, 16,* 315–320.

Conger, J.J., & Petersen, A.C. (1984). *Adolescence and youth. (3rd edition).* New York: Harper and Row.

Connelly, V. (1993). The influence of instructional technique on the reading strategy of beginning readers. Poster presented at the *VIth European Conference on Developmental Psychology,* Bonn, Germany.

Cox. M. V. (1991). *The child's point of view (2nd edition).* Hemel Hempstead: Harvester.

Cox, M.V. (1993). *Children's drawing of the human figure.* Hove: Lawrence Erlbaum Associates Ltd.

Curcio, F. (1978). Sensori-motor functioning and communication in mute autistic children. *Journal of Autism and Childhood Schizophrenia, 8,* 281–292.

Darwin, C. (1859). *The origin of species.* London: John Murray.

Darwin, C. (1871). *The descent of man: Selection in relation to sex.* London: John Murray.

Darwin, C. (1872). *The expression of emotions in men and animals.* London: John Murray.

Dasen, P. (1972). Cross-cultural Piagetian research: A summary. *Journal of Cross Cultural Psychology, 3,* 29–39.

DeCarie, T.G. (1969). A study of the mental and emotional development of the thalidomide child. In B.M. Foss (Ed.), *Determinants of infant behaviour, Vol. IV.* London: Methuen.

De Casper, A.J., & Fifer, W. (1980). Of human bonding: Newborns prefer their mothers' voices. *Science, 208,* 1174–1176.

DeFrancis, J. (1989). *Visible speech: The diverse oneness of writing systems.* Honolulu: University of Hawaii Press.

Dennis, W., & Dennis, M.G. (1940). The effect of cradling practice upon the onset of walking in Hopi Indians. *Journal of Genetic Psychology, 56*, 77–86.

Dennis, W., & Najarian, P. (1957). Infant development under environmental handicap. *Psychological Monographs, 7,* 1–7.

De Vries, J.I.P., Visser, G.H.A., & Prechtl, H.F.R. (1984). Fetal motility in the first half of pregnancy. In H.F.R. Prechtl (Ed.), Continuity of neural function from prenatal to postnatal life. London: Spastics International Medical Publications.

DeVries, R. (1969). Constancy of genetic identity in the years three to six. *Monographs of the Society for Research in Child Development, 34* (127).

Diamond, A. (1988). Differences between adult and infant cognition: Is the crucial variable presence or absence of language? In L.Weiskrantz (Ed.), *Thought without language*. Oxford: Clarendon Press.

Dockrell, J., & McShane, J. (1992). *Children's learning difficulties: A cognitive approach*. Oxford: Blackwell.

Doctor, E., & Coltheart, M. (1980). Children's use of phonological encoding when reading for meaning. *Memory and Cognition, 8*, 195–209.

Donaldson, M. (1978). *Children's minds* Glasgow: Fontana.

Dore, J. (1978). Conditions for the acquisition of speech acts. In I. Markova (Ed.), *The social context of language*. New York: John Wiley.

Dore, J. (1985). Holophrases revisited: Their "logical" development from dialogue. In M.D. Barrett (Ed.), *Children's single-word speech*. Chichester: John Wiley.

Dromi, E. (1987). *Early lexical development.* Cambridge: Cambridge University Press.

Dunlea, A. (1989). *Vision and the emergence of meaning*. Cambridge: Cambridge University Press.

Dunn, J. (1984). *Sisters and brothers.* London: Fontana.

Dunn, J. (1987). The beginnings of moral understanding: Development in the second year. In J. Kagan & S. Lamb (Eds.), *The emergence of morality in young children*. Chicago, IL: University of Chicago Press.

Dworetzky, J. P., & Davis, N.J. (1989). *Human development: A lifespan approach*. St Paul, MN: West Publishing.

Edelmann, G.M. (1992). *Bright air, brilliant fire: On the matter of the mind*. New York: Basic Books.

Eibl-Eibesfeldt, I. (1989). *Human ethology*. New York: De Gruyter.

Eimas, P.D. (1985). The perception of speech in early infancy. *Scientific American, 204*, 66 –72.

Eimas, P.D., Siqueland, E., Jusczyk, P., & Vogorito, J. (1971). Speech perception in infants. *Science, 171*, 303–306.

Elliot, C.D., Murray, D.J., & Pearson, L.S. (1983). The British abilities scales. Windsor, UK: NFER-Nelson.

Erikson, E.H. (1968). *Identity: Youth in crisis*. New York: Norton.

Estes, B.W., & Combs, A. (1966). Perception of quantity. *Journal of Genetic Psychology, 108*, 333–336.

Fantz, R.L. (1961). The origins of form perception. *Scientific American, 204*, 66–72.

Fantz, R.L. (1965). Visual perception from birth as shown by pattern selectivity. *Annals of the New York Academy of Sciences, 118*, 793–814.

Fischer, K., & Lazerson, A. (1984). *Human development from conception to adolescence*. New York: W.H. Freeman.

Flavell, J.H. (1993). *Cognitive development (3rd edition)*. London: Prentice-Hall.

Flavell, J.H., Flavell, E.R., & Green, F.L. (1983). Development of the appearance reality distinction. *Cognitive Psychology, 15*, 95–120.

Fogel, A. (1991). *Infancy.* New York: West Publishing.

Folven, R.J., Bonvillian, J.D., & Orlansky, M.D. (1984/85). Communicative gestures and early sign language acquisition. *First Language, 5,* 129–144.

Fouts, R.S. (1972). Use of guidance in teaching sign language to chimpanzees. *Journal of Comparative and Physiological Psychology, 80,* 515–522.

Fraiberg, S. (1974). *Insights from the blind.* New York: Basic Books.

Freedman, D. (1974). *Human infancy: An evolutionary perspective.* Hillsdale, NJ: Lawrence Erlbaum Associates Inc.

Freeman, D. (1983). *Margaret Mead and Samoa: The making and unmaking of an anthropological myth.* Cambridge MA: Harvard University Press.

Freeman, N., & Janikoun, R. (1972). Intellectual realism in children's drawings of a familiar object with distinctive features. *Child Development, 43,* 1116–1121.

Freud, S. (1938). Three contributions to the theory of sex. In A.A. Brill (Ed.), *The basic writings of Sigmund Freud.* New York: Random House.

Frith, U. (1985). Beneath the surface of developmental dyslexia. In K. Patterson, M. Coltheart, & J. Marshall (Eds.), *Surface dyslexia.* London: Lawrence Erlbaum Associates Ltd.

Frith, U. (1989). *Autism: Explaining the enigma.* Oxford: Blackwell

Fryer, D. (1985). Stages in the psychological response to unemployment: A (dis)integrative review. *Current Psychological Research and Reviews, Fall,* 257–273.

Fryer, D. (1990). The mental health costs of unemployment: Towards a social psychological concept of poverty. *British Journal of Social and Clinical Psychology, 7,* 164–175.

Fryer, D. (1992). Editorial: Introduction to Marienthal and beyond. *Journal of Occupational and Organizational Psychology, 65,* 257–268.

Furth, H.G., & Kane, S.R. (1992). Children constructing society: A new perspective on children at play. In H. McGurk (Ed.), *Childhood social development: Contemporary perspectives.* Hove: Lawrence Erlbaum Associates Ltd. (pp. 149–171).

Fuson, K.C. (1988). *Children's counting and concepts of number.* New York: Springer.

Gaines, R., Mandler, J.M., & Bryant, P.E. (1981). Immediate and delayed recall by hearing and deaf children. *Journal of Speech and Hearing Research, 24,* 463–469.

Gallahue, D.L. (1982). *Understanding motor development in children.* Chichester: John Wiley.

Gallistel, R., & Gelman, R. (1991). Preverbal and verbal counting and computation. In S. Dehaene (Ed.), *Numerical cognition.* Oxford: Blackwell.

Galton, F. (1869). *Hereditary genius.* London: Macmillan.

Gardner, B.T., & Gardner, R.A. (1971). Two-way communication with an infant chimpanzee. In A.M. Schrier & F. Stollnitz (Eds.), *Behavior of nonhuman primates, Vol. 4.* New York: Academic Press.

Gardner, H. (1978). *Developmental psychology: An introduction.* Boston, MA: Little, Brown and Co.

Gardner, H. (1983). *Frames of mind: The theory of multiple intelligences.* New York: Basic Books.

Gardner, R.A., & Gardner, B.T. (1974). A vocabulary test for chimpanzees. *Journal of Comparative Psychology, 98,* 381–404.

Garvey, C. (1977). *Play.* Cambridge, MA: Harvard University Press.

Gelman, R. (1991). Epigenetic foundations of knowledge structures: Initial and transcendent constructions. In S.Carey & R. Gelman (Eds.), *The epigenesis of mind: Essays on biology and cognition.* Hillsdale, NJ: Lawrence Erlbaum Associates Inc.

Gesell, A., Ilg, F.L., & Bullis, G.E. (1949). *Vision: Its development in infant and child.* New York: Paul B. Heober.

Gibson, J.J. (1966). *The senses considered as perceptual systems*. London: George Allen & Unwin.

Gibson, E.J., & Spelke, E.S. (1983). The development of perception. In J.H. Flavell & E.M. Markman (Eds.), *Cognitive development. Vol. III: Handbook of child psychology*. Chichester: John Wiley (pp.1–76).

Gilligan, C. (1982). *In a different voice*. Cambridge, MA: Harvard University Press.

Girotto,V., & Light, P. (1992). The pragmatic bases of children's reasoning. In P. Light & G.E. Butterworth (Eds.), *Context and cognition*. Hemel Hempstead: Harvester (pp. 134–156).

Gladwin, E.T. (1970). *East is a big bird*. Cambridge, MA: Harvard University Press.

Goldfield, B.A., & Reznick, J.S. (1990). Early lexical acquisition: Rate, content, and the vocabulary spurt. *Journal of Child Language, 17*, 171–183.

Golomb, C. (1992). *The child's creation of a pictorial world*. Oxford: University of California Press.

Goodenough, W.H. (1953). *Native astronomy in the central Carolines*. Museum Monographs. Philadelphia University Museum, University of Philadelphia.

Goodnow, J., & Collins, W.A. (1990). *Development according to parents*. Hove: Lawrence Erlbaum Associates Ltd.

Goswami, U. (1993). *Analogical reasoning in children*. Hove: Lawrence Erlbaum Associates Ltd.

Goswami, U., & Bryant, P. (1990). *Phonological skills and learning to read*. Hove: Lawrence Erlbaum Associates Ltd.

Gould, S.J. (1977). *Ontogeny and phylogeny*. Cambridge MA: Harvard University Press.

Greenfield, P.M. (1993). Representational competence in shared symbol systems: Electronic media from radio to video games. In R.R. Cocking & K.A. Renninger (Eds.), *The development and meaning of psychological distance*. Hillsdale, NJ: Lawrence Erlbaum Associates Inc.

Gregory, S., & Barlow, S. (1988). Interactions between deaf babies and their deaf and hearing mothers. In B. Woll (Ed.), *Language development and sign language*. Bristol: International Sign Linguistics Association.

Griffiths, R. (1954) *The abilities of babies*. London: University of London Press.

Groen, G.J., & Parkman, J.M. (1972). A chronometric analysis of simple addition. *Psychological Review, 79*, 329–343.

Groos, K. (1901). *The play of humans*. London: Heinemann.

Haeckel, E. (1874). *The evolution of man*. (Translated and published 1906). London: Watts & Co.

Hagen, M.A. (1985). There is no development in art. In N.H. Freeman & M.V. Cox (Eds.), *Visual order: The nature and development of pictorial representation*. Cambridge: CUP (pp. 59–77).

Haith, M.M. (1980). *Rules that babies look by: The organisation of newborn visual activity*. Hillsdale, NJ: Lawrence Erlbaum Associates Inc.

Harlow, H., McGaugh, J.L., & Thompson, R.F. (1971). *Psychology*. San Francisco, CA: Albion Publication Co.

Harris, M. (1992). *Language experience and early language development: From input to uptake*. Hove: Lawrence Erlbaum Associates Ltd.

Harris, M., Barrett, M., Jones, D., & Brookes, S. (1988). Linguistic input and early word meaning. *Journal of Child Language, 15*, 77–94.

Harris, M., & Beech, J. (1994). Reading development in prelingually deaf children. In K. Nelson & Z. Reger (Eds.), *Children's language, Vol. 8*. Hillsdale, NJ: Lawrence Erlbaum Associates Inc.

Harris, M., Jones, D., & Grant, J. (1983). The nonverbal context of mothers' speech to children. *First Language, 4,* 21–30.

Harris, M., Jones, D., & Grant, J. (1984/85). The social-interactional context of maternal speech to children: An explanation for the event-bound nature of early word use? *First Language, 5,* 89–100.

Harris, M., Jones, D., Brookes, S., & Grant, J. (1986). Relations between the non-verbal context of maternal speech and rate of language development. *British Journal of Developmental Psychology, 4,* 261–268.

Harris, P.L. (1989). *Children and emotion.* Oxford: Blackwell.

Hayflick, L. (1980). The cell biology of human ageing. *Scientific American, 242,* 58–65.

Hinde, R.A. (1982). *Ethology.* Glasgow: Fontana.

Hobson, R.P. (1993). *Autism and the development of mind.* Hove: Lawrence Erlbaum Associates Ltd

Hofer, M. (1981). *The roots of human behaviour.* San Francisco, CA: Freeman.

Holmes, J. (1993). *John Bowlby and attachment theory.* London: Routledge.

Hood, B., & Willatts, P. (1986). Reaching in the dark to an object's remembered position in 5 month old infants. *British Journal of Developmental Psychology, 4,* 57–65.

Hughes, M. (1986). *Children and number: Difficulties in learning mathematics.* Oxford: Blackwell.

Inagaki, K. (1990). The effects of raising animals on children's biological knowledge. *British Journal of Developmental Psychology, 8,* 119–131.

Ingram, N., & Butterworth, G.E. (1989). The young child's representation of depth in drawing: Process and product. *Journal of Experimental Child Psychology, 47,* 356–379.

Inhelder, B., & Piaget, J. (1958). *The growth of logical thinking from childhood to adolescence.* New York: Basic Books.

Jahoda, M. (1981). Work, employment and unemployment: Values, approaches and theories in social research. *American Psychologist, 36,* 184–191.

Johnson, M. (1993). *Brain development and cognition: A reader.* Oxford: Blackwell.

Johnston, F.E. (1986). Somatic growth in the pre-school years. In F. Falkner & J.M. Tanner (Eds.), *Human growth: A comprehensive treatise, Vol. 2.* New York: Plenum Press.

Kail, R. (1990). *The development of memory in children.* New York: W.H. Freeman.

Kalnins, I., & Bruner, J.S. (1974). Infant sucking used to change the clarity of a visual display. In L.J. Stone, H.T. Smith, & L. Murphy (Eds.), *The competent infant.* London: Tavistock.

Kampfe, C.M., & Turecheck, A.G. (1987). Reading achievement of prelingually deaf students and its relationship to parental method of communication. *American Annals of the Deaf, 132,* 11–15.

Kaye, K. (1982). *The mental and social life of babies: How parents create persons.* Chicago, IL: University of Chicago Press.

Keating, D. (1980). Thinking processes in adolescence. In J.Adelson (Ed.), *Handbook of adolescent psychology.* NY: John Wiley.

Kellogg, R. (1969). *Analyzing children's art.* Palo Alto, CA: National Press Books.

Kimura, Y., & Bryant, P.E. (1983). Rhyme, rime and the onset of reading. *British Journal of Developmental Psychology, 1,* 129–144.

Kohlberg, L. (1966). A cognitive developmental analysis of children's sex role concepts and attitudes. In E. Maccoby (Ed.), *The development of sex differences.* Stanford, CA: Stanford University Press.

Kohlberg, L. (1982). Moral development. In J.M. Broughton & D.J. Freeman-Moir (Eds.), *The cognitive developmental psychology of James Mark Baldwin.* Norwood, NJ: Ablex.

Kozulin, A. (1990). *Vygotsky's psychology.* Hemel Hempstead: Harvester.

Kuhl, P., & Meltzoff, A.N. (1982). The bimodal perception of speech in infancy. *Science, 218,* 1138–1141.

Kuhl, P.K., & Miller, J.D. (1978). Speech perception by the chinchilla: Identification functions for synthetic VOT stimuli. *Journal of the Acoustical Society of America, 63,* 905–917.

Kyle, J., & Allsop, J. (1982). *Deaf people and the community.* Final Report to the Nuffield Foundation.

Landau, B., & Gleitman, L.R. (1985). *Language and experience: Evidence from the blind child.* Cambridge, MA: Harvard University Press.

Langer, S. (1969). *Philosophy in a new key, 5th edition.* Cambridge, MA: Harvard University Press.

Lee, N D., & Aronson, E. (1974). Visual proprioceptive control of standing in human infants. *Perception and Psychophysics, 15,* 529–532.

Leslie, A.M. (1991). The theory of mind impairment in autism: Evidence for a modular mechanism of development? In A. Whiten (Ed.), *Natural theories of mind.* Oxford: Blackwell.

Leung, E.H.L., & Rheingold, H. (1981). Development of pointing as a social gesture. *Developmental Psychology, 17,* 215–220.

Levinson, D.J. (1986). A conception of adult development. *American Psychologist, 41,* 3–13.

Lewis, C. (1986). *Becoming a father.* Milton Keynes: Open University Press.

Light, P. (1988). Context, conservation and conversation (first published 1986) Reprinted in K. Richardson & S. Sheldon (Eds.), *Cognitive development to adolescence.* Hove: Lawrence Erlbaum Associates Ltd.

Lloyd, B., & Duveen, G. (1990). A semiotic analysis of the development of the social representation of gender. In G. Duveen & E. Lloyd (Eds.), *Social representation and the development of knowledge.* Cambridge: Cambridge University Press.

Locke, J. (1690). *An essay concerning human understanding.* London: Tegg (23rd edition).

Lucariello, J. (1987). Concept formation and its relation to word learning and use in the second year. *Journal of Child Language, 14,* 309–332.

Lundberg, I., Olofsson, A., & Wall, S. (1980). Reading and spelling skills in the first school years predicted from phonemic awareness skills in kindergarten. *Scandinavian Journal of Psychology, 21,* 159–173,

Luquet, G.H. (1927). *Le dessin enfantin.* Paris: Delachaux et Niestle.

Luria, A.R. (1959). The directive function of speech development and dissolution. Part I: Development of the directive function of speech in early childhood. *Word, 15,* 341–352.

Maccoby, E. E. (1980). *Social development: Psychological growth and the parent–child relationship.* New York: Harcourt Brace Jovanovich.

MacFarlane, A. (1975). Olfaction in the development of social preferences in the human neonate. In *Parent Infant Interaction (CIBA Foundation Symposium 33).* Amsterdam: Elsevier.

Marsh, G., Friedman, M.P., Welch, V., & Desberg, P. (1980). A cognitive-developmental approach to reading acquisition. In G.E. MacKinnon & T.G. Waller (Eds.), *Reading research: Advances in theory and practice, Vol. 3.* New York: Academic Press.

Masur, E.F. (1982). Mothers' responses to infants' object-related gestures: Influences on lexical development. *Journal of Child Language, 9,* 23–30.

Matarazzo, J.D. (1972). *Wechsler's measurement and appraisal of adult intelligence.* Baltimore: Williams & Wilkins (5th ed.).

McGraw, M.B. (1943). *The neuromuscular maturation of the human infant*. New York: Hofner.

McShane, J. (1979). The development of naming. *Linguistics, 13*, 155–161.

Mead, M. (1963). *Coming of age in Samoa*. Harmondsworth: Penguin (original publication 1928).

Mead, M. (1963). *Growing up in New Guinea*. Harmondsworth: Penguin (original publication 1930).

Mehler, J., & Dupoux, E. (1994). *What infants know*. Oxford: Blackwell.

Meltzoff, A.N., & Borton, R.W. (1979). Intermodal matching by human neonates. *Nature, 282*, 403–404.

Meltzoff, A.N., & Moore, M.K. (1977). Imitation of facial and manual gestures by human neonates. *Science, 198*, 75–78.

Millar, S. (1975). Visual experience or translation rules? Drawing the human figure by blind and sighted children. *Perception, 43*, 63–71.

Mills, A.E. (1987). The development of phonology in the blind child. In B. Dodd & B. Campbell (Eds.), *Hearing by eye: The psychology of lip reading*. Hillsdale, NJ: Lawrence Erlbaum Associates Inc.

Money, J., Hampson, J.G., & Hampson, J.L. (1955). An examination of some basic sexual concepts: The evidence of human hermaphroditism. *Bulletin of Johns Hopkins Hospital, 97*, 301–319.

Morss, J. R. (1990). *The biologising of childhood*. Hillsdale, NJ: Erlbaum.

Moss, P., Bolland, G., Foxman, R., & Owen, C. (1986). Marital relations and the transition to parenthood. *Journal of Reproductive and Infant Psychology, 4*, 57–67.

Muir, D., & Field, J. (1979). Newborn infants orient to sounds. *Child Development, 50*, 431–436.

Nash, R. (1990). *Intelligence and realism*. Basingstoke: Macmillan.

Nelson, K. (1973). Structure and strategy in learning to talk. *Monographs of the Society for Research in Child Development, 38*.

Nelson, K. (1987). What's in a name? Reply to Seidenberg and Petitto. *Journal of Experimental Psychology (General), 116*, 293–296.

Nelson, K.E., & Bonvillian, J.D. (1978). Early language development: Conceptual growth and related processes between 2 and 4.5 years. In K.E. Nelson (Ed.), *Children's language, Vol. 1*. New York: Gardner.

Nelson, K., & Lucariello, J. (1985). The development of meaning in first words. In M. Barrett (Ed.), *Children's single-word speech*. Chichester: John Wiley.

Nunner-Winkler, G., & Sodian, B. (1988). Children's understanding of moral emotions. *Child Development, 59*, 1323–38.

Parke, R. (1981). *Fathering*. Glasgow: Fontana .

Perner, J. (1991). *Understanding the representational mind*. Cambridge, MA: MIT Press.

Petitto, L. (1988). Knowledge of language in signed and spoken language acquisition. In B. Woll (Ed.), *Language development and sign language*. Bristol: International Sign Linguistics Assoc.

Petitto, L.A., & Seidenberg, M.S. (1979). On the evidence for linguistic abilities in signing apes. *Brain and Language, 8*, 162–183.

Piaget, J. (1923). *The language and thought of the child*. (Translated and published 1926) London: Kegan Paul.

Piaget, J. (1924). *Judgment and reasoning in the child*. (Translated and published 1926) London: Kegan Paul.

Piaget, J. (1932). *The moral judgment of the child*. New York: Harcourt Brace.

Piaget, J. (1951). *Play, dreams and imitation in childhood*. London: Heinemann (first published in French 1945).

Piaget, J. (1952). *The origins of intelligence in children*. New York: Harcourt Brace (first published in French 1936).

Piaget, J. (1954). *The construction of reality in the child*. New York: Basic Books (first published in French 1937).

Piaget, J. (1970). *Genetic epistemology.* Columbia, OH: Columbia University Press.

Piaget, J. (1971). *Biology and knowledge.* Edinburgh: Edinburgh University Press.

Piaget, J. (1973). *The child's conception of the world.* London: Paladin Books (first published 1929. London: Routledge & Kegan Paul).

Piaget, J., & Inhelder, B. (1956). *The child's conception of space.* London: Routledge & Kegan Paul.

Piaget, J., & Inhelder, B. (1969). *The psychology of the child.* London: Routledge & Kegan Paul.

Piaget. J., Inhelder, B., & Szeminska, A. (1960). *The child's conception of geometry.* London: Routledge & Kegan Paul (first published in French 1948).

Piaget, J., & Szeminska, A. (1952). *The child's conception of number.* London: Routledge & Kegan Paul (first published in French 1941).

Plunkett, K., & Sinha, C. (1992). Connectionism and developmental theory. *British Journal of Developmental Psychology, 10,* 209–254.

Pope, M.J. (1984). *Visual proprioception in infant postural development.* Unpublished PhD thesis, University of Southampton.

Premack, D. (1986). *Gavagai! or the future history of the animal language controversy.* Cambridge, MA: MIT Press.

Preyer, W. (1882). *The mind of the child.* (Vols. 1 & 2). (Translated and published 1892/1914). New York: Appleton.

Radford, J. (1990). *Child prodigies and exceptional early achievers.* Hemel Hempstead: Harvester.

Ramsay, D.S. (1980). Onset of unimanual handedness in infants. *Infant Behaviour and Development, 2,* 69–76.

Raven, J. (1962). *Coloured progressive matrices.* London: H.K. Lewis.

Reese, H.W., & Smyer, M.A. (1983). The dimensionalization of life events. In E.J. Callahan & K.A. McCluskey (Eds.), *Life span developmental psychology: Non-normative life events.* New York: Academic Press.

Reissland, N. (1988). Neonatal imitation in the first hour of life—observations in rural Nepal. *Developmental Psychology, 24,* 464–469.

Rheingold, H.L., & Cook, K.V. (1975). The contents of boys' and girls' rooms as an index of parents' behaviour. *Child Development, 46,* 459–463.

Rogoff, B., & Waddell K.J. (1982). Memory for information organized in a scene by children from two cultures. *Child Development, 53,* 1224–1228.

Romanes, G.J. (1892). *Darwin and after Darwin.* London: Longmans & Co.

Rousseau, J.J. (1762). *Emile.* (1974 edition). London: Dent.

Rubel, E.W. (1985). Auditory system development. In G. Gottlieb & N.A. Krasnegor (Eds.), *Measurement of audition and vision in the first year of postnatal life* (pp. 53–90). Norwood, NJ: Ablex

Russell, J. (1978). *The acquisition of knowledge.* London: Macmillan.

Rutter, M., & Rutter, M. (1992). *Developing minds: Challenge and continuity across the lifespan.* Harmondsworth: Penguin.

Sakamoto, T., & Makita, K. (1973). Japan. In J. Downing (Ed.), *Comparative reading.* New York: Macmillan.

Sarason, S.B., & Doris, J. (1979). *Educational handicap, public policy and social history.* New York: Free Press.

Savage-Rumbaugh, E.S. (1986). *Ape language: From conditioned responses to symbols.* New York: Columbia University Press.

Savage-Rumbaugh, E.S. (1987). Communication, symbolic communication and language: Reply to Seidenberg and Petitto. *Journal of Experimental Psychology (General), 116,* 288–292.

Savage-Rumbaugh, E.S., McDonald, K., Sevcik, R.A., Hopkins, W.D., & Rupert, E. (1986). Spontaneous symbol acquisition and communicative use by pygmy chimpanzees (*Pan paniscus*). *Journal of Experimental Psychology (General), 115,* 211–235.

Savage-Rumbaugh, E.S., Murphy, J., Sevcik, R.A., Brakke, K.E., Williams, S.L., & Rumbaugh, D.M. (1993). Language comprehension in ape and child. *Monographs of the Society for Research in Child Development, 58,* (3 & 4, Serial No. 233).

Saxe, G.B. (1981). Body parts as numerals: A developmental analysis of numeration among the Oksapmin in Papua New Guinea. *Child Development, 52,* 306–316.

Saxen, L., & Rapola, J. (1969). *Congenital defects.* New York: Holt, Rinehart & Winston, Inc.

Scarr, S., & Dunn, J. (1987). *Mother care—other care.* Harmondsworth: Penguin.

Schaffer, R. (1977). *Mothering.* Glasgow: Fontana .

Schaffer, R. (1984). *The child's entry into the social world.* London: Academic Press.

Schaie, K.W. (1990). Developmental design revisited. In H.W. Reese & S.H. Cohen (Eds.), *Life span developmental psychology: Methodological issues.* Hillsdale, NJ: Lawrence Erlbaum Associates Inc.

Schiff, W. (1986). *Perception: An applied approach.* Acton, MA: Copley.

Schliemann, A.L., & Nunes, T. (1990). A situated schema of proportionality. *British Journal of Developmental Psychology, 8,* 259–268.

Seidenberg, M.S., & Petitto, L.A. (1979). Signing behaviour in apes: A critical review. *Cognition, 7,* 177–215.

Seidenberg, M.S., & Petitto, L. (1987). Communication, symbolic communication and language: Comment on Savage-Rumbaugh et al. *Journal of Experimental Psychology (General), 116,* 279–287.

Selfe, L. (1976). An autistic child with exceptional drawing ability. In G.E. Butterworth (Ed.), *The child's representation of the world.* New York: Plenum Publishing Corp.

Selfe, L. (1983). *Normal and anomalous representational drawing ability in children.* London: Academic Press.

Seymour, P.K., & Elder. L. (1986). Beginning reading without phonology. *Cognitive Neuropsychology, 3,* 1–36.

Siegal, M. (1991). *Knowing children: Experiments in conversation and cognition.* Hove: Lawrence Erlbaum Associates Ltd.

Sigman, M., & Ungerer, J.A. (1984). Attachment behaviour in autistic children. *Journal of Autism and Developmental Disorders, 14,* 231–244.

Sinclair, D. (1978). *Human growth after birth (3rd edition).* Oxford: Oxford University Press.

Skinner, B.S. (1957). *Verbal behavior.* New York: Appleton-Century-Crofts.

Slater, A. (1989). Visual memory and perception in early infancy. In A. Slater & G. Bremner (Eds.), *Infant development.* Hove: Lawrence Erlbaum Associates Ltd.

Slater, A., & Morrison, V. (1985). Shape constancy and slant perception at birth. *Perception, 14,* 337–344.

Smith, N.V., & Tsimpli, I.-M. (1991). Linguistic modularity? A case-study of a "savant" linguist. *Lingua, 84,* 315–351.

Snow, C.E. (1977). Mothers' speech research: From input to interaction. In C.E. Snow & C.A. Ferguson (Eds.), *Talking to children: Language input and acquisition.* Cambridge: Cambridge University Press.

Spelke, E., & Cortelyou, A, (1981). Perceptual aspects of social knowing: Looking and listening in infancy. In M.E. Lamb & L.R. Sherrod (Eds.), *Infant social cognition.* Hillsdale, NJ: Lawrence Erlbaum Associates Inc.

Spelke, E., & Owsley, C.J. (1979). Intermodal exploration and knowledge in infancy. *Infant Behaviour and Development, 2,* 13–24.

Starkey, P., Spelke, E., & Gelman, R. (1983). Detection of intermodal numerical correspondences by human infants. *Science, 222,* 179–181.

Steiner, J. (1979). Human facial expression in response to taste and smell stimulation. In H. Reese & L.P. Lipsitt (Eds.), *Advances in Child Development and Behaviour, 13,* 257–295.

Super, C.M. (1976). Environmental effects on motor development: A case of African infant precocity. *Developmental Medicine and Child Neurology, 18,* 561–567.

Super, D.E. (1957). *The psychology of careers.* New York: Harper & Row.

Swisher, M.V., & Christie, K. (1988). Communications using a sign code for English: Interaction between deaf mothers and their infants. In B. Woll (Ed.), *Language development and sign language.* Bristol: International Sign Linguistics Association.

Tanner, J.M. (1978). *Foetus into man.* London: Open Books.

Terrace, H.S. (1979). *Nim.* New York: Alfred A. Knopf.

Terrace, H.S. (1985). In the beginning was the "name". *American Psychologist, 40,* 1011–1028.

Thelen, E. (1984). Learning to walk: Ecological demands and phylogenetic constraints. In L.P. Lippsitt & C. Rovee-Collier (Eds.), *Advances in Infancy Research, 3.* Norwood, NJ: Ablex.

Thelen, E. (1989). Self organization in developmental processes. In M. Gunnar & E. Thelen, Systems and development: *The Minnesota Symposia in Child Psychology.* Hillsdale, NJ: Lawrence Erlbaum Associates Inc.

Thines, G., Costall, A., & Butterworth, G.E. (1990). *Michotte's experimental phenomenology of perception.* Hillsdale, NJ: Erlbaum.

Thorstad, G. (1991). The effect of orthography on the acquisition of literacy skills. *British Journal of Psychology, 82,* 527–537.

Tizard, B., & Hodges, J. (1978). The effect of early institutional rearing on the development of 8 year old children. *Journal of Child Psychology and Psychiatry, 16,* 61–73.

Turner, P. J. (1991). Relations between attachment, gender and behaviour with peers in pre-school. *Child Development, 62,* 1475–1488.

Vaillant, G.E. (1977). *Adaptation to life.* Boston, MA: Little, Brown & Co.

Valsiner, J. (1988). *Developmental psychology in the Soviet Union.* Brighton: Harvester.

Van Geert, P. (1993). A dynamic systems model of cognitive growth: Competition and support under limited resource conditions. In L.S. Smith & E. Thelen (Eds.), *A dynamic systems approach to development: Applications.* Cambridge, MA: MIT Press.

Verweij, E. (1988). *Devleopment of grasping in full term and pre-term infants.* Unpublished master's thesis, Free University, Amsterdam.

Vinter, A. (1986). The role of movement in eliciting early imitation. *Child Development, 57,* 66–71.

Volterra, V. (1981). Gestures, signs and words at two years: When does communication become language? *Sign Language Studies, 33,* 351–362.

Volterra, V., & Caselli, M.C. (1985). From gestures and vocalisations to signs and words. In W. Stokoe & V. Volterra (Eds.), *SLR '83.* Silver Spring, MD: Linstok Press.

Von Hofsten, C. (1983). Foundations for perceptual development. In L.Lipsitt, & C. K. Rovee-Collier (Eds.), *Advances in infancy research, 2.* Norwood, NJ: Ablex.

Vygotsky, L.S. (1961). *Thought and language.* Boston, MA: MIT Press.

Vygotsky, L.S. (1971). *The psychology of art.* Boston, MA: MIT Press.

Vygotsky, L.S. (1976). Play and its role in the mental development of the child. In J.S. Bruner, A. Jolly, & K. Sylva (Eds.), *Play*. Harmondsworth: Penguin (first published 1933).

Vygotsky, L.S. (1988). The genesis of higher mental functions. Reprinted in K. Richardson & S. Sheldon. *Cognitive development to adolescence*. Hove: Lawrence Erlbaum Associates Ltd.

Waddington, C.H. (1957). *The strategy of the genes*. London: George, Allen & Unwin.

Walker, S. (1984). *Learning theory and behaviour modification*. London: Routledge.

Walkerdine, V. (1988). *The mastery of reason*. London: Routledge.

Walton, G.E., & Bower, T.G.R (1991). Newborn preferences for familiar faces. Paper presented at a *Meeting of the Society for Research in Child Development*, Seattle, WA.

Watson, J.B. (1919). *Psychology from the standpoint of a behaviorist*. Philadelphia, PA: J.B. Lippincott.

Watson, J.B. (1930). *Behaviourism*. New York: W.W. Norton

Watson, J.B., & Rayner, R. (1920). Conditioned emotional reactions. *Journal of Experimental Psychology, 3*, 1–14.

Wechsler, D. (1967). *Wechsler intelligence scale for children*. New York: Psychological Corporation.

Wellman, H.M., Cross,D., & Bartsch, K. (1987). Infant search and object permanence: A meta analysis of the A not B error. *Monographs of the Society for Research in Child Development, 51*.

Werker, J.F., & Tees, R.C. (1984). Cross-language speech perception: Evidence for perceptual reorganization during the first year of life. *Infant Behavior and Development, 7*, 49–63.

Wertheimer, M. (1961). Psychomotor coordination of auditory and visual space at birth. *Science, 134*, 1692.

White, B.L., Castle, P., & Held, R. (1964). Observations on the development of visually directed reaching. *Child Development, 35*, 349–364

Winnicot, D. (1971). *Playing and reality*. New York: Basic Books.

Woods, S.S., Resnick, L.B., & Groen, G.J. (1975). An experimental test of five process models for subtraction. *Journal of Educational Psychology, 67*, 17–21.

Wynn, K. (1992). The origins of numerical knowledge. *Mind and Language, 7*, 315–332.

Zelaso, P.R. (1984). Learning to walk: Recognition of higher order influences? In L.P. Lippsitt & C. Rovee-Collier (Eds.), *Advances in Infancy Research, 3*. Norwood, NJ: Ablex.

Zelaso, P.R., Zelaso, N.A., & Kolb, S. (1972). Walking in the newborn. *Science, 177*, 1058–1059.

# Author index

Duveen, G., 145
Edelmann, G.M., 253
Eibl-Eibesfeldt, I., 43
Eimas, P.D., 74–75
Elder, L., 201
Elliot, C.D., 217
Erikson, E.H., 29, 236–237, 243, 250
Estes, B.W., 211
Fantz, R.L., 64, 103
Field, J., 70
Fifer, W., 54
Fischer, K., 147
Flavell, J.H., 28, 175
Fogel, A., 55, 56
Folven, R.J., 128–129, 137
Fouts, R.S., 122
Foxman, R., 248
Fraiberg, S., 81, 83, 106
Franco, F., 128
Freedman, D., 105
Freeman, D., 226
Freeman-Moir, D.J., 9
Freeman, N., 150
Freud, S., 11, 28, 29, 146, 236–239, 242
Friedman, M.P., 200
Frith, U., 157, 159, 200–201, 203
Fryer, D., 251
Furth, H.G., 143
Fuson, K.C., 211–212
Gaines, R., 207
Gallistel, R., 212, 213
Galton, F., 218–219
Gardner, B.T., 122
Gardner, H., 147, 218
Gardner, R.A., 122
Garvey, C., 145

Gelman, R., 210, 212, 213
Gesell, A., 13, 78
Gibson, J.J., 60–62, 100–101
Gilligan, C., 243
Girotto, V., 228
Gladwin, E.T., 232
Gleitman, L.R., 134–135
Goldfield, B.A., 130
Golomb, C., 148, 152
Goodenough, W.H., 232
Goodnow, J., 247
Goswami, U., 202, 207, 230
Gould, S.J., 7
Grant, J., 126
Green, F.L., 212–213
Greenfield, P.M., 22, 186, 254
Gregory, S., 136
Griffiths, R., 78–79
Groen, G.J., 212–213
Groos, K., 139
Grover, L., 127
Haeckel, E., 7
Hagen, M.A., 153, 157
Haith, M.M., 53–54
Hall, G.S., 10–11
Hampson, J.G., 238
Hampson, J.L., 238
Harlow, H., 24, 26
Harris, M., 126, 128, 130, 131, 136, 207
Harris, P.L., 197
Harris, T., 27, 110
Hayflick, L., 241
Held, R., 83
Hicks, L., 100
Hinde, R.A., 105
Hobson, R.P., 157, 159, 160

Hodges, J., 110
Hofer, M., 43, 44
Holmes, J., 25, 27
Hood, B., 96
Hooker, D., 44
Hopkins, B.N., 86
Hughes, M., 152–153
Ilg, F.L., 13
Inagaki, K., 177
Ingram, N., 150–151
Inhelder, B., 16, 150, 166, 228, 229
Jahoda, M., 251
James, W., 58
Janikoun, R., 150
Jarrett, N.L.M., 100, 127, 128
John-Steiner, V., 173
Johnson, M., 253
Johnston, F.E., 115
Jones, D., 126, 131
Jusczyk, P., 74-75
Kail, R., 184
Kalnins, I., 77
Kampfe, C.M., 136, 207
Kane, S.R., 143
Kaye, K., 117, 118
Keating, D., 227
Keating, D.P., 210, 211
Kellogg, R., 148
Kessen, W., 51
Kimura, Y., 202, 204–206
Kohlberg, L., 147, 194–196, 198
Kolb, S., 80
Koptynskya, H., 189–190
Koslowski, B., 82
Kozulin, A., 22
Kuhl, P., 72
Kuhl, P.K., 75
Kyle, J., 136
Landau, B., 134–135
Langer, S., 117

Lazerson, A., 147
Lee, N D., 82
Leslie, A.M., 159–160
Leung, E.H.L., 127
Levinson, D.J., 243
Lewis, C., 249
Light, P., 169, 174, 228
Lloyd, B., 145
Locke, J., 5, 59, 67
Lucariello, J., 130
Lundberg, I., 206
Luquet, G.H., 149–150, 151, 153
Luria, A.R., 183–184
MacFarlane, A., 55
MacGarrigle, J., 173–174
McGaugh, J.L., 24
McGraw, M.B., 79
MacKeith, S.A., 143–144
McShane, J., 130, 213–214
Makita, K., 204
Mandler, J.M., 207
Markman, E.M., 129
Marsh, G., 200
Masur, E.F., 129
Mead, M., 226
Meltzoff, A.N., 67–68, 72, 73
Michotte, A., 96–97
Millar, S., 149
Miller, J.D., 75
Mills, A.E., 72, 135
Molyneux, W., 59, 67
Money, J., 238
Moore, M.K., 65, 72
Morrison, V., 63
Morss, J. R., 58–59
Moss, P., 248
Muir, D., 70
Mullin, J.T., 71
Murray, D.J., 217

# Subject index

accommodation, 10, 18
addition, 212
adolescence, 4–5, 225–40
 and culture, 226–7, 231–3
 Freud's theory, 236–8
 gender identity, 238–9
 Piaget's formal
     operational reasoning,
     227–31
 reasoning *vs.* adult
     reasoning, 234–6
adulthood, 5, 241–52
 biological and physical
     development, 242–3
 definition of, 242
 employment and
     unemployment, 250–1
 marriage and parenting,
     246–50
 reasoning *vs.* adolescent
     reasoning, 234–6
 theories of, 243–6
affine projection, 155
ageing, 241
alphabetic strategy for
     reading, 201–2
alphabetic writing, 200
Alzheimer's disease, 245
American Sign Language
     (ASL), 137
analogic reasoning, 229–31
animism, 167–8, 176–7
Apgar scale, 43
Arabic numerals, 208
arithmetic, 212–15
artistic ability, 218
 *see also* drawing

assimilation, 10, 18
attachment, Bowlby's
     theory, 24–7, 107–10
autism, 157–60

babies *see* infancy; neonate;
     parenting
balance, 81–2
behaviourism, 11–13, 120
benchmarks, 246
bereavement, 248
biogenetic law, 10
biology, 5–6, 253
birds
 imprinting, 107
 releasing stimuli, 105
birth, 42–3
 and culture, 55–6
blindness
 and drawing, 149
 and language
     development, 134–6
 and reaching, 83
Bowlby's theory of
     attachment, 24–7, 107–10
brain development, 183,
     253
Brazil, 215, 231, 233
Brazleton scale, 43
British Ability Scales
     (BAS), 217
British Sign Language
     (BSL), 137

canalisation, 19
career, 243
centrations, 165

child care, 109
childbirth, 42–3
 and culture, 55–6
childhood, early, 115
 cognitive development,
     163–80
 language development,
     119–37
 Piaget's pre-operational
     reasoning, 163–72
 play and drawing, 139–62
 symbols, 116–38
 Vygotsky's language and
     thought, 172–4
 *see also* infancy
childhood, middle, 183–4
 cognitive development,
     184–98
 intelligence testing,
     214–21
 literacy, 199–207
 moral development, 192,
     194–8
 numeracy, 208–14, 215
 Piaget's concrete
     operational reasoning,
     184–98
 schooling, 199, 220–1
chimpanzees, language
     learning, 122–4
China, 55
 written language, 200,
     204, 205
choice algorithm, 212–13
classical conditioning, 11
classification, 185, 187
clinical methods, 33

fear, learned *vs.* innate, 11,
  12
fertilisation, 43, 44
fetal alcohol syndrome, 47
fetus, 38, 39–43
 hearing, 54
 movement, 43–50
formal operational stage of
  development, 19, 227–31
 and concrete operational
  stage, 227–8
 criticisms of, 228–31
 transition to, 228, 229
fortuitous realism, 149
fractions, 213
Freud's theory of
  development, 11
 adolescence, 236, 237,
  238–9
 gender identity, 146,
  238–9
 personality development,
  237
 stages, 28, 29

gender identity
 in adolescence, 238–9
 and play, 145–7
genetic epistemology, 16
genius, 218–19
German measles, 39
Germany, 109
germinal stage of
  development, 37–8
gerontology, 241
gestures, 117, 119
Gibson's theory of
  perception, 60–2
gradients, texture, 61–2
grammar, 119–20
grandparents, 249–50
grasp reflex, 47
grasping, 83–6
grief, 248
growth, physical, 42

adolescence, 225–6
adulthood, 242–3
early childhood, 115
infancy, 77
middle childhood, 183
pre-natal, 37–9, 42
gustation, 55

habituation method of
  demonstrating
  constancy, 63, 65
handedness, 86
hands, control of, 83–6
health, and mental
  abilities, 245
hearing
 impaired, 136–7
 neonate, 54–5
 and vision, 70–4
heredity, *vs.* environment,
  5–6, 11–14, 219
hierarchical integration, 85
homeorhesis, 44
homeostasis, 44
Hopi Indians, 80
hypotheses, 227
hypothetico-deductive
  reasoning, 228

iconic signifiers, 119, 149
identification, 146
*idiots savants*, 218
imagination, 140
 paracosms, 143–4
imitation, infants, 72–3
imprinting, 107
 *see also* attachment
indexes, 117, 118–19
India, 55
infancy
 attachment, 107–10
 cognitive development,
  88–111
 motor development,
  77–87

neonate (*q.v.*), 42–3, 50–5
number discrimination,
  210–11
perceptual development,
  58–76
Piaget's sensori-motor
  period, 88–102
pre-natal development
  (*q.v.*), 37–50
 vision, 51–3
information processing
  models, 253
initiation rituals, 238
intellectual realism,
  149–50
intelligence testing, 8–9,
  32–3, 214–21
 and culture, 217, 219–20
 genius, 218–19
 and other talents, 218
 and schooling, 220–1
 Wechsler scales, 216–17
IQ, 9, 216–17
 effects of schooling on,
  220–1
Iran, 80
Italy, 199–200, 203

Japan
 infant socialisation, 109
 learning to read, 203–6
 phoneme recognition, 74,
  75
 pregnancy and
  childbirth, 56
 written language, 200,
  203–4
job, 250–1

kana, 203–4
kanji, 200, 203, 204
Kipsigi tribe, 80
!Kung San people, 226

language, 119

of faces, 103–4, 105
fetus, 47, 54
Gibson's theory, 60–2
hearing and vision, 70–4
infancy, 58–76
neonate, 50–5, 104
Piaget's theory, 59–60
sensory impairment, and
  language
  development, 134–7
size and shape constancy,
  62–5
of speech, 74–5
study methodology, 64
vision and touch, 58–9,
  65–9
personality development,
  Erikson and Freud,
  236–8, 243
persons, knowledge of,
  102–7
and attachment
  formation, 107–10
development of mental
  models, 106–7
face recognition, 103–4,
  105
smiling, 105–6
phonemes, distinction
  between, 74–5
phonology
  awareness of, 206–7
  and orthography, 199
phylogeny, 7
Piaget's theory of
  development, 15–21
  animism, 167–8, 176–7
  concrete operations stage,
    184–92
  conservation problems,
    164, 173–4, 184–5, 186–7
  dreams, 168
  egocentrism, 165–7, 170–2
  formal operations stage,
    227–31

language development,
  124
logical operations, 185–9
moral reasoning, 192,
  194–8
perception, 59–60
play, 141–3, 146
pre-operational stage,
  116, 163–79
representation, 88, 90, 95,
  116
sensori-motor period,
  88–102
space, conception of, 150
symbols, 90, 116
Pinyin, 200
play, 139–40
and gender identity, 145–7
with objects, 140–4
in Piaget's theory, 141–3,
  146
rules of, 194, 197
symbols in, 139–47
transitional objects, 144
and zone of proximal
  development, 23, 140–1
pointing, 127–9
and counting, 211
population growth, 55
posture control, 81–3
pre-natal development,
  37–48
embryo, 38, 39, 43–4
fetus, 38, 39–43
germinal stage, 37–8
pre-operational stage of
  development, 19, 116,
  163–5
animism, 167–8, 176–7
conservation problems,
  164
critique of, 169–72
egocentrism, 165–7
pregnancy, 247
prematurity, 42

primary circular reactions,
  88, 89, 92
projective geometry, 156,
  157
psychosocial stages of
  development, 236–8
puberty, 225, 238
Pulawat navigators, 231,
  232

Raven Coloured
  Progressive Matrices,
  219, 220
reaching and grasping,
  83–6
reading see literacy
recapitulation, 7, 10, 16
reconstructive
  imagination, 140
reflexes
  fetus, 47
  neonate, 43, 49
  Piaget's theory, 88, 89, 92
reinforcement, in language
  development, 120–1
releasing stimuli, 105–6
reliability of intelligence
  testing, 214–15
representation (Piaget),
  88, 90, 95, 116
research, methodology,
  30–1, 32–3
roles, 192–3
Roman numerals, 208
rooting reflex, 43
rubella, 39
rules, 194, 196–7

saccades, 53
Samoa, 226
scaffolding, 80
schooling, 199–222
  intelligence testing,
    214–21
  literacy, 199–207